HUNTLAND

*The Historic Virginia Hunt Country House,
the Property, and Its Owners*

Marc Leepson

This book is dedicated to Sharon Smith Peterson and

her great-grandmother, Mattie McQuay Berryman,

and to the memory of their ancestors,

the enslaved women and men of the Benton family

who built New Lisbon, later Huntland, and continued to live and work on

the Benton family properties until after emancipation.

SHARON SMITH PETERSON

Mattie McQuay Berryman

MARAL S. KALBIAN

Sharon Smith Peterson

Huntland Press, LLC

ISBN 979-8-218-18492-6

Distributed by University of Virginia Press

UNIVERSITY *of*
VIRGINIA PRESS

CONTENTS

PROLOGUE

Christmas Morning 2007 dawned cold, gray, and dreary in the Northern Virginia Piedmont—the farm-dotted rolling hills between the famed Blue Ridge and Bull Run mountains. Betsee Parker—accomplished horse woman, ordained Episcopalian minister, committed preservationist and philanthropist, and recently widowed with a young child—made her way to Huntland, the historic country property in Middleburg she had purchased seven weeks earlier.

"I had this notion that it was mine now, and we hadn't begun restoring it—it was completely derelict and shut down—and I decided that it would be fun to go out there that morning," she said in 2019.[1]

Her daughter, Rosie, was away. She was alone at her home in nearby Delaplane Manor, "and I thought I would go out there and see how quiet it was. The quiet of the land is so lovely there because there are dirt roads around it and at [nearby] Foxcroft the girls weren't in school, so that road was very quiet. I just wanted to hear how quiet it was."

Parker—who grew up in Minneapolis and had worked for nearly two years as a volunteer at the New York City Medical Examiner's Office at Ground Zero at the former World Trade Center following the 9/11 attacks—walked up to the one-time pristine house and stood on the front stairs taking in the horse country quiet and gazing across the wide front lawn.

"As I panned looking to the right," she said, "I looked down into the sunken garden and I saw this funny little narrow column of smoke coming up by the side of the porch. I couldn't believe my eyes. I had no idea what it was. At first, I thought, 'Is somebody smoking a cigarette back there?'"

It wasn't cigarette smoke, Betsee Parker quickly realized. An electric wire leading into the house was completely on fire. "It was in full flame," she said, "not just a smoker, full flame." On Christmas morning. With no one else on the grounds of the estate.

"I thought the only thing I could do was call a local fire department and the closest one I knew of was in Philomont, five miles away. So I rang the fire station and told them there was a fire here and they came out that morning and put it out."

If Betsee Parker hadn't happened by that cold, dreary Christmas morning, it's very likely that historic Huntland would have burned to the ground. "I don't know who [else] would have seen it if there had been a fire because no one was living across the road at the time and no one was on the land living there," she said.

"Strangely enough, I happened to be here when the wiring caught fire—and if I had not been, I believe it could have been catastrophic. It frightens me when I think about it."

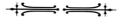

The catastrophe averted, Betsee Parker, with her farm manager and master carpenter Jerry Coxsey superintending, soon began meticulously repairing, restoring, and preserving Huntland, along with its one-of-a-kind hound kennels and stables. On December 24, 2013, nearly six years after the place came dangerously close to burning to the ground, the National Park Service added Huntland to the National Register of Historic Places.[2]

"With sweeping vistas across fields devoted to cultivation for nearly two centuries, Huntland includes at its core an 1830s dwelling built by a master brick mason, William Benton, Sr.," the Park Service National Register nomination noted.[3] William Benton came to these shores from England early in the 19th century. He is best known for superintending the building of Oak Hill, the home of President James Monroe near the small village of Aldie, Virginia, not far from Huntland, in the early 1820s.

William Benton went on to build several other structures in the Middleburg area, including a house he named New Lisbon on 171 acres he purchased in 1833. He and members of his large family lived at New Lisbon, which was finished in 1834, for the rest of the 19th century. His heirs added surrounding acreage over the decades, and sold the New Lisbon property—referred to in some real estate documents as "James Benton's Farm"—in 1900 to the recently widowed Annie Gregg Leith. She paid $8,161 for the house and some 272 acres.

On January 1, 1912, Annie Leith sold New Lisbon to Joseph B. Thomas, the son and grandson of Gilded Age millionaires. Thomas, who grew up in New York City and Connecticut, graduated from Yale in 1903 and was strongly interested in polo, dog breeding, yachting, and foxhunting—among other things. He bought New Lisbon and its 272 acres for $20,000. He promptly changed its name to Huntland, and immediately set about redoing the house.

Joe Thomas subsequently bought adjoining acreage, enlarging Huntland's landholdings to more than 411 acres. He completely remodeled the house and designed and built what would become one of the nation's most extensive and elaborate fox hound kennels and horse stables.

Thomas "converted and enlarged a relatively modest but stately brick Virginia country dwelling into a Colonial Revival-style masterpiece," the NPS historic designation— written by the architectural historian Maral S. Kalbian—notes.[4] "At the same time, Thomas, an expert on all elements of the foxhunting world, constructed arguably one of the most sophisticated kennels and stables to accommodate horses and hounds associated with point-to-point foxhunting in the region."[5]

Thomas hired the noted New York City architectural firm Peabody, Wilson & Brown to turn William Benton's New Lisbon into a Colonial Revival treasure. Although he was not a professional architect, Joe Thomas designed the kennels and stables in 1912-13. He worked with a young Northern Virginia architect, Claude Haga of M.D. Morrill Associates, on designing the buildings on the property that accommodated the horses and hounds. The grounds were designed—most likely by Peabody, Wilson & Brown—to include, as the NPS report notes, "elements such as gates, walls, and terraced gardens reminiscent of English manor estates."

Joe Thomas, as we will see, more or less gave up on Huntland in 1920, less than ten years after he bought the place, and moved back to New York City (and his Connecticut farm). He sold Huntland in June 1927 for $200,000 to William and Gwendolyn Denys Robinson, who were living in Washington, D.C., at the time. The Robinsons did not move into Huntland, and sold it just three years later, in 1930, the year the couple divorced and Gwendolyn Robinson remarried.

The new owners were Thomas Hunt and Mildred Donnell Talmadge, a young, upper-crust couple who lived in New York City. The Talmadges owned Huntland for six years, but they never lived there. In 1936, in the depths of the Great Depression, they relinquished the place to a New York bank, which picked Huntland up for $80,000 at an auction on the front steps of the Loudoun County Courthouse in Leesburg.

The Bank of New York and Trust Company sold Huntland two years later, in July 1938, to Colin MacLeod, a horseman from Boston, for $75,000. Unlike the Robinsons and the Talmadges, Colin MacLeod, his wife Katherine, and their son Colin "Sandy" MacLeod, Jr. moved into the house at Huntland and lived there most of the year.

The MacLeods stayed at Huntland for seven years. They moved to Dunvegan, a large home and horse farm Colin MacLeod built in nearby Upperville, Virginia, in 1945. The MacLeods then sold Huntland for $150,000 to Fred B. Prophet, a highly successful Detroit-based businessman who owned a nationwide industrial food services company. Prophet and his wife Vera split their time at their home in Palm Beach, Florida, and at Huntland. They sold the latter in February 1948 to Countess Priscilla Dickerson Gillson de la Fregonniere and her husband, Count Guy de la Fregonniere.

She was an American who lived for many years in England and France; he was French. They had married just a year before buying Huntland. The couple moved in, but also spent time at their lavish home in Nassau in the Bahamas. The de la Fregonnieres (sometimes referred to as "the Count and Countess") raised and trained race horses at Huntland, and continued the cattle operations that had being going on there since the 1840s.

On December 4, 1954, the de la Fregonnieres sold Huntland to George R. Brown of Houston, Texas, who with his brother Herman (who became Huntland's co-owner in 1957), ran Brown & Root, the giant government contracting firm. In 1954 George Brown was looking for a place near Washington, D.C., to use as his base of lobbying operations and he bought Huntland sight unseen.

The Brown family would own the property until 1990. During the fifties and sixties Huntland was the country hub for countless social and political gatherings of many Washington lobbyists and politicians, most of them from Texas. The most prominent (and powerful) figures among them were President Lyndon B. Johnson and Lady Bird Johnson, President John F. Kennedy and Jacqueline Bouvier Kennedy, and Speaker of the House Sam Rayburn. LBJ had been the beneficiary of the Brown brothers' campaign fund largess since

1937 when he won a seat in a special election to the House of Representatives, kicking off a remarkable political career that ended with him becoming the 36th President of the United States in November 1963.

LBJ's close political and personal relationship with George and Herman Brown continued throughout his twelve years in the House of Representatives, twelve additional years in the Senate (1949-61), including his tenure as Majority Leader, and his time as Vice President and President of the United States (1961-69). Johnson visited Huntland scores of times when the Browns owned it. After LBJ acceded to the presidency in November 1963 following the assassination of President John F. Kennedy, some locals took to calling Huntland the "summer White House."

On July 2, 1955, Sen. Lyndon Johnson arrived for one of his frequent visits to Huntland, intending to spend the long Fourth of July weekend in the peace and quiet of the Middleburg countryside. That plan evaporated not long after he walked in the front door complaining of severe chest pains. At first, Johnson put it down to indigestion. But another weekend guest, Sen. Clinton Anderson of New Mexico, realized Johnson was having a heart attack.

A Johnson aide managed to contact Middleburg's only doctor, James "Jimmy" Gibson, who examined the Senator and told him he needed to get to a hospital as quickly as possible. Dr. Gibson summoned Middelburg's one and only ambulance—which doubled as the town's hearse. It soon roared off to Bethesda Naval Hospital fifty miles to the east. The town's undertaker drove the ambulance/hearse, Dr. Gibson sat in the front seat next to him, and Brown aide Frank "Posh" Oltorf was in the back with LBJ. Johnson survived, but at one point the doctors had given him a 50-50 chance to live.

The other notable event that took place during the Browns' ownership of Huntland came in the spring and summer of 1962 when the house hosted secret negotiations between representatives of the Republic of Indonesia and the Netherlands, the country's former colonial ruler. The discussions at Huntland focused on settling a long-simmering disagreement on the fate of what was known then as Netherlands New Guinea (or West New Guinea)—the Dutch-controlled half of the large island in the Indonesian archipelago that had remained under Dutch control when the Netherlands turned the other half over to the Republic of Indonesia in 1949.

With the threat of war a strong possibility after thirteen years of intermittent, fruitless negotiations, a small fleet of limousines containing delegations led by the Dutch Ambassador to the United States and the Indonesian Ambassador to the then Soviet Union rolled out from Washington to Middleburg on March 20 for the first of a series of secret negotiations.[6]

The man who moderated the hush-hush discussions, Ellsworth Bunker, had been U.S. Ambassador to Argentina, Italy, and India during the Truman and Eisenhower administrations.[7] In this case, Bunker acted as a private citizen, although it was understood by all that he was acting on behalf of the Kennedy Administration. The diplomats had formal sessions in the mornings and afternoons, followed by cocktails, dinner, and dips in the Browns' swimming pool.

The sides reached an agreement on July 31, in which the Dutch agreed to cede West New Guinea to Indonesia after more meetings at Huntland. War averted, the Dutch would turn their portion of the island over to a UN protectorate in 1963. Indonesia's foreign minister arrived in New York on Aug. 12, 1962. Three days later the agreement was signed at the UN.

The Brown brothers' heirs held on to Huntland until 1990. In September that year, they sold the property, along with about 125 additional nearby acres, to the industrialist Roy Ash and his wife Lila. The price tag: a staggering $7.6 million, what was believed to have been the highest amount ever paid for a property in Middleburg.[8]

Roy Ash, who was born in Los Angeles in 1918, in 1953 co-founded Litton Industries, which grew into a multi-billion-dollar conglomerate, at one point controlling more than a hundred different companies. He later served as Director of the Office and Management and Budget under Presidents Nixon and Ford, and was instrumental in creating the Environmental Protection Agency in 1970.

In the late 1980s and early 1990s Roy Ash purchased several other large properties in the Middleburg area. That included Llangollen, a historic 1,100-acre estate at the foot of the Blue Ridge Mountains formerly owned by John Hay Whitney and his wife Liz Whitney Tippett.

Roy and Lila Ash—who did not live at Huntland, but rented out the house and other buildings—sold the 129-acre parcel that contained the house, kennel, and barns in May 2007 to a family partnership for $7.3 million. The partnership soon put the property back on the market and sold Huntland to Betsee Parker in November. A few years later, she acquired the balance of the property from the Ashes.

⊹══ ══⊹

Largely absentee owners had Huntland for decades when Betsee Parker bought it at the end of 2007. "The Browns did not live here [full time]," Parker said. As for repairs and maintenance, "there was a tremendous amount of work to be done to make it livable. All the buildings had fallen into complete dereliction."[9]

The good news today, in 2023, is that the 1834 house and the early 20th century kennels and stables have been carefully restored and preserved to their original magnificence.

Betsee Parker's "devotion to historical accuracy and attention to detail is reflected in her meticulous restoration of Huntland," Maral S. Kalbian said. "The property was in complete disrepair when Betsee purchased it and saved it from demolition by neglect. I can't recall ever seeing such attention paid to period details. Betsee is not only keenly observant, but she takes the time to research a subject and make the best possible decision. It's quite remarkable. Betsee has also restored several other important historic landmarks in the Piedmont region of Virginia, and in some cases, given relevant historic buildings to nonprofits."[10]

What follows is a history of Huntland that starts in the 1830s with William Benton and his family's long-term tenure, and chronologically covers the state of the house and grounds—and its owners—into the start of the third decade of the 21st century.

It's a story full of intriguing and colorful characters, beginning with self-made, multi-talented William Benton and his children. It focuses on the Bentons, the mercurial Joe Thomas, the powerful Brown Brothers, and the accomplished polymath, Betsee Parker. It's an American historic preservation story with more than a few twists and turns—and with a happy ending.

CHAPTER ONE
William Benton at Oak Hill

"I wish to hear from you without delay to know in what way it is to end."

—William Benton to James Monroe, January 20, 1824

Details about the early ownership of the property we know today as Huntland are cloudy. Loudoun County Deed and Will Books indicate that Charles Green of what was then Fairfax County[11] owned the property as early as 1741, about fifteen years after the first Europeans began to settle there. Sometime after that date, it appears that Green sold 150 acres of that land to William Savage of nearby Prince William County, who conveyed it after 1757 to William Smith and his wife Margaret of Loudoun County. Then, in April of 1773, the Smiths likely sold the land to Simon Hancock, a prominent citizen of Fairfax County who later served as a captain in the Continental Army during the Revolutionary War and who lived not far away near Mount Gilead in Loudoun County.[12]

What is clear from the deed books is that on May 5, 1775—just sixteen days after the Battles of Lexington and Concord in Massachusetts and the start of the Revolutionary War—Simon Hancock and his wife Mary sold that land, where Huntland sits today, to George Johnston, who is identified in the official colonial land records as "of Bucks County, in the Province of Pennsylvania."[13] The price: two hundred pounds of Virginia Continental Currency.[14] Eighteen months later, in late November 1776, Johnston, who had subsequently moved to Loudoun County, joined the Continental Army.[15]

The Johnston family held on to the property until 1811, when Hugh and James Johnston, the executors of the estate of George Johnston, sold the acreage to Jeremiah William Bronaugh (1779-1856). Born in Loudoun County, Jeremiah Bronaugh married Elizabeth Hope Mitchell in Georgetown (then an incorporated city adjoining Washington, D.C.) in 1810.[16] The following year, on March 21, 1811, Jeremiah Bronaugh purchased the property for $3,122.50.[17]

Jeremiah and Elizabeth had been married on May 22, 1810, by the Rev. Walter Dulany Addison, a notable Washington, D.C., clergyman who was then the rector of St. John's Episcopal Church in Georgetown. They had seven children, all of whom were born in Georgetown.

There are no records indicating that the Bronaughs built a house on their property in Loudoun County. Given that fact—and that the family owned several other parcels of land in Loudoun and that they lived in Georgetown—it's all but certain that they purchased the property as a land-banking investment. If so, they didn't make much of a profit.

1

On January 2, 1833, the Bronaughs, who were still paying a mortgage on the land to the Bank of the United States, sold the property for $3,277.07, only about $150 more than they paid for it twenty-two years earlier. When later surveyed, the tract turned out to contain 171.5 acres.

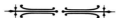

The new owner of the property was William Benton, Sr. A master brick mason and builder, Benton was born on Christmas Day 1788 in England in the village of Lisbon in Lincolnshire, about 125 miles northeast of London. It appears that he came to these shores as a young man very early in the 19th century, most likely in 1801.[19]

According to one newspaper obituary, Benton spent his "early" years in America in Spotsylvania County, Virginia. In the summer of 1814, responding "to the cause of his adopted country," as the obituary put it,[20] Benton decided to join the American military to fight against England in the War of 1812. The twenty-four-year-old signed up for a six-month enlistment in Stevensburg in nearby Culpeper County on August 4, 1814, joining Capt. Charles C. Allen's Company of the 33rd Virginia Militia Regiment.

Private Benton first served as an assistant quartermaster at Camp Seldon on the shores of the Potomac River in Stafford County with Col. Robert Crutchfield's detachment of Brig. Gen. William Madison's 1st Brigade of Virginia Militia.[21] He stayed in the military for 136 days, receiving an honorable discharge in Fredericksburg on December 17, 1814, a week before British and American negotiators signed the Treaty of Ghent ending the war.[22] William Benton had been promoted to corporal after his time at Fort Seldon, and later performed his quartermaster duties at Camp Federal Springs south of Richmond and in Washington, D.C., and the adjacent town of Bladensburg, Maryland.

Sometime in 1815, Benton, according to his obituary, "took charge of the Willis estate, bordering upon Fredericksburg." Strong evidence exists that William Benton, indeed, did work for Col. Byrd Charles Willis (1781-1846) at his farm, Willis Hill. The property sits just outside Fredericksburg, near Ferry Farm, George Washington's boyhood home along the Rappahannock River. Byrd Willis' father, in fact, was a boyhood friend of George Washington. What's more, Byrd Willis' wife Mary was a granddaughter of the Father of our Country's younger sister, Betty Washington Lewis.[23]

The earliest known evidence of the connection between William Benton and James Monroe is a reference in a May 17, 1817, letter Monroe wrote to Byrd Willis from the President's House (what most people then, including James Monroe, called the White House) barely two months after he was sworn in as the nation's fifth chief executive.[24] In it, President Monroe told Willis that he had learned that William Benton was "in your service, but that you would let me hire him."

"When I left you in Fredericksburg," Monroe wrote to Willis, "I understood of Mr. Benton that he would make a visit to my farms in Loudoun to examine the present state and capacity," and "to enter into an agreement if he was so disposed," to manage the farm.[25]

The "farms" in Loudoun Monroe referred to is the property that came to be known as Oak Hill just outside the village of Aldie on present-day U.S. Route 15, a few miles southeast of Huntland. Monroe became part owner of Oak Hill in 1794, the year he resigned his U.S. Senate seat after President Washington appointed him U.S. Minister (Ambassador) to France. Monroe joined with his uncle, Judge Joseph Jones of Fredericksburg, and purchased the 4,400-acre property from Col. Charles Carter, Jr. of Ludlow in Stafford County.[26]

Judge Jones died in 1805. His son, Joseph Jones, Jr., inherited his father's portion of the land. When the younger Jones died three years later, James Monroe became executor of his and his father's estates, and inherited the entire property.

In that year, 1808, Monroe had returned to Virginia as a private citizen after having served as U.S. Minister to England for four years in the Jefferson Administration. He was living at his Highland Farm in Albemarle County, not far from Thomas Jefferson's Monticello, and decided he didn't need the large property (now around 2,000 acres) a hundred miles north in Loudoun. So, in late 1809 and early in 1810, Monroe placed an advertisement in several newspapers, including the Richmond *Enquirer* and the Leesburg *Washingtonian*, offering the land for sale.

The ad noted that the property, "on which the late Judge Jones resided, in Loudoun county, with about 25 SLAVES, and the stock of Horses, Cattle and Hogs on the estate," containing "nearly two thousand acres... 35 miles from Alexandria, and forty from George-Town" would be divided into tracts... to suit the convenience of purchasers."[27]

When the land didn't sell, Monroe reconciled himself to holding on to the property. That resolve hardened in 1811 after he became Secretary of State, and solidified in 1816 after being elected President of the United States. During his time as Secretary of State—which included the August 1814 British invasion of Washington during the War of 1812—and during his presidency James Monroe and his family regularly came out to Oak Hill in rural Loudoun County. After a full-day's carriage ride covering about forty miles, James, his wife Elizabeth, and their children decamped at the farm and settled into in a wood-framed, six-room cottage on the property.

In 1817, Monroe hired William Benton away from Col. Willis. Benton moved up from Fredericksburg to Oak Hill to replace a man named Thomas Slaughter who had been managing the estate and overseeing the farming operations for about a year.[28] Benton and his family moved into the cottage, sharing it with the Monroes when they were in Loudoun—usually during the summers and early fall.

On December 18, 1818, William Benton married Sarah Hyde of Spotsylvania County, Virginia. Family lore has it that she was his first cousin, the daughter of his uncle, Daniel Hyde.[29] Less than a year later, on September 18, 1819, the Bentons welcomed a son into the world at Oak Hill. They named him James Monroe Benton. William and Sarah had three more sons—William Hyde (born at Oak Hill in February 1821), Richard, and Thomas—and two daughters, Eliza and Sarah.

William Benton worked for James Monroe at Oak Hill for the next six years. Biographers and historians have described Benton as Monroe's "steward, counsellor and friend,"[30] and his estate or farm manager.[31] One obituary referred to him as "an intimate friend of President Monroe."[32]

Whether or not the two men were friends, there is plenty of evidence that William Benton counseled James Monroe on the upkeep of the massive grounds and the structures on the property, which included the cottage and at least five other buildings. He certainly managed the varied farming ventures there, taking care of the livestock and managing all the crops, as well as the orchard and hundreds of acres of meadows, pastures, and fields. From his first days at Oak Hill, Benton also oversaw the purchasing, hiring, housing, and clothing and feeding of the enslaved people at Oak Hill owned by President Monroe.

In a May 8, 1818, letter from the White House to Benton at Oak Hill, President Monroe laid out some of the work he wanted Benton to do. Monroe told his manager/overseer to "attend to the improvements for our accommodation when we come up," including "plaistering [sic] the house," "putting plank in the kitchen loft," and enlarging the yard "eastward."

The "greatest attention should be paid," Monroe wrote, to "the meadows," which he relied on "for grass [to] support the horses & other stock, and the stock cattle...." The meadows, he said, should "be put in the best order, by cutting up the broom straw &c." Corn was to be planted and the horses on the farm should "be got in good order, which is so necessary to carry on the business well."[33]

As for the cattle, Monroe suggested to Benton in November that "the purest way" for him to "make a profit" from the cattle operations on the farm, "is to purchase and sell after making fat, stock cattle."[34]

In 1820 James Monroe decided to build a large two-story brick house with a huge columned portico on the property—with the bricks made on site at Oak Hill.[35] It appears that construction began the following year, and was completed either in late 1822 or early the next year. "The home... is a stately mansion of the old Virginia style surrounded by a grove of magnificent oaks, locusts, and poplars, covering several acres," a 1937 federal Works Project Administration Report noted. "A wide Greek portico, overlooking privet gardens, fronts south with massive Doric columns, nine feet in circumference. Simple but solidly and beautifully built. The bricks were all burned on the place, and all the inside work was cut out by hand."[36]

It sometimes has been said that Thomas Jefferson designed the main house at Oak Hill. That is not true. However, Jefferson did discuss his ideas about what the house should look like with James Monroe, an old friend and colleague.[37] In June 1820 Thomas Jefferson presented what he later called an "unintelligible sketch" of the house's outlines to James and Elizabeth Monroe. Later that month he mailed another version, "drawn at large," as he put it, so that the Monroes, he said, "may take some hints from it for a better plan of your own."[38]

Two other men—George Bomford and James Hoban—contributed much more significantly to the final design of the Monroe home at Oak Hill, which today is on the National

Register of Historic Places. Bomford (1780–1848), a West Point graduate who helped rebuild the U.S. Capitol in 1815-19 following the War of 1812, sent a set of plans to Monroe in January 1821.[39] Hoban (c. 1762-1831), the Irish-born architect who designed the White House in 1792 and later helped superintend the building of the U.S. Capitol, worked closely with Monroe on virtually every aspect of the design and construction of Oak Hill.

Aside from contributing to the house's design, Hoban "handled the contracting with the carpenters, maintained the accounts for that work, undertook the final 'measure' or inspection" and advised Monroe "on matters like when to plaster," the Oak Hill National Register nomination noted. The daily supervision of all construction, though, "fell to William Benton."[40]

William Benton stayed on at Oak Hill for nearly two years after the house was built, continuing to oversee the extensive farming operations. That included even mundane tasks such as trying to find the owner of two wayward animals that wandered onto the property late in 1822. Benton's search included placing an ad in a Leesburg newspaper called *Genius of Liberty*, headlined "Two Estrays." In it, Benton, acting as "agent of James Monroe," asked the owners of a "Brindle Bull with a white face, belly, tail and back," and a "Red & White STEER, with a white face, and short horns turned down" to "come forward, pay charges, and take them away."[41]

The phrase "pay charges," is telling in two respects. First, for years James Monroe had been in difficult financial straits, having spent large amounts of his own money during his time in France and England and as president. Second, his not inconsiderable correspondence with William Benton beginning in 1820 often deals with financial matters. In a July 18, 1820, letter to Benton, for example, written from his Highland farm in Albemarle County, Monroe proposed that Benton manage that property as well as Oak Hill—but then pointed out that he couldn't afford to increase Benton's wages if he did.[42] Two years later, in August 1822, Monroe wrote to Benton saying that because of his financial losses at Oak Hill and Highland, he wanted to reduce his farm manager's salary.[43] Early the next year, Monroe for the first time seriously considered firing his farm manager because he couldn't afford him. In an October 1823 letter from Monroe to his son-in-law Samuel Gouverneur, the President said that Benton would be leaving his employ at the end of the year.[44]

That did not happen, though, until April 1824. For the first four months of that year, Benton and Monroe were almost constantly squabbling over money matters. That months-long dispute over money led directly to the termination of their relationship—and indirectly to William Benton purchasing the property that would become Huntland nine years later.

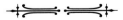

Early in 1824 George Hay—a Loudoun attorney who had married James Monroe's daughter Eliza in 1810—wrote to his father-in-law at the White House questioning the financial dealings of his manager at Oak Hill. Word got back to Oak Hill and on January 20 Benton wrote a letter to Monroe in Washington, forcefully rebutting a series of what he called Hay's "insinuations." That included an allegation that Benton had clandestinely removed two wagons' worth of goods from Oak Hill. Or, as Benton put it, that he "packed in the night... and took two waggons to carry me away."[45]

Benton explained to Monroe that wagons indeed had left the property one night, but that he used them to move a family then living on the farm to a neighbor's place. It took place at night, Benton said, because he had "but one day's notice" to make the move and that day "several persons called on me to settle their accounts." That prevented him from "packing all our items during the day," Benton said, and he was forced to finish the work in the dark. He told Monroe he defied his accuser "or any other person, to prove one dishonest or disconsiderate act in me."

Benton also brought up other Oak Hill financial matters dealing with bills that were due, a thrashing machine, oxcart wheels and blacksmith work, as well as a note at the Bank of Leesburg "for which I am your endorser." He told Monroe that he wanted all that financial business settled so that his mind "may be entirely at ease to attend my own farm and family."

The "farm" Benton mentioned was a 250-acre property known as Spring Hill north of the town of Middleburg—and near what is now Huntland—that he had purchased in 1822. Although he would not finish building the large main residence there until the early 1830s, there were other buildings on the farm where the Benton family most likely lived after they left Oak Hill in 1824.[46]

In the "six years that I have lived with you," Benton told Monroe in that January 20, 1824, letter, you have "been kind and friendly; therefore to injure you in any respects shall be the last alternative." But George Hay's allegations amounted to "an impeachment and insult," Benton said, and suggested that "all of my conduct [be] inspected either in court or by two persons chosen by you and myself," and that he preferred "the latter."

He ended the letter by saying: "I wish to hear from you without delay to know in what way it is to end."

Three months of disagreements followed, dealing almost entirely with money matters. Two local lawyers—as Benton suggested—agreed to serve as arbitrators or referees.[47]

William Benton submitted a six-part declaration to the lawyers in March stating his case. He described an arrangement dating from the end of 1818, in which Monroe agreed to pay Benton "interest on wages" and that the President "never" objected to that arrangement.

"I took for granted" that Monroe was "satisfied" with his work, Benton said. But when crops failed and "other misfortunes" hit Monroe at his Highland farm in 1823, "he wrote to me as though I ought to deduct 300 Dollars from my salary to make up for his losses in Albemarle."[48]

Benton testified that the "great charges" against him had been brought "since I left the farm & by an interested and designing man who knows that every dollar he can keep out of my pocket would go in his own." Benton said that he believed that Monroe actually owed him $705.64, "which I conceive to be my just due with interest from" the last bill he paid on December 20, 1823.

"I am sorry to find that Mr. Monroe should so far descend from the dignity of his station to make charges that he well knows [were] never intended to be made," Benton told the lawyers. As his "agent," he said, "I do not wish to be [dunned] for Mr. Monroe's debts. I wish to have the whole matter settled in such a manner as to prevent any controversy hereafter."

I "regret much," he said, "that Mr. Monroe has suffered for his name to be used for so base a purpose... I cheerfully submit the whole affair to your consideration as I well know that justice will be done to both parties."

Less than a week later James Monroe stated his case in a letter he wrote most likely to Major William Noland, a friend who was helping him make his case with the referees. Monroe wrote that he did not know "how truly" the statements made against Benton were, and that he never doubted Benton's honesty, nor "his employment of the poor in the neighborhood to work for his family & paying them with provisions." My "wish," he said, "always has been not to touch his character, in any questionable point, but always to presume favorably of him."

Still, Monroe pointed out what people had told him, such as Benton's "consumption of my provisions," and his "entertainment of company out of the line of an overseer or manager." He also cited Benton's "absence from the [property], even when on the farm." These absences, Monroe said, "are fair grounds of charges to be brought forward."

He went on to say that he had been unhappy with Benton's management for years. "I gave him many proofs of my dissatisfaction at his conduct," but, "having good wishes for him... and always hoping that hints would answer the object... and so much occupied with public duties as not to be able to look very closely unto my affairs, I bore these things much longer than I ought to have done." But, Monroe said, he was forced to act when he found "that I was likely to be ruined by bad crops, continual drafts for money, his expensive living, [and] the loss of horses [and] cattle."

Building the large house, Monroe said, "cost more than I expected considerably, but I always allowed him credit for it, as some workmen say more than deserved." Oak Hill—"that large property—has been a heavy burden on me."

Echoing Benton, Monroe concluded: "My earnest hope is that the affair be now settled finally. I shall be satisfied with whatever the arbitrators decide."[49]

The affair was settled to both parties' satisfaction early in April. The settlement ended William Benton and James Monroe's personal and business relationship.

CHAPTER TWO
The Bentons at Spring Hill and New Lisbon

"One of the best farmers and most reliable men in the State of Virginia."

—*The Southern Planter* magazine, on William Benton, July 1857

William and Sarah Benton and their children and grandchildren would live on his two farms—New Lisbon (Huntland) and Spring Hill (Benton)—from the time William Benton stopped working for James Monroe at Oak Hill in 1824 until the last days of the 19th century. U.S. Census and Loudoun County records do not clearly spell out which family members lived in which dwellings on the properties since both were recorded as a single land holding under William Benton's name until 1870.

However, other documents show that for most of that time William and Sarah (who died in 1854) lived on Spring Hill farm and that their son James Monroe Benton and next oldest, William, Jr., and their families lived at New Lisbon—sometimes called simply Lisbon— for significant periods of time from the mid-1830s until it was sold by William Benton's grandchildren in 1900. Those documents include William Benton's 1866 will and an 1870 Loudoun County Deed Book entry formally giving James Monroe Benton title to the "New Lisbon Division."[50]

A March 1827 local newspaper notice offering a horse for rent at "five dollars the season" written by Daniel Hyde—most likely William Benton's father-in-law—refers to William Benton's farm. But the ad does not spell out the exact farming property, saying only that the Benton farm is "near the Pot House, Loudoun County."[51]

The Pot House is an 18th-century building in the center of a small hamlet named for it. The two-story dwelling also contained a "Kiln House" in which local potters and bricklayers produced earthen ware and bricks.[52] The property lies at the intersection of what is now Foxcroft Road (State Route 626) and Pot House Road (Route 745). That area is sometimes called Leithtown in honor of the Leith family, which owned large portions of the surrounding land for many decades.

Both of William Benton's farms were near the Pot House. New Lisbon/Huntland is contiguous to the Pot House crossroads on the northwest corner. In fact, the main entrance to Huntland today is off Pot House Road near its junction with Foxcroft Road. The Spring Hill property is less than a mile south of the intersection on the eastern side of Pot House Rd.

The 1830 Census lists William Benton as the head of his household in the Bloomfield section of Loudoun County. It is all but certain that the entire family was living somewhere on Spring Hill farm from 1824 until Benton built the house that would become known as Huntland at New Lisbon sometime between 1833 and 1834.[53]

The only names listed on the 1830 Census are those of the heads of families. Other members of households are not listed by name, only by sex, race, and age bracket. So the Benton household, according to the Census, was made up of William Benton, along with ten other free white persons and sixteen slaves.[54]

William Benton—when he and his family were living at Spring Hill and at New Lisbon—did not confine his bricklaying and construction to the buildings on those properties. He also was responsible for other brick buildings in the area. That includes four local churches:

- The United Methodist Church in the nearby village of Unison (circa 1832)
- The parsonage at Emmanuel Episcopal Church in Middleburg (1843)
- The Middleburg Free Church, which later became Middleburg Baptist Church (1847)
- The Middleburg United Methodist Church (likely 1857)

There also is evidence that William Benton oversaw additions to what is known as the Brick House at a property called Locust Lawn. That building became part of Foxcroft School when that all-girls boarding school opened in 1914.

William Benton also presided over a substantial agricultural operation on his two Middleburg farms. *Southern Planter* magazine accurately described him in 1857 as "one of the best farmers and most reliable men in the state of Virginia."[55]

Benton was a prominent member of the Agricultural Society of Loudoun, Fauquier, Prince William and Fairfax, serving in 1827 as a member of its Committee on Crops.[56] New Lisbon and Spring Hill sat amid a booming Loudoun County agricultural economy. Agricultural activity had dominated the rural county since before the Revolutionary War. Loudoun farmers contributed so much corn and wheat to the Continental Army, in fact, that it was one of several areas in the colonies that became known as the "Breadbasket of the Revolution."[57]

Loudoun County agricultural census records clearly show extensive farming operations at New Lisbon and Spring Hill in the 1840s, '50s and '60s. By 1860, seventy percent of the farms' combined nearly 1,000 acres were under cultivation. The county valued the two farms at $52,000, among the highest in the district. The Bentons owned dozens of horses, cattle, sheep, and oxen. The county placed the value of the livestock at $5,000 in 1860—the equivalent of more than $180,000 in 2023. The milk cows that year produced 400 pounds of butter. The crops yielded more than 5,000 bushels of wheat and corn and some 200 tons of hay.[58]

Significant amounts of slave labor contributed to Benton's agricultural operations. Census slave schedules show that William Benton had sixteen enslaved people in 1830, twenty-two in 1840, and twenty in 1850. Of that 1850 number, twelve were older than eighteen, and almost certainly would have been working in the fields, tending farm animals, and helping in his bricklaying and construction business. In 1860, Benton had twenty-nine enslaved people. Twelve were men over eighteen and twelve were boys under fifteen. The household also included five enslaved women over the age of eighteen.[59]

Benton was by no means alone in Loudoun County and the Commonwealth of Virginia in his dependence upon slave labor. Virtually all landowners in the county—and throughout the state—used enslaved people to do the manual labor on their farms. James Monroe, for example, had dozens of slaves on his farms at Loudoun and Albemarle counties. One of William Benton's jobs at Oak Hill starting from early 1818, in fact, was working with enslaved people.[60] County records show that on at least one occasion, in August of 1820, acting as Monroe's agent, William Benton sold an enslaved person—in this case a man named Bill, to James Saunders.[61]

In 1860, a year before the start of the Civil War, over a quarter of Loudoun's population was made up of enslaved African Americans. The Census that year counted 5,501 slaves in Loudoun and 1,252 free Blacks out of a total population of 21,774. Virginia—the nation's fifth most populous state with nearly 1.6 million people—was home to more than 490,000 enslaved individuals.[62]

Benton family lore has it that although they owned slaves, the family did not believe in the institution of slavery. Stories passed down to the present Benton generations also say that their ancestors taught trades to all or some of the enslaved people at New Lisbon and Spring Hill, and that some were taught to read and write, which was in essence illegal in the slave-holding state of Virginia.[63] Other Benton family stories say that William Benton was against secession, even though his oldest son, James Monroe Benton, served in the Confederate Army.

The Benton family stories also have it that formerly enslaved people at New Lisbon stayed on the farm after the Civil War. One formerly enslaved family, the McQuays, settled on property close to New Lisbon and Spring Hill sometime after the war.[64]

Another handed-down story is that New Lisbon served as a refuge for runaway slaves, especially in the 1850s, and that a tunnel leading from Pot House Road to the house was used to spirit enslaved people north toward freedom—a tunnel that was part of the famed (and figurative) Underground Railroad. However, the Loudoun County Benton slave schedules show that between 1850 and 1860 the number of enslaved people the family owned stayed about the same.

The tunnel, which appears to have been installed in the 1910s, today is filled in. According to local lore, Secret Service agents did so in the 1960s as a security measure because Lyndon Johnson visited Huntland frequently when he was Vice President when the Brown Brothers owned the house.

No primary-source evidence (letters, journals, diaries, newspaper articles, or official documents) exists buttressing any of these stories. That does not necessarily mean that those tales are not true or that they do not contain grains of truth. In fact, it's likely that every story is based on some facts.[65]

When he was in his seventies William Benton became a director of the Middleburg and Plains Station Turnpike Company. The company formed in 1867, three years before Virginia was readmitted to the Union after the end of the Civil War, when the Virginia General Assembly passed a bill authorizing the company to raise funds to improve the eight-mile country road that ran from Middleburg south to the Manassas Gap Railroad station in The Plains. The idea was to turn the road into a turnpike, complete with a toll house.

That winding country road, now known as State Route 626, stretches from U.S. Route 50 (Washington Street) in the center of the Town of Middleburg to U.S. Route 55 in the center of the small town of The Plains. It begins as The Plains Road in Middleburg, then—about a mile outside of town—becomes Halfway Road, which winds its way about seven more miles to the old railroad station in The Plains.[66]

Benton also was active politically. Not long after the Whig Party formed in 1834, William Benton became a member of that relatively short-lived (1834-55) major political party, a coalition of northerners and southerners that came together united in opposition to the policies of President Andrew Jackson.[67] The Whig Party was popular in Loudoun, especially among its prominent citizens, including William Benton and his son James Monroe Benton.

In the summer of 1839 William Benton was appointed to the Loudoun County Whig Committee of Vigilance and Correspondence, along with a few dozen other prominent local men. The following year Benton became one of five members of the Whig Party committee appointed to superintend the elections in Union—later known as Unison—not far from Spring Hill and New Lisbon.

In 1840, Benton strongly supported the Whig ticket of William Henry Harrison and John Tyler ("Tippecanoe and Tyler, too") against Democratic incumbent President Martin Van Buren. Harrison had gained fame for his role in putting down an Indian uprising at the Battle of Tippecanoe in 1811. His campaign dealt with few national issues, concentrating instead on building Harrison's image as a war hero and a man of the people. As former Virginia Governor, Senator, and U.S. Secretary of War James Barbour put it at the 1839 Whig Party National Convention that nominated Harrison: The party stood for "One Presidential term; the integrity of the public servants; the safety of the public money; and the general good of the people."[68]

William Benton took part in a January 1840 Whig Party public dinner in Leesburg honoring Charles Fenton Mercer (1778-1858). A prominent lawyer who lived in the village of Aldie not far from Oak Hill, Mercer graduated from Princeton, served in the Virginia General Assembly, fought in the War of 1812, and was elected to twelve terms in the U.S. House of

Representatives. Mercer also was known as one of the founders—and strongest supporters—of the American Colonization Society. The group officially formed in Washington, D.C., in 1816. Its other founding members included James Monroe, Andrew Jackson, Daniel Webster, Henry Clay, and Francis Scott Key.[69] The ACS worked for decades to send free Blacks to a new colony in West Africa that would become the nation of Liberia.

At the Leesburg tribute dinner, William Benton offered one of many toasts to Harrison and to Mercer, a fellow Whig. Benton praised Mercer for his leadership of the Chesapeake & Ohio Canal Company, which formed in the late 1820s to build a twenty-mile canal from central Loudoun to the Potomac River at Edwards Ferry north of Leesburg. The canal, Benton said in his toast, "will be a living monument to the memory of our distinguished friend and guest, Charles Fenton Mercer, when party bickering shall be forgotten."[70]

With the demise of the Whig Party in 1855, it appears that William Benton and his son James allied themselves with the Know Nothing Party. The strangely named party had formed in 1848 as the secret Order of the Star Spangled Banner, an anti-immigrant nativist political organization, in the wake of the large number of primarily Irish and German Catholics who came to this country in the mid-1840s. The group had passwords, signs, and phrases of recognition and was open only to Protestant adults who pledged their belief in God.

The 1856 Know Nothing presidential candidate was former President Millard Fillmore, who had acceded to the nation's highest office with the death of President Zachary Taylor in 1850. Fillmore did not receive the Whig presidential nomination in 1852 and attempted a comeback as a Know Nothing in 1856. In August that year James M. Benton invited his father to attend a political event for Fillmore in Springfield in northern Virginia.

"There is to be a great Fillmore Barbeque at Backlick" next Thursday, James Benton wrote to his brother William on August 15. "Tell Father to come down on the next Wednesday on the stage to attend it. There will be some very distinguished speakers there."[71]

In 1855, William Benton received eighty acres of land from the federal government for his service in the War of 1812 in the form of a General Land Office Land Warranty or "Bounty Land." He had applied for that veterans benefit after Congress had passed a law in September 1850 granting "bounty land to certain officers and soldiers who have been engaged in the military service of the United States."[72] After attesting in 1871 that he had disposed of the eighty acres, Benton received a veterans survivor's pension of eight dollars a month, which began on February 14 of that year.[73]

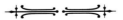

The Civil War came to Loudoun County not long after Virginia seceded from the Union in April of 1861. The county's delegates to the Virginia Secession Convention, John Janney and John A. Carter, had voted against the state leaving the Union in the final vote on April 17. In the special referendum that soon followed, however, Loudouners voted by more than two-to-one (1,626 to 726) in favor of the Ordinance of Secession. In the northern sections of Loudoun where many Quakers lived, most people voted to stay in the Union. However, in central and in Southern Loudoun where the Bentons lived, the voters heavily favored secession.[74]

The town of Middleburg, a hotbed of Confederate sentiment, was well known during the war for being the center of what became known as "Mosby's Confederacy." In the four-county area in and around Loudoun and Fauquier, CSA Col. John Singleton Mosby and his men of the 43rd Battalion of Virginia Cavalry conducted hit-and-run, guerrilla-type raids on Union troops beginning early in 1863.

One of the first battles of the Civil War took place in Loudoun County, at Ball's Bluff on October 21, 1861, along the Potomac River near Leesburg. In the next three and a half years, some of the bloodiest fighting in the war played out in Virginia in massive engagements at Manassas, Fredericksburg, Chancellorsville, The Wilderness, Spotsylvania Courthouse, Cold Harbor (outside Richmond), and Petersburg.

Countless smaller skirmishes and battles also were fought throughout the Commonwealth. That included several days of serious fighting near Spring Hill and New Lisbon during a series of cavalry, artillery, and infantry skirmishes in Unison, Mountville, and Philomont six weeks after the bloody September 17, 1862, Battle of Antietam in Maryland.[75]

On October 28, sharp skirmishing broke out not far from the Benton farms when J.E.B. Stuart's cavalrymen routed a Union force of a hundred troops in Mountville. The fighting, which included artillery barrages, continued in Aldie that day and in Philomont the following day. It intensified in Unison on October 30 and ended when the Union Army drove Stuart and his men over Ashby's Gap and into the Shenandoah Valley.

Stuart's orderly retreat was not a defeat. He had succeeded in his mission: to delay the Union Army's belated effort to attack Robert E. Lee's retreating Army of Northern Virginia after Antietam. Abraham Lincoln famously stripped Union Commanding Gen. George McClellan of his command in November in Rectortown after it took McClellan more than a month to decide to go after Lee in Virginia.

Fighting again came very close to the Benton farms in late June 1863 as Lee's Army of Northern Virginia headed north in the Shenandoah Valley on its way to what would become the three-day Battle of Gettysburg that began on July 1. Stuart and his cavalry once again played the main role in the fighting. This time Lee dispatched Stuart east of the Blue Ridge Mountains to keep the Union high command from learning that he was leading his army into Maryland and Pennsylvania.

Stuart, in one of the first battles of the Gettysburg Campaign, engaged Union forces for three blazingly hot days—June 17, 18, and 19—of sometimes intense and brutal fighting in and around the towns of Aldie, Middleburg, and Upperville. Some 21,000 men engaged in the fighting. Around 1,400 were killed, wounded or missing in action when the firing stopped on June 19. Stuart then once again retreated over the Blue Ridge Mountains at Ashby's Gap, and again accomplished what he and Lee set out to do: to keep Union generals in the dark about Lee's Army of Northern Virginia's intentions, nothing less than a second Southern invasion of the North.[76]

On the morning of June 19, the final day of the fighting in Middleburg, Union Army Brigadier Gen. John Buford arrived in town. His commanding officer, Gen. Alfred Pleasanton, ordered Buford to take two brigades of his cavalrymen—some 3,500 men—north of the center of town to try to outflank Stuart. The men wound up riding up Pot House Road where they ran into a small contingent of Confederate pickets at Benton's Bridge over Goose Creek. A brief fight ensued, then Buford moved the main body of his troops past Spring Hill and up to the Pot House crossroads adjacent to New Lisbon.

Buford, West Point Class of 1848, then found himself facing the men of the 5th Virginia Cavalry (Col. Thomas Munford's brigade) under the command of Col. Thomas L. Rosser and the 7th Virginia (Gen. William "Grumble" Jones' brigade) under Col. Thomas A. Marshall, Jr.[77] A short fight ensued, but Rosser—with orders from Stuart to delay, not fully engage, the enemy—retreated under an artillery barrage.

Fierce fighting took place later on the afternoon of June 19 in Millville when Buford's men ran into part of Col. John Chambliss' Confederate cavalry brigade. The fight there lasted until sunset when the three days of fighting ended.

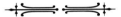

Family stories have it that during the Civil War New Lisbon "was ravaged by both Union and Confederate soldiers," as Anna Lee Jeffery Peterson, a great-great granddaughter of William Benton, put it in a 2010 letter.[18] "Soldiers, cold and hungry would take animals to slaughter for food and the silver," she wrote. "The soldiers demanded meat." On one occasion soldiers "saw a young girl cradling her pet goose in her arms in the house. An officer grabbed the goose from her arms and wrung its neck to the girl's horror. The goose was cooked and eaten by soldiers. The child was heartbroken."

On "another occasion when soldiers invaded Huntland," Anna Peterson said, an enslaved woman "lay on the couch" with all of the family's silver stowed "under her dresses and skirts." A Union officer burst into the house and confronted the woman, who "feigned advanced pregnancy." The silver "she had under her skirts was never found by the soldiers."

Peterson went on to say that during the war "slaves and livestock successfully hid in the tunnel under Huntland to avoid being stolen."

Union and Confederate troops regularly looted and burned private property during the Civil War—including in Loudoun County where both sides marched and rode through its towns, villages, and countryside throughout the entire war. Union marauding reached a peak in Loudoun in November and December 1864, when Gen. Philip Sheridan, acting on orders from Commanding Gen. U.S. Grant, ordered Maj. Gen. Wesley Merritt's 1st Cavalry Corps Division of Sheridan's Army of the Shenandoah to wreak havoc among Loudoun's Confederate-friendly populace.

In what became known as the Burning Raid of 1864, Merritt's cavalrymen spent five days rampaging throughout Loudoun's towns and rural countryside. "Orders were to burn every barn, haystack, corncrib or anything which contained supplies of forage or subsistence for troops, excepting dwelling houses, and drive of [sic] all stock of whatever description they could find," Union soldier Edwin Havens of the 7th Michigan Cavalry Regiment wrote to his sister in Michigan a few days after the troops left Loudoun.

Before long, he said, "we could see the flames rising from every hand. The boys loaded themselves with turkeys, geese, chickens, flour, bacon, apples, and everything they could lay hands on... we marched to Upperville burning everything that was not inhabited driving in a large drove of stock and capturing several bushwackers."[79]

As Havens indicated, when they were done, the Union troops had slaughtered or driven off thousands of hogs, cattle, sheep, and horses; burned down more than two hundred barns and mills; and torched tens of thousands of bushels of grain and countless hay fields.

The marauders hit the area around Middleburg and the Benton farms on November 29. "We have had a terrible day today," Catherine Hopkins Broun, who lived with her family at Sunny Bank Farm outside Middleburg, wrote in her diary that day. "Expecting every moment to be burned up. The barns all around us are on fire, burning all the hay, corn and wheat, driving off all the cattle. Sheep, hogs, &c., &c. We put all of our valuables around us, packed trunks, &c., &c."

At 8:00 that night, she wrote, "the whole heavens are illuminated by the fires burning and destroying as they go. Mr. Benton's mill and large barn filled with corn and hay looked terrific."[80]

Broun's eyewitness testimony gives credence to Anna Peterson's family story that Union troops ravaged Huntland (New Lisbon) and Spring Hill. And, as she wrote, it is all but certain that the Bentons tried to hide their enslaved people and livestock when Union soldiers were in the vicinity.

One member of the family, James Monroe Benton, joined the Confederate Army and took part in the war. On April 20, 1861, six days after Union troops lowered the American flag at Fort Sumter, William Benton's oldest son enlisted in the fight against the North. At the relatively advanced age of 41, James Benton reported for duty on July 1 as a Private in the Quartermaster Department of Company F in Capt. Edward H. Powell's 6th Regiment of Virginia Cavalry.[81] His unit was attached to the 1st Brigade of the Army of the Potomac, nicknamed "Bonham's Brigade," for its commandeering general, Milledge Luke Bonham of South Carolina. Benton's unit took part in the First Battle of Manassas on July 21.

James M. Benton, his wife Margaret A., and their five young children (Sarah, Emma, Hannah, William H., and Margaret "Maggie" Catlin, according to the 1860 U.S. Census) were living in the house at New Lisbon when the war broke out. In 1857 James Benton had purchased a 188-acre farm in Fairfax County.[82] Family lore has it that William Benton set his son "up in business near Alexandria," as James M. Benton's grandniece Grace Benton put it in 1962.[83]

A few months before James Benton enlisted in the Confederate Army, he moved his wife and children to the Fairfax County farm. Grace Benton referred to the farm as "Aspen Hill" and described it as "one of the big estates in Fairfax County between Annandale and Alexandria." For the first time in nearly three decades no members of the Benton family lived at New Lisbon.[84]

CHAPTER THREE
An Institution of Rare Merit

"He was one of the few remaining folks that connect us with the olden time."
—The *Washingtonian* newspaper on the death of William Benton, August 1881

When the James Benton family moved to Fairfax, they leased New Lisbon for the next five years to Rev. Dr. James A. Haynes, a Baptist minister in Middleburg. Rev. Haynes took the opportunity to use the house (and perhaps other structures on the farm) to operate the New Lisbon Female Institute, a boarding and day school for girls. As early as 1832, Haynes advertised for a teacher in local newspapers. The curriculum at the school included English, Latin, Greek, and French. He charged $85 for board and tuition for each five-month session. Piano lessons cost an additional $20.[85]

The Rev. Haynes boarding school followed in the footsteps of two other educational institutions at New Lisbon in the days before the state of Virginia mandated free public schools. In 1839, Benjamin Hyde Benton, a nephew of William Benton, began operating what he called the Lisbon Institution, a boarding school for boys, in a structure referred to as a "school house" on the farm. Benjamin H. Benton ran the school and served as its principal for most of the next fourteen years.

"In this institution are taught the Branches usually taught in the best English Schools," he said, in an 1845 newspaper advertisement. That included Latin and Greek; astronomy "with the use of the Globes," algebra; plane, solid, and analytical geometry; plane and spherical trigonometry; "methods of calculating and using Logarithms; and the theory and practice of Surveying, Levelling, Plotting, Mechanical and Architectural Drawing, &c, &c."[86]

The school offered "Scientific Lectures," Benjamin Benton explained, "illustrated by several hundred highly interesting experiments." The "academy," he said also had a "cabinet of Minerals, Shells, Fossils, Geological Specimens, &c." The school's workshop offered a wide range of tools, including a turning lathe so students could devote their "leisure moments" to working in "wood, iron, brass, or steel; brazing, soldering, filing, screw cutting, screw turning, casting in brass, galvanic, silvering, &c."

Tuition ranged from $12 to $32, depending on the "branches studied." Board was $68 for each ten-month session. The boarding students, however, had to supply their own towels and have all their clothes "conspicuously marked" with their names "in full." The school charged an extra $10 for laundry, and provided textbooks, "when required," at "moderate prices."

Benjamin H. Benton's Lisbon Institution proved to be a big success. Its founder and principal, who was born in 1815, gave the credit to two people, Ludwell Luckett—a descendant of the founders of the Northern Loudoun County hamlet of Lucketts—and William Benton. Luckett and his uncle "brought [the school] into existence," Benjamin H. Benton enthused in 1844 five years after it opened, "administered to its wants—nourished it in infancy—stood by it in difficulties—protected it in weakness—and forsook it not in its growth." He ended his testimonial with an effusive exhortation: "as a faithful child to devoted parents, so may it, in healthful maturity, place a crown of honor on their aged heads."[87]

Six years after Benjamin Benton wrote those words, in 1850, he turned the school over to Professor W.B. Carr, who changed its name to the New Lisbon Boarding School.[88] At first, the school, which also included day students, flourished.[89] But that institution lasted only a few years. It ceased operations sometime between 1853 and 1854. Carr went on to become principal of Leesburg Academy, a classical Latin grammar school for boys in downtown Leesburg.

However, within a year after Carr's school shut its doors, another boarding school—this one for young women—took up the educational mantle at New Lisbon. In March 1854 E.H. Greer announced that her new school, the New Lisbon Female Seminary, would begin in September in the "commodious and pleasantly located buildings formerly occupied at a Boarding House for the Male Academy."[90]

Mrs. Greer, as she referred to herself, would serve as the principal. She had started another school—the Upperville Female Institute—the year before, in September 1853, in a new brick building in the village of Upperville, just west of Middleburg that had "been fitted up, so as to make the School as pleasant as possible to those attending." In that endeavor she had one assistant, a man she referred to as Mr. S. Willson, A.B.[91]

At the new New Lisbon Female Institute in Middleburg Mrs. Greer employed Helen Benedict, who taught French, piano and organ, as well as drawing and painting. The ten-month school year of two, twenty-one week terms started that September. Board and tuition, "including lights and washing," was $75 per term. For an extra $10 each, female students could take Latin, French, music, and drawing and painting.

It appears that the two women ran the Female Institute at New Lisbon until Rev. J.A. Haynes took it over in 1861 when he leased the farm from James M. Benton.

James Anthony Haynes was born on December 13, 1822, near Bruington, a small town northeast of Richmond in Central Virginia. He was tutored at home and then attended Richmond College (also known as the Virginia Baptist Seminary, and now part of the University of Richmond) and Columbian College (now part of George Washington University), graduating in 1843. Haynes then took a job as the principal of Bruington Academy, a private prep school in his hometown. A year later, he decided to become a physician. He went back to Washington, D.C., to study at the National Medical College (now the George Washington University School of Medicine) from 1844-45. Haynes finished his medical education when he journeyed north to Pennsylvania and graduated from Jefferson Medical College in Philadelphia in 1846.[92]

Dr. Haynes practiced medicine in his hometown for two years, married Mary Mason, and moved to Berryville in Clarke County in the Northern Shenandoah Valley on the west side of the Blue Ridge Mountains. After working for seven years as a doctor in Berryville, J.A. Haynes made a big career change. He gave up medicine for religion after being ordained as a Baptist minister by the Berryville Baptist Church. In addition to his Baptist preaching, Rev. Haynes also was the principal at the Clarke Female Seminary school in Berryville—"a seminary for young ladies," as his 1880 obituary put it.[93]

In 1857, two years after he went into the ministry, Rev. Haynes helped organize the Mountain Baptist Church in Bluemont atop the Blue Ridge, and also played a role in starting a Baptist church in nearby Charles Town, West Virginia. He subsequently preached at Middleburg Baptist Church and Ebenezer Baptist in Bluemont, as well as the Long Branch Baptist Church just outside of The Plains.

While serving at the Baptist Church in Middleburg near the end of 1860 (or in early 1861) Rev. Haynes opened the second iteration of the girl's boarding school at New Lisbon. After the Civil War ended in 1865 and the James Benton family returned to New Lisbon, Haynes ran a School for Young Ladies in the town of Middleburg until 1876 as he continued his duties as Middleburg Baptist's pastor.

During the war, Union troop movements and skirmishing disrupted church life so much that by the spring of 1863 it couldn't afford to buy wood to heat its building. In April 1863, Dr. Haynes volunteered to forgo his salary, but continued to serve as the church's minister. After the war, the twenty-six formerly enslaved African-American members of the church left Middleburg Baptist and in 1867 formed Shiloh Baptist Church a few blocks away. Middleburg Baptist Church had accepted enslaved African Americans as members from its beginnings in 1847. However, they needed to have "permission forms" from their owners in order to be members and were segregated by race at all church functions, including being relegated to sitting in the balcony during services.[94]

J.A. Haynes, who received an honorary Doctor of Divinity from Richmond College in 1877, died suddenly of a heart attack at age 57 on March 30, 1880. He is buried at Sharon Cemetery adjacent to the Middleburg Baptist Church, where a group of Benton family members, including William Benton and his son James M., also lie at rest.

Benjamin Hyde Benton married Margaret Isabella Gulick on September 10, 1839.[95] He became a man of science in his early twenties, giving a lecture on the steam engine, for example, in 1840 when he was twenty-five years old. He is listed in the 1840 Census as an engineer and the head of a household in Loudoun County that included his wife and two enslaved people, a woman and a young girl.[96] In 1842, the young scientist and educator filed with the U.S. Patent Office for a new type of surveying instrument, "a quadrant with a geometrical table and a graduated arch and two limbs connected by a joint," as he put it in his application. Benj. Hyde Benton—as he often referred to himself—received that patent on December 12.[97]

In 1854 he joined with two Loudoun farmers— his brother-in-law James Hixon Gulick, and Harmon Bitzer, who also was a stonemason and builder—in a pioneering educational endeavor: the Loudoun County Agricultural Institute and Chemical Academy, the first college-level agricultural school in Virginia, and one of the first in the United States.

The school opened in March the following year in a three-and-a-half story, stucco-and-stone building that Bitzer built on a large tract of land owned by Gulick that once was part of James Monroe's Oak Hill farm in Aldie. "Professor Benton," as Benjamin H. called himself in the school's newspaper advertisements, served as principal.

"It is not to be a Manual Labor School," he pointed out, "but a course of practical instruction" in math, chemistry—including "agricultural chemistry" and soil and mineral analysis—along with "other branches useful to" business."[98]

Aside from classroom work and laboratory experiments, the students also were instructed in the "practical application of their studies to the everyday affairs of life" in the school's workshop, gardens, and fields, Benton said in 1855. To that end, Benjamin Benton taught a wide variety of subjects, including "the properties of soils, the requirements of plants, the composition of minerals, the utility of different kinds of rocks, laws of mechanical forces, calculations of the strength of materials used for building and other purposes, surveying farms, levelling water courses, layout roads, making maps, mechanical drawing, calculations, required in the construction of machinery, &c."

The students learned and lived in a serene pastoral setting, Benton pointed out in his ads. The Institute's location, he said, had "all the advantages of purity of water, salubrity of atmosphere, and beauty of scenery."[99]

He set tuition at $200 for the ten-month term, although sons of preachers and editors received a $50 per term discount. Tuition in this case included room, board, and "washing, fuel and lights." Books were for sale "at store prices," and students were expected to pay in cash. Benton also let farmers in the area know they were welcome to bring soil samples to the Institute and have the students analyze them.

Soon after opening, Benton and James Gulick shortened the school's name to the Loudoun Agricultural Institute. The first reviews were raves. Benjamin Benton "deserves much credit for his indomitable energy and perseverance in establishing an institution of such rare merit among us," S.B.T. Caldwell of Purcellville wrote in a December 1855 letter to the editor of *Country Gentleman* magazine.

Benton, the head of the school, Caldwell said, was "as well versed in Theoretical and Practical Chemistry, and its application to agriculture and every day affairs of life, as any man in our country." Caldwell characterized James Gulick as "a good practical agriculturalist" and "a gentleman raised upon the soil and familiar with the complicated details of farming."[100]

More glowing words came in an *Alexandria Gazette* report on the Institute's July 18,

1856, commencement exercises. The day "will long be remembered by those so fortunate to attend," an anonymous *Gazette* correspondent wrote. The ceremonies began at 9:00 a.m. when Benjamin Benton, speaking from a stand erected for the occasion in "a beautiful grove adjoining the Institute," welcomed the crowd and introduced several speakers. They included T.J. Kincheloe, who spoke on "the importance of Chemistry," and J.B. Conklin, who offered his insights on "the relation of Science to Commerce."

Everyone then enjoyed "an elegant" picnic "spread out in an adjoining grove." A one-hour intermission followed, during which visitors examined the school's "unsurpassed" laboratory and workshop. Then came more orations back at the grove, followed by the awarding of prizes to "the successful students."

The Institute, the writer said, "is yet in its infancy" under "the charge of Benj. Hyde Benton." The "people of his county should be proud of such an Institute in their midst. They should endeavor to cherish and maintain it... by sending their sons, so that a pure practical knowledge of things may be imparted to them that will eventually prove a blessing."[101]

The Institute, however, soon began to flounder. Most likely because of the severe worldwide economic downturn known as the Panic of 1857, tuition dropped to $80 in January 1858, and board and lodging to $50, although the school added a class in ancient and modern languages for an extra $10. Payments had to be made in advance, either in cash or an interest-bearing note.[102]

By the end of that year, Benton and Gulick had dissolved their partnership in the venture and announced they would auction off all of the property on the farm. That included the animals, farm implements, household goods and furniture, scientific instruments, and books.[103]

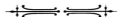

John Hixon Gulick lost his life during the Civil War on March 27, 1864. Benjamin Hyde Benton left Middleburg after the war. In the early 1870s he started another school, a Polytechnic Institute, in the small Virginia Shenandoah Valley town of New Market, the site of a notable May 15, 1864, Civil War battle. A Richmond newspaper correspondent visiting New Market in 1873 wrote glowingly of "Prof. B. Hyde Benton" and the school. Benton is "a thoroughly educated gentleman and superior practical teacher," the article noted.

The course of study at New Market Poly emulated Benton's Loudoun Institute curriculum, as it was heavy on the sciences, with lectures, laboratories, and workshops. "It is just the place where young men should go who wish for really useful, practical education in the sciences as well as literature and the classics," the correspondent gushed.

A "visit to this institution will furnish more interesting entertainment than any theatre or museum, and better instruction. This city, and the state, may well be proud of it, and all will honor themselves by sustaining and encouraging it liberally."[104]

Benjamin Benton ran the school in New Market until 1879. He next surfaced in Washington, D.C., in 1880, where he taught mathematics and civil engineering in the

Polytechnic Department of the National University at 14th Street and New York Avenue. In 1883 he gave private lessons in "practical mathematics" and business at what he called "Prof. Benton's School of Mathematics" and in surveying at "Prof. Benton's School of Engineering" in downtown Washington not far from the National University.[105]

Benjamin Hyde Benton's time in the nation's capital ended in tragedy. On June 13, 1883, a young boy stumbled across his body in a wooded area on the Virginia side of the Potomac River's old Aqueduct Bridge connecting Georgetown and Rosslyn. An empty pint flask, "which evidently contained liquor," a Washington newspaper reported, was in his pocket."[106] Next to his badly decomposed body was an "ebony cane with a silver head. On the head of the cane was engraved, 'Prof. B.H.B., March 30, 1873.'"[107]

The cause of death was not known, the newspapers said, "although it is thought that he took poison and committed suicide, "as he had several times stated that his dead body would be found sometime on the Virginia shore. The day before he left home a bottle of laudanum was taken from him, and that night he refused to eat his supper, stating that he had eaten all he ever would. He was suffering from some mental aberration."[108]

Benjamin Hyde Benton is buried at Congressional Cemetery in Washington.

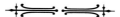

Meanwhile, in Middleburg, after the Civil War ended in 1865—at around the same time that Benjamin Hyde Benton left town—James Monroe Benton moved his family back to New Lisbon farm. His father, 81, was living close by in retirement at Spring Hill farm (now known as Benton) with his son William H. and his wife Sallie Benton and their four children, William C., Edwin, Mary, and Clara.[109]

According to the 1870 Census, three adult white women—the Census categorized people by race—also lived on Spring Hill farm. One of them, Bettie Hansbrough, 26, was listed as "teaching school." The other two—Catharine Gibb, 46, and Mary Clark, 38—were, in Census terminology, "without occupation."

James and Margaret Benton lived at New Lisbon and spent time at their second home in Fairfax. They had six children, ranging in age in 1870 from nine to twenty. Bettie, the eldest, was a schoolteacher. The others—Emma, Hannah, Margaret, William Hyde, and Alice—attended school. The household also included Cornelia Hutchinson, nineteen, the family's cook.

In 1880, a year before he died, ninety-one-year-old William Benton was still at Spring Hill, living with his son William and his family, as well as his forty-seven-year-old son Thomas H. Benton. Also on the farm: nine African Americans, all of whom were listed on the 1880 Census as "servants." The group included Charles and Robert McQuay, both twenty-six and evidently twins.

William Benton died at Spring Hill on July 28, 1881. Family stories have it that he was vigorous until his last days, and that his death resulted from injuries he sustained after falling off a horse. In one version he "fell from a colt he was breaking and died."[110]

Grace Benton wrote in 1962 that her great uncle died "after he lingered for several months with a broken hip. There was a limb over a gate that he wanted cut off. Being impatient, he took a saw and rode a young horse (colt) to do the job himself. After getting the limb off, in mounting his horse, the horse lunged and threw him."[111]

Whether or not these family stories were true, it is a fact that William Benton lived a long, fruitful life, becoming one of Loudoun County's most productive, prosperous, and well-regarded figures in the mid- and late 19th century. Benton was "one of the few remaining folks that connect us with the olden time," a laudatory obituary in the *Washingtonian* newspaper noted, "having lived in the age of all the Presidents, save Washington and the elder Adams."

＋══ ══＋

In December 1883 two wedding celebrations took place at New Lisbon. In the span of thirty-six hours James and Margaret Benton's son, William Hyde Benton, married Annie Bentley Gordon, and their daughter Margaret (Maggie) Catlin Benton married Oscar Beavers.

On Tuesday morning, December 5, a party of twenty people from Middleburg piled into buggies and made their way west to Bluemont (then called Snickersville) and over the Blue Ridge to the small hamlet of Castleman's Ferry on the Shenandoah River in Clarke County. There they joined about a hundred other guests for the 11:30 a.m. wedding of William Hyde Benton, 24, to Annie Bentley Gordon, 22, in her father's home. The Rev. F.A. Strother performed the ceremony. Then came a lavish "wedding dinner," as one observer writing in the Alexandria *Gazette* put it.[112]

Late that afternoon the newly married couple left the Gordon home and headed to New Lisbon where they would be setting up housekeeping. "Along the route," the *Gazette* reported, "the good people of Loudoun gave the bride a hearty welcome."

At 7:00 p.m. the following day, Wednesday, December 6, 1883, Oscar L. Beavers, 30, and Maggie Benton, 24, stood under "a beautiful floral bell" in the parlor at New Lisbon. A local minister then pronounced them husband and wife in front of about 150 guests. A wedding banquet followed in honor of both newly married couples. The party went on to the wee hours the next morning.

Both brides, the *Gazette* observer wrote, "and their maids were dressed in white with all the adornments which befitted the occasion."

＋══ ══＋

Just before the Civil War James Monroe Benton had taken an interest in Camp Meetings, in which Protestant churches—primarily, but not exclusively Methodists—sponsored annual days-long summer "meetings" in cotton canvas tents in rural areas during which the ministers and evangelists preached the gospel, music was played, and food and drink (but not alcohol) consumed. Folks showed up in their Sunday-best clothes. In the summer of 1859, for example, James M. Benton helped put on the Fairfax Camp Meeting. In 1872, he helped set in motion an annual Camp Meeting at New Lisbon on a twelve-acre area of the farm that would be called Benton's Woods—an institution that continued for more than two decades into the twentieth century.

In 1872 the Methodist Episcopal Church South in Leesburg[113] formed a committee to start an annual Camp Meeting "in the woods of Jas. M. Benton, esq.," as a newspaper ad put it.[114] E.C. Broun, a lay member of the congregation, chaired the committee. The advertisement urged church members and friends to "tent with us" on the New Lisbon farm beginning on Friday, August 17, 1872. Vendors (then commonly known as "sutlers") were warned not to sell their wares within a mile of the religious encampment.

All did not go well, though. On Saturday evening at around 6:30 the heavens opened up and the rain didn't stop for two days. People said it hadn't rained that heavily in Middleburg for two years. But the deluge didn't dampen the spirits of the assembled. When the ground dried, the preaching continued and members of four other local Methodist districts—Goose Creek, Bull Run, Blue Ridge, and Beaver Dam—joined the Leesburg church at the meeting.

The tents "are good," one observer reported, "and withstand the pressure of the rain. All are cheerful."[115]

A year later, on Friday, August 15, 1873, the second Benton Woods Camp Meeting, with "large and comfortable boarding tents," opened. The Rev. Henry H. Kennedy of Middleburg held the title of Preacher in Charge of the meeting, in which campers paid a dollar a day (or fifty cents a meal) to take part. Accommodations in the spacious tents were extra.[116]

For the second straight year, though, the weather turned nasty. Heavy rain fell that first night, and things stayed wet and cloudy for the next few days. On Sunday the *Loudoun Mirror* reported that "while there was a goodly number of tents on the ground, the attendance was unusually slim." Some sermons "were dispensed with," although an "able" one was "preached in one of the tents" by Rev. James Duncan."[117]

It rained again for two days during the 1874 Camp Meeting that began August 20. Nevertheless, one Methodist bishop, David Seth Doggett, and seven ministers preached throughout the week and observers counted at least seventy-five tents. Services took place inside tents on the rainy day of August 23, resulting "in one conversion and four penitents."[118] When heavy rain struck for the third straight year—this time on the last night of the 1875 Camp Meeting—a vote was taken to decide whether or not to close the meeting. The attendees voted overwhelmingly to continue.

That meeting, however, was marred by the shooting of "a negro by a white man," as a newspaper account put it, at around 7:00 on the night of August 18. "The negro, who hails from Aldie," the newspaper article said, "was suspected of selling liquor, and was arrested by constable Taylor and left in charge of a young man named Thomas Bundle, from whom he attempted to escape. Bundle fired three times, only one shot taking effect. The doctors reported the wounded man to be in a dying condition... The name of the man who was shot is Jones."[119]

Another African-American man was shot and killed by a white man—a not unheard of occurrence in the Jim Crow South—at the 1878 Benton's Woods Camp Meeting.[120]

The rain and mud—and the occasional altercation—by no means ended the Benton Woods Camp Meetings. The Leesburg Methodist Church stopped running the camps in the 1880s. But a new organization, the Loudoun Camp Meeting Association, took over and put one on annually for the next fifty years. By the early twentieth century the Benton Woods Camp meeting had become one of the most popular in the South.

As the years passed, tents grew larger and more elaborate—some even had two levels, complete with balconies—and a few wooden cottages were added. Well-known Methodist ministers and bishops from throughout the South traveled to Middleburg to preach and take part in the festivities. By 1898, the Benton Woods Camp Meeting area featured an enormous tabernacle tent that seated 2,000 people for services. At least 3,000 showed up to take part in the last day of that year's meeting.[121]

The numbers continue to increase in the early 1900s. Some 6,000 flocked to the twelve-day 1904 meeting, which began on Friday, August 12.[122] Aside from daily services in the big tent, the meeting that year included a Women's Christian Temperance Union convention, along with a reunion of Confederate Civil War veterans. The veterans heard two lectures, on the lives of CSA Generals Robert E. Lee and Stonewall Jackson. The Benton Woods camp, a *Baltimore Sun* reporter said, "is the largest in Northern Virginia and one of the few survivals of the old-time Methodist camp-meeting."[123]

Soon the camp added an Old Soldiers Day as more and more Confederate veterans and their descendants—members of local camps (chapters) of the recently formed Sons of Confederate Veterans and the United Daughters of the Confederacy[124]—flocked to the meetings. At the 1907 meeting, a large number of SCV and UDC camps took part in what one observer called an "elaborate programme, consisting of music and addresses." [125] In 1909, the *Richmond Times-Dispatch* reported that as many as 10,000 people from "all sections of the country and surrounding places" showed up for Old Confederate Soldiers Day festivities at [the camp meeting at] Benton Woods.[126]

The organizers built a new tabernacle tent seating 3,000 in time for the 1911 camp meeting. That gathering featured a day devoted to the temperance movement led by the Anti-Saloon League and the Women's Christian Temperance Union, along with another big Old Soldiers Day commemoration on a Tuesday.

The 1911 meeting may have marked the Benton's Woods Camp Meeting's apogee. By the time Prohibition began in 1920, attendance had declined significantly. The last one took place in 1928. In 1930, the new owners of Huntland, Gwendolyn and William Robinson, had the 3,000-seat tabernacle tent torn down and they dismantled every other structure in the woods. The Robinsons sold the lumber from the structures to a carpenter in Upperville for $500.[127]

Today—in 2023—there are no above-ground traces of the Benton's Woods Camp Meeting on the Huntland property.

James Monroe Benton, who inherited New Lisbon following his father's death in 1881, died on July 13, 1895. The property then went to his six adult children. Three years later, in August 1898, the children of J.M. Benton sold the New Lisbon property to their youngest sibling, Alice, who was born in 1861 and had married C. Webb Monroe. The price for the house and its 272 acres: $3,627.[128] Less than two years later, in 1900, Alice and Webb Monroe sold New Lisbon to Annie Gregg Leith for $8,161.[129]

Anne (Annie) Gregg was born in 1837. She married Theodoric Bryant Leith, a farmer who was four years her senior, most likely around 1866. They had two sons, Walter and Robert, and six daughters before Theodoric Leith died in 1896.[130] Walter Leith, described in the 1910 Census as a farmer, ran the farming operations at New Lisbon for his mother during the twelve years that the widowed Annie Leith and her family lived there.

According to 1899 insurance documents, the brick main house was insured for $3,000. Her possessions, including a piano, were valued at $375. Other structures on the property included a barn with a shed extension, a corn house, and a tenant house. The property was described as being in "Leithtown, known as New Lisbon."[131]

On New Year's Day 1912, seventy-four-year-old Annie Leith sold the farm to Joseph Brown Thomas—the New York City renaissance man who in two years would turn New Lisbon into Huntland and extensively and expensively remodel the William Benton house, and transform the farm into one of the most lavish, extensive fox-hunting facilities in the nation, if not the world.

CHAPTER FOUR
A Pretty Cocky Little Ostrich

"Mr. Thomas was a man of gifted imagination and towering personality."

—Horace A. Laffaye, *Polo in the United States: A History*

They called Joseph Thomas' grandfather "Captain Thomas." Not for any military command he had, but for his international maritime exploits captaining merchant ships.

Captain Joseph Brown Thomas was born on June 23, 1811, in Pittston, Maine, a small town on the Kennebec River south of Augusta, the son of Samuel and Betsey Brown Thomas. His grandfather, also named Samuel Thomas, a farmer, fought in the Continental Army in the Revolutionary War at the Battle of Bunker Hill, family lore has it.[132]

Captain Thomas grew up in Pittston, a shipbuilding and seafaring town. He followed local tradition and left home at fourteen to seek his fortune at sea. He soon did just that. By the time Joseph Brown Thomas hit his mid-twenties, he had command of a merchant ship. In the next twenty-five years he captained and built a fleet of his own ships.

The thirty-nine-year-old Captain struck gold (so to speak) in 1850, when he sailed his ship, the *Thomas Watson*, to San Francisco, and promptly unloaded the cargo for a huge profit. Thomas took those proceeds and left the seafaring life behind to settle in the booming Gold Rush city. He started an extremely successful shipping business and soon expanded into banking and real estate. A strong supporter of the Union during the Civil War, Joseph Thomas helped found the Bank of California in 1864 and headed the San Francisco Board of Trade for many years.

In 1866, the year after the Civil War ended, Joseph B. Thomas decided to spend a good chunk of the money he'd made. He left California, treating his wife Martha and his sons Joseph B. Jr., 17, and Washington B., 9, to a two-year European tour. The Thomas family toured the Continent, and returned to the United States in 1868—but not to San Francisco. Captain Thomas decided to relocate back to New England, and moved the family into a huge house he bought in the Charlestown section of Boston.

In 1870, Joseph B. Thomas started another business—one that would dwarf his other commercial ventures and elevate him (and later his two sons)—into Gilded Age millionaire status. With a group of five other entrepreneurs he went into the lucrative sugar-refining business, starting the Standard Sugar Refinery of Boston Corporation. The men capitalized their venture with $150,000. Two years later, with J.B. Thomas as its president, the company was worth $1 million.[133]

Standard Sugar Refinery of Boston bought up other local sugar refineries, including Boston Sugar Refinery, which had been around since the mid-1830s, and became one of the giants of the sugar industry in the United States, rivaling large refineries in Brooklyn, Philadelphia, Baltimore, and in Louisiana and California.[134] In 1887, Thomas merged his company into the American Sugar Refining Company, later known as the Sugar Trust. By 1890, with Captain Thomas as its vice president, American Sugar controlled nearly all of the nation's sugar production and had net assets of nearly $12 million.[135]

Captain Joseph B. Thomas died of heart failure after a bout of pneumonia on January 13, 1891, at age 79, at his home in Boston. His "years upon the sea were those of the best days of American ships and American sailors," as his obituary the next day in *The Boston Post* put it, "and he belonged to that class of sea captains which is now nearly extinct."

His assets, the *Post* reported, "it is supposed, will inventory between $25 and $30 million."[136]

The Captain's two sons inherited the bulk of their father's vast wealth. His younger son, Washington Butcher Thomas, who was thirty-three when his father died, would take a leading role in American Sugar, rising to become its president and board chairman in 1911.

Washington B. Thomas was born on August 14, 1857, in his father's hometown, Pittston, Maine.[137] After graduating from Williston Seminary prep school in Northampton, Massachusetts, (now Williston Northampton School), he started college at Harvard in 1875. Washington B. went to work in his father's Boston refinery in 1879, the year he graduated from Harvard. That first job, in the sales department, was in "a very modest and humble capacity," Washington Thomas said in 1911.[138]

In the summer of 1883, four years after going to work at Standard Sugar, Washington Thomas married Caroline Wadleigh, the daughter of Bainbridge Wadleigh, a lawyer and one-term Republican U.S. Senator from New Hampshire. After his father's death in 1891, Washington B. Thomas took control of Standard Sugar, which had been part of the American Sugar conglomerate for four years. In 1893, he moved into a seat on American Sugar's Board of Directors. He soon became a driving force in American Sugar—and began reaping significant financial rewards.[139]

He served as the company's vice president in 1900. After the death of American Sugar's founder, Henry O. Havemeyer, in 1907, Washington Thomas—"one of the best-known citizens of Boston," according to *The New York Times*[140]—became its largest stockholder.[141] He went on to serve as president of American Sugar from 1908-1911, then was tapped to be Chairman of the Board at a salary of $25,000 a year—roughly equivalent to $750,000 in 2023.[142]

An avid golfer and sailor, Washington B. Thomas headed the United States Golf Association (the sport's governing body) in 1899 and 1900 and the Eastern Yacht Club in Marblehead, Massachusetts, the home of his auxiliary schooner *Arbella*, in 1909.[143] He and his wife Caroline divided their time between his home in Boston, their summer homes in Beverly and Manchester-By-The-Sea, Massachusetts, and New York in the first three decades of the twentieth century—when they were not traveling the globe.

"I was abroad for four months in the spring of 1905," W.B. Thomas wrote in 1914, "for the same period in 1907 and for two months in the autumn of 1911." More than a few ocean-liner crossings followed in the next fifteen years.

Washington B. Thomas died in Boston on May 29, 1929, following what was described as a "brief illness." The headline of his brief obituary in one Washington newspaper was "Capitalist Dead at 72."[145]

Washington Butcher Thomas' older brother, Joseph Brown Thomas, Jr., was forty-one when their father Captain Thomas had died in 1891. An 1870 graduate of Wesleyan University in Middletown, Connecticut, Joseph Jr. went to work in his father's sugar-refining business right out of college, as his younger brother would do nine years later. But Joseph B. Thomas, Jr. didn't start in sales as Washington B. Thomas did. He began his business career as the superintendent of the Standard Sugar Refinery, a job he would hold for eleven years. In 1890 he took over as president.

On April 14, 1875, Joseph B., Jr. married Anna Hill, who was born in New York and grew up in South Norwalk, Connecticut. Four years later the couple moved into a spacious, four-story brick home on Marlborough Street in Boston that his father had bought. The Thomas family employed four household workers: a Canadian cook; two maids, and a coachman.[146] Anna Thomas—whose great grandfather, Ebenezer Hill of Fairfield, Connecticut, served in the Revolutionary War—gave birth to her first child on January 3, 1879. They gave him the same name as his father and grandfather: Joseph Brown Thomas.

In 1891, the year his father died and his younger brother Washington took over Standard Sugar, Joseph B. Thomas, Jr., then in his early fifties, took an early retirement and moved to New York City with his wife and twelve-year-old son Joe. They soon began living a life of leisure in a large, opulent apartment at the up-scale Savoy Hotel, which opened with great fanfare in June of 1892 at Fifth Avenue and 59th Street.

The Savoy's "magnificently furnished and decorated rooms," *The New York Times* reported, included a banquet hall illuminated by 800 bronze figures in niches "carrying incandescent electric lights." A corner suite was an "exact reproduction" of Marie Antoinette's apartment in the Petit Trianon chateau at Versailles. Three of the large public rooms on the second floor were decorated in the style of Louis XVI, and one "in the style of the First Empire."

Mr. and Mrs. Joseph B. Thomas' names regularly appeared in the society pages of the New York newspapers, attending performances at the Metropolitan Opera House, hosting events at the famed Delmonico's steakhouse, and taking part in countless other private social functions.[147] He belonged to the University, New York Yacht, Seawanhaka Corinthian Yacht, and other clubs. In 1897, he was elected to the Board of Directors of St. Andrew's Golf Club in Westchester County and became Board president in 1900.

The couple often traveled abroad and had a summer place in Jamestown, Rhode Island. Joseph B. Thomas also was a "keen fisherman," who was known to journey to Newfoundland for salmon fishing,[148] and who made an annual summertime visit to a rustic but luxurious "sporting camp" at Moosehead Lake in Maine.[149]

Joseph Brown Thomas, Jr., died of cancer at his apartment in the Savoy Hotel on August 4, 1909, at age sixty. He left behind his wife Anna—who died at age sixty-nine in 1916—and his two sons:

Ralph Hill Thomas, who was born in Boston on January 6, 1882.

And his older brother, Joseph Brown Thomas, whom friends and family called Joe.

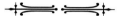

Joe Thomas—who inherited a $100,000 annual trust fund when his father died—lived a life of privilege from the day he came into this world. He grew up in luxury at the Thomas home in Boston, the family's country place in Rhode Island, and later in his parents' lavish apartment in the Savoy in Manhattan.[150] When he was seven he sat for a portrait by the noted Scottish artist Harrington Mann. Accounts of his early schooling differ,[151] but it's all but certain that he attended the Berkeley School in New York. A private, all-boys prep high school in Manhattan, it was founded in 1880 by the Harvard classics scholar John S. White. Next stop for Joe Thomas: Yale, where he thrived in and out of the classroom for four years.

Before that, in the summer of 1899, Joe Thomas and his younger brother Ralph took up competitive sailing at their father's yacht club at Oyster Bay on Long Island Sound. According to one report, Joe first crewed on a yacht called the *Constance* that took part in the International Challenge Cup at Lake St. Louis, Missouri, that summer. After that, Joe and his brother "with the *Paprika*, won eighteen races out of nineteen starts."[152]

Joe made the track team in his freshman year at Yale, ran hurdles for four years, and served as the team captain in his 1902-03 senior year. A highlight: coming in third in the 220-yard hurdle race in the 1903 national Intercollegiate Meet.[153] Another: inviting the Yale track team to train for the 1901 International Games with teams from Oxford and Cambridge universities at a farm his family had acquired in Simsbury, Connecticut.[154] A member of the Yale Polo Club, Joe arranged to have more than twenty new Yale Polo Club ponies boarded at the Simsbury farm in the spring of his senior year.[155]

Joe Thomas' other collegiate extracurricular activities included managing the university's many musical organizations (the Banjo, Mandolin, and freshman Glee Clubs, among others), co-chairing the Junior Promenade Committee (a dance held during prom week), serving as Rear Commodore of the Yale Corinthian Yacht Club, and being elected to Yale's exclusive Scroll and Key secret society.

He had one rough patch during his four years at Yale. In the summer between his junior and senior years Joe Thomas came down with typhoid fever. When school started in September it was not certain he was well enough to return to classes. But he persevered, recovered, and reclaimed his captaincy of the track team by the spring. No surprise that a few months later Joseph B. Thomas was voted Hardest Worker of the Yale Class of 1903.[156]

When he graduated in the spring of 1903, Joe Thomas—tall (six feet, one) handsome, athletic, smart, ambitious, adventurous, wealthy, and well-connected—immediately set about pursuing his passions: polo, yachting, dog breeding, international travel, fox hunting, business, and the opposite sex—among other things. When asked three years later what his thoughts centered on as he pondered what to do after graduation, Joe wrote, half tongue in cheek:

"Once upon a time in the dark ages, about the year 1903, there flutter[ed] forth from Alma Mater's protecting wings, a pretty cocky little ostrich who has ever since been rushing around in an attempt to capture those evasive will o' the wisps, Fame and Fortune."[157]

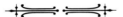

Joe Thomas would achieve much in his life, including some fame and continued fortune. It could have involved—of all things—breeding and showing chickens. In 1899, while still an undergraduate at Yale, at the family country place in Connecticut Joe Thomas began raising a rare breed called the Houdan, which had been developed in France and brought to the United States in the 1860s. Joe entered one of his Houdan hens that year in the eleventh annual New York Poultry and Pigeon Association Exhibit in New York's Madison Square Garden—and came home with a first-place ribbon.[158]

Although he showed up at Madison Square Garden to judge the Houdan classes at the 1906 poultry show, Joe soon lost interest in chickens. He then became fascinated with a rare breed of another animal, the Russian Wolfhound. Also known as the Borzoi (meaning "fast" in Russian), these large, greyhound-like hunting dogs had been fixtures among the Tsarist Russian nobility since the 17th century.

The "wolf dogs of the Muscovites," one dog expert enthused in 1931, "are magnificent creatures" with "speed, great strength and killing powers."[159]

The first Borzois came to this country in the late 1880s. Joe bought several of them while he was in college. But he became convinced they were inferior specimens and decided to go to Europe to bring a superior kind of Borzoi known as the "ancient type" to the U.S. and breed them at the farm in Connecticut. Those dogs were a new type of Borzoi bred in the early 1880s to combine "great beauty, physical stamina, swiftness, and tenacity."[160] They were popularized by the Russian Grand Duke Nicholas Nikolaevich (1856-1929), a cousin of Tsar Nicholas II (another Borzoi fancier), and a committed hunter and Borzoi breeder.[161]

In 1903, having "read everything I could find on the subject," Joe later wrote, "I came to the conclusion that in America there were no hounds that fulfilled the requirements of the Russian standard." He also noted his disappointment with "the repeated failure of the breed to reproduce itself with any kind of regularity." He was "so much perplexed in regard to this matter," he said, that on July 1, 1903, the freshly minted Yale graduate boarded an ocean liner and headed off to England to search for the perfect Borzoi.[162]

After spending a couple of weeks "visiting every prominent breeder in England," Joe decided he had to go to Russia. By early August he was in St. Petersburg, only to be disappointed by what he saw at the Imperial Kennels. That led to a trip to Moscow, then a wild ride "across the trail of the steppes" in a carriage drawn by three horses to pay a visit to two Borzoi kennels in southern Russia, including one on the 25,000-acre Woronzova estate where the Grand Duke bred his ancient-type Borzois. His kennel contained "the finest collection of dogs of any one breed we have ever seen," Joe Thomas said, "a hundred grown hounds, all stamped with the mark of the 'ancient type.'"

He bought four "ancient-type" Borzois, including a dog that became a future champion, Bistri of Perchina, and Sorva of Woronzova, "said to be the finest wolfhound outside Russia and valued at $3,000," *The New York Times* reported.[163] Thomas shipped the dogs to this country aboard a steamer that sailed from Hamburg to New York.[164] He then brought the dogs to Connecticut, where he and two partners set up an extensive, 4,000-square-foot breeding operation called Valley Farm Kennels a mile from the farm at Simsbury.[165]

Joe returned to Russia in 1904, this time with his brother Ralph, where they hunted "the hare, the fox, and the wolf" with the Grand Duke at "his enormous estate of Perchina," Joe wrote. He made a third trip in 1911, during which he bought two more dogs to bring home.

The next year Joe Thomas published *Observations on Borzoi: Called in America Russian Wolfhounds: In a Series of Letters to a Friend*, his first book. The short book "gives a striking picture" of Borzois, "with more accurate historical data of [their] Russian environment than has probably appeared elsewhere," Henry T. Allen wrote in the book's Introduction.[166]

Joe Thomas, Allen said, "has expended more time and energy in fixing a correct type of this picturesque hound than any American, and probably more than anyone in Europe, barring a very few in Russia. The results achieved by him in popularizing and developing the Borzoi in the United States solely for the love of the hound and for sport, the large numbers of fine specimens imported and bred by him, his travels in Russia... clearly make the writer of this book an authority on the subject."

On November 3, 1903, Joe met with other Borzoi boosters in New York and came up with guidelines for a new Russian Wolfhound "Specialty Club for the amelioration of the breed," as he put it in his book. On February 10, 1904, during the annual Westminster Kennel Club show at Madison Square Garden, the Russian Wolfhound Club of America was formally organized with Joe as Secretary-Treasurer.[167] By October he had become the club's president.

Beginning in 1904, Thomas' Valley Farm began produced a string of show-winning Borzois. By 1906, they had some 300 dogs, and took home ribbons at the Westminster Kennel Club and other dog shows for many years. As one show dog expert put it: Joe Thomas "dominated the show rings."[168]

He was not shy about talking up the breed—and his kennel. Soon after coming home from his first trip, for example, he gave a talk at the Simsbury Free Library called "Country

Life in Russia."[169] Never hesitant to travel, Joe and six other men made a "sporting trip" to Texas in December 1906, arriving in San Antonio by train with eleven horses and twenty of his Russian Wolfhounds. They proceeded to cross the state "coursing jackrabbits and racing their ponies against any and all ranch ponies," one newspaper correspondent wrote. They also used their dogs to hunt mountain lions, coyotes, and timber wolves. The expedition, the newspaper said, was "a novel one, as nothing like it has ever been attempted before."[170]

In January 1907, Joe Thomas announced that he would open a Russian Wolfhound kennel in Gillette, Wyoming, and that thirty of his dogs would compete in the Westminster Kennel Club show the following February. The dogs would make the journey from Connecticut to New York City by train, he said, and would "occupy an entire car." [171]

Although he remained interested in dogs for the rest of his life, Joe Thomas soon tired of Borzois and sold his kennel to his partners a few years after his hounds competed at Westminster in 1908. "Thomas all but disappeared from the breed," one observer noted, "appearing only once more in Borzoi circles, this to judge the breed at the 1936 Westminster Kennel Club show."[172]

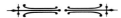

Even during the years he devoted himself to Borzois, Joe Thomas hardly ignored his other passions. In 1905, for example, he became one of the twenty-six founders of the Dalmatian Club of America, which had its headquarters in Philadelphia.

Spending most of his time at Simsbury—he also rented office space in New York City at 1 Madison Avenue, near the Flatiron Building, and later on Wall Street[173]—Joe had memberships in the Taconic Polo Club in Hartford and the Hartford Country Club, which fielded a polo team. In 1909, he helped reorganize the Point Judith Country Club's Polo Club in Narragansett, Rhode Island. That same year he and another member of the Taconic Polo Club took a trip to "the West," and came home with, a Connecticut newspaper reported, "a fine string" of polo ponies, including nineteen that Joe Thomas bought.[174]

The first United States Open Polo Championship, in 1904, took place in the Bronx. It was Joe's idea. A tournament "open to all, the Open Championship, arose in the fertile mind of Joseph B. Thomas," the polo historian Horace Laffaye wrote. "Mr. Thomas was a man of gifted imagination and towering personality."[175] The tournament, now considered the most prestigious in the U.S., was not played again until 1910, after which Joe presented the first U.S. Open Polo Championship perpetual trophy to the winning team.

Joe Thomas had a very full social life in his post-undergraduate years. In June 1906 he threw a giant party at the farm in Simsbury. In what *The Hartford Currant* called "undoubtedly the most unusual private entertainment ever given in this state," Joe dreamed up an elaborate cowboys-and-Indian-themed shindig. The invitation read: "A stupendous Pow Wow and Potlash will be holden [*sic*] near the Tepee of Chief Joseph under the Totem of the Great White Dog in the Vale of Tuxia know to the Whites as Simsbury, an hour before the Sinking of the Sun."[176]

That cheeky invitation went on to ask his young polo and horse show friends to come in costume—and they did. Joe (AKA "Chief Joseph") greeted them at the farm's gate decked out in war paint and feathers astride a pony. The "coming of each guest was announced by the chief," a New York newspaper reporter noted, "who rode pell-mell up the hill to the clubhouse, firing his rifle and shouting an Indian welcome."[177] Outside the clubhouse Joe created a mock Indian village.

The party also featured an appearance by Thunder Cloud, billed as "a full blooded Sioux Indian," a covered wagon drawn by a "yoke of oxen," a mock cowboys vs. Indians battle, pony races, and a feast of clams, oysters, lobsters, crabs, sweet and white potatoes, corn on the cob, chicken, and bluefish steamed "in true clambake style." The evening ended with Thunder Cloud leading a ghost dance around a bonfire.

Later that year, in September, Joe—the vice president of the Simsbury Agricultural Society—produced an elaborate "pastoral ball" in a newly dedicated exhibition hall at the local fairgrounds. The evening started with fireworks, then a "grand march" lead by Joe himself before the dancing began to the strains of the Foot Guard Orchestra of Hartford.

"Interest in the fair had practically died out when Mr. Thomas came to Simsbury," a speaker announced to the crowd during a dancing lull. But Joe "had revived the interest and by his energy had created a greater interest than ever before." He called for three cheers for "Our Joe." They "were heartily given."[178]

Joe's energy and accomplishments did not go unnoticed by local Republican Party officials. A party caucus nominated him for a seat in the Connecticut House of Representatives three days before the November 6, 1906, elections. Joe won, but kept a low profile in Hartford, sitting on just two committees: Roads, Bridges, and Rivers, and Assignment of Seats. He was the prime sponsor of just one bill. It dealt with—no surprise—dogs.[179]

+≈·≈+

Joe Thomas left Connecticut politics behind in the spring of 1910—less than a year after his father's death—and bought two mid-19th-century brownstones on the same block in New York City. But not just any block. Joe chose East 19th Street between 3rd Avenue and Irving Place near Gramercy Park. When Joe came on the scene, the architect Frederick Sterner had recently moved into one of the block's brownstones and had extensively and extravagantly remodeled it.

Sterner, one architectural journalist wrote, "sparked a wave of renovations on the block. Within a few years, several rebuilders changed the East 19th Street block into one of tinted windows, iron balconies, Arts and Crafts style tilework, flower boxes and projecting tile roofs, mostly in the Mediterranean style..."[180] Joe hired Sterner to redo his buildings, and soon the street became known as "Block Beautiful."

Joe Thomas converted one of the buildings (132 E. 19th St.) he bought on the block—a large, three-story structure—into an apartment house.[181] He kept the second house, an ornate, five-story, 19th century Jacobean-style building, and had Sterner (who lived directly

36

across the street) go to work on it. Joe shared that dwelling (135 E. 19th St.) with his recently widowed mother. It had six bedrooms, multi-colored brick on the outside, gargoyles on the roof, a huge living room known as "the Italian Room" featuring an enormous stone fireplace, and an extensive wine cellar.

The eccentric artist, muralist, and screen painter Robert Winthrop Chanler moved into a Sterner-remodeled double townhouse on the block in 1911. He made that building—which he dubbed "The House of Fantasy"—into his home and studio. Not surprisingly, Joe Thomas befriended his neighbor and hired him to help decorate his house. Chanler came up with a series of ornate, Chinese-like screens adorned with polo scenes for Joe's den.[182]

The beautiful, artsy block of East 19th Street was a fitting home for the fashionable, art-loving, polo-playing, fox-hunting socialite Joe Thomas. Not long after he moved in, Joe "invited his friends to see two pre-Elizabethan miracle plays at his residence" put on by the American Dramatic Guild, *Town & Country* reported in a page featuring a reproduction of a 1908 painting of Joe by the noted society portrait artist Robert MacCameron.[183]

In 1911, not long after he moved to New York City, Joe Thomas turned his eyes south, to the rolling hills of the Northern Virginia Piedmont, soon to be known as Hunt Country. Joe had done some fox hunting in Connecticut and elsewhere; had single-mindedly bred and popularized the Russian Wolfhound in the U.S.; and had just put his architectural stamp on an up-scale property in New York City. Now he was about to do nearly the same things—but on a much larger scale—in Virginia.

On January 1, 1912, Joseph B. Thomas bought the New Lisbon house and its surrounding 272-plus acres for $20,000 from Annie Leith. He promptly changed the property's name to Huntland, and almost immediately set about restoring William Benton's 1834 house and creating what would soon become one of the most extensive and elaborate foxhunting facilities in the nation—if not the world.

CHAPTER FIVE
A Mecca for Horsemen and Huntsman

If "there is a 'Hound Haven' on earth, it is at Huntland."

—Bit and Spur, magazine May 1913

When Joe Thomas bought Huntland in 1912, he immediately set about redesigning the sturdy Federal-style brick home and its surrounding farm into an English estate dedicated to foxhunting and to the science of developing and breeding quality foxhounds. He came to the right place. Foxhunting and other types of equestrian activities had long been a part of life throughout Virginia, especially in the Middleburg area of the state in western Loudoun and northern Fauquier counties.

Col. Richard Henry Dulany—widely recognized as the pioneering figure in foxhunting in the Northern Virginia Piedmont[184]—bred fox hounds as a teenager in the 1830s on his family property, Welbourne, located between Upperville and Middleburg. He went on to found one of the first foxhunting clubs in the country, the Piedmont Fox Hounds, in 1840.[185]

Foxhunting had "from time immemorial" been the "chief sport" in Loudoun County, the popular author and journalist Walter A. Dyer only slightly exaggerated in a 1908 *Country Life in America* magazine article on the subject. "Originally," Dyer pointed out, "the hunt was a very informal affair and sometimes a rather wild one, but within recent years the more orderly English form of fox-hunting has been adapted to Loudoun conditions, though none of the good local traditions have been destroyed."[186]

Foxhunting "is indigenous" to Virginia, *Town and Country* magazine reported in 1912. The magazine noted that virtually every farmer in the state owned a few foxhounds— meaning there were "literally thousands" of them in Virginia; that all farm owners bred horses; and that most Virginia landowners hunted "in one fashion or another." Foxhunting in Virginia, the article concluded, "is the heritage of all, like air and water."[187]

A noted early-twentieth-century journalist, Mayme Ober Peak, wrote a valentine to fox hunting in the Middleburg-Upperville area in a long 1920 *Spur* magazine article. The Northern Virginia Piedmont, she wrote, "has always been a hunt-loving section, with the best-bred foxhounds in the country." The area's "fame as a hunting center—meaning, of course—organized hunting—only dates back about ten years" when "it became a Mecca for horsemen and huntsmen."[188]

Middleburg became that mecca not long after what Ober Peak described as "a celebrated trial meet" took place in Upperville in 1905, to test "the stamina of the American and English breeds of foxhounds." That celebrated meet did much more than that. Later known as the Great Hound Match, the much-ballyhooed event is widely credited with sparking an influx of new, well-heeled foxhunters to the Middleburg area, and in doing so turned its rolling hills, open pastures, stone walls, and wooden fences into the nation's foxhunting center—soon to become known as "Hunt Country."[189]

The Great Hound Match took place during the peak of fox-hunting season, from November 1-15, 1905. It pitted A. Henry Higginson and his pack of English hounds against Harry Worcester Smith and his American-bred foxhounds. The two Massachusetts foxhunters made a thousand-dollar bet on which pack would perform the best and thereby be deemed the superior breed of foxhound. After two weeks of hunting, a panel of judges ruled that the American hounds outperformed Higginson's English foxhounds. But the wager and the judges' verdict receded in importance as the two-week event brought international media attention, virtually all of it rhapsodizing about the scenic beauty of the area and its perfect fox-hunting attributes.

The Match—with Welbourne as Ground Zero—attracted "prominent sportsmen from all parts of the country, who were struck by the beauty of the Blue Ridge section and its special adaptation to the hunt," Ober Peak wrote. She extolled the area's "wide, rolling pastures separated by low stone fences," leaving "plenty of space between for galloping." Ditches had "firm banks for take-off and landing," she pointed out. The "innumerable mountain streams," along with "the wealth of cover" and the "lack of obstacles such as high fences, barbed wire and posted land," she said, "all made this an unsurpassed hunting ground."

When the event ended, the area's "sporting possibility" became "a sporting reputation," as the historian Andrew C. Baker aptly put it. In the following decades, he said, "wealthy northerners" bought "large tracts of land, turning the region into one of the wealthiest in the country."[190] Aside from the pleasing landscape, the northern newcomers also were attracted to Hunt Country by the fact that the more temperate climate in Northern Virginia usually allowed foxhunting from the fall through the spring, and that local farmers and landowners in general were fine with fox hunters galloping across their farms and fields.

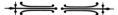

The Piedmont Fox Hounds received official recognition from the National Steeplechase and Hunt Association, the sport's governing body, in 1904, two years before Col. Dulany's death.[191] Harry Worcester Smith then became its first officially recognized Master of Fox Hounds.

The following year, 1905, the five-year-old Orange County Hunt moved from Orange County, New York, about seventy-five miles north of New York City, to new facilities in the southern portion of Hunt Country, in The Plains. John R. Townsend was chosen the Orange County Hunt's Master of Hounds. Following a dispute over hunting territory, Townsend and several other men formed the Middleburg Hunt in 1906 with a ten-by-fifteen-mile foxhunting territory lying primarily north and east of the town of Middleburg.

Joe Thomas burst upon the Hunt Country fox-hunting scene a few years before he purchased New Lisbon Farm. The National Sporting Library reports that he made an appearance at the 1905 Great Hound Match in the company of Harry Worcester Smith.[192] It appears that Joe made a return trip in 1908 or 1909. He was among the horse-loving "wealthy northerners" who in 1911—the year that he decided to buy New Lisbon—checked into what was billed as a "hunting inn" that Rosalie Haxall Noland had begun operating in 1908 at her Burrland Farm between Middleburg and The Plains.[193] Visitors could rent the furnished, twelve-room house and its horse stables for $150 a month or $700 for six months.[194]

"This handsome residence, furnished with all modern conveniences and ample stable accommodations can be leased for the hunting season or winter," a Burrland 1910 ad proclaimed. "It is within reach of the Loudoun and Warrenton Hunts and in the heart of the country over by the Piedmont and Orange Co., N.Y., hounds."[195] Visitors could bring their own horses or rent either fox-hunting or pleasure-riding horses from Noland at the "only real 'hunting inn' in the United States," as *Bit and Spur* magazine put it in 1912.[196]

Joe Thomas evidently found the Burrland operation so accommodating that sometime in 1912 he leased the place while he was turning New Lisbon into Huntland on the other side of Middleburg. The entrepreneurial Thomas even made an agreement with Rosalie Noland to take over the operations at the Burrland country inn for a few months in the fall of 1912.[197]

Always a peripatetic type, Joe, who was 33, also spent considerable amounts of time that year traveling. He was among "the Long Island smart set," the *New York Times* reported, who frequented the exclusive Piping Rock Club, a country club that had opened the previous year on Long Island's North Shore.[198] Piping Rock featured an eighteen-hole golf course and extensive horse show grounds. Joe spent a good part of the summer of 1912 playing polo at Point Judith Polo Club in Narragansett, Rhode Island. He stayed in a rented, up-scale cottage at Narragansett Pier.[199]

Aside from riding and socializing in New York and Rhode Island that year—not to mention starting to build what soon would become a renowned world-class fox-hunting facility at Huntland—Joe Thomas decided that the American Kennel Club, which was founded in 1884 as the governing body of the nation's dog clubs, needed a member club devoted to foxhounds. So he convened a meeting on March 9, 1912, at Burrland for, as the meeting's minutes put it, "the purpose of organizing an American Fox Hound Club, the object being to encourage the systematic breeding and general use of American fox hounds in the United States."[200]

Joe chaired the meeting at which a small group of like-minded foxhunting enthusiasts adopted bylaws and a constitution, agreed to apply for active membership in the American Kennel Club, and elected officers. Daniel Cox Sands, a fellow New Yorker who had purchased Spring Hill Farm in 1907 from the Benton heirs (and renamed it "Benton"), was chosen as president. Joe joined the group's executive committee. He took over as president in 1915, and led the club for the next four years.

His ambition from the time he decided to buy New Lisbon, Joe Thomas later said, was "to see the Piedmont country become recognized as on a par with the best [foxhunting] in America."[201] In his fertile mind, that meant fashioning an English-style foxhunting estate at Huntland. So Joe bought up additional land adjoining the 272 acres he had purchased from Annie Leith. Then in January 1912,[202] Joe bought a 44-plus-acre tract that William Benton, Jr. had sold to William C. Rawlings in 1885.[203] He subsequently acquired a second parcel from Rawlings.[204] When he purchased eight-plus acres from Daniel Sands in 1914, and an additional one-acre parcel at the Pot House Road/Foxcroft Road intersection, Joe Thomas brought his Huntland holdings to just over 413 acres.[205]

With the land in place, Joe jumped neck-deep into drawing up the final plans and building what *Bit and Spur* called perhaps "the most complete kennel for the use of sporting dogs ever constructed in this country, and second to none abroad...."[206] If "there is a 'Hound Haven' on earth," the magazine proclaimed, "it is at Huntland." The "architecture of the kennels is Eighteenth Century, there is every canine convenience and luxury, the buildings are within a rectangle of cement and brick, which forms a pleasing contrast."[207]

Joe later wrote that the inspiration for his design of the Huntland foxhound kennels, which were completed in the fall of 1912, came during his first visit to Europe in 1903 and subsequent trips in 1904 and 1911. He visited "dozens of famous kennels in England, France, Belgium, and Russia" during those three sojourns, Joe wrote in his 1928 book *Hounds and Hunting Through the Ages.* He also managed, he claimed, to have inspected "the really good hound kennels in America"—not to mention reading "everything obtainable on the subject."[208]

He put that experience and knowledge to use spending "many months" working on the plans for an innovative, upscale kennel. It would be the home of his private foxhound-breeding operation, as well as home for the Piedmont and Middleburg foxhound packs and the Piedmont Beagles, which Joe naturally helped run, serving as the group's secretary in 1915. The kennel, which was completed in the fall of 1912, was designed to accommodate as many as 160 hounds.

"If hounds are to be kept at all," Joe wrote in his foxhunting book, "certainly they should be kept in the best possible way. If a remarkable, or even a respectable, pack is the objective, a well-designed, handy kennel kept in a neat, workmanlike manner is essential."[209]

Joe's "Hound Haven" at Huntland certainly fits the definition of "well-designed." All the walls and floors are made of poured reinforced concrete—an innovative building technique in 1912—with cream-colored cement stucco exterior walls that included "handmade brick pilaster supporting arches," as Joe put it. The entire building—with the exception of the cypress-shingled roof—is fireproof. All of the pipes are hidden inside walls; all the floors contain drains and each room has a sewer connection.

Joe had the roof shingles stained black and the shutters painted black around the windows. On several walls and at the entrance of the square structure he had "admonitions on kennel management" placed on panels with raised lettering. Joe took those words of fox-hunting wisdom from the 18th century English poet William Somerville's epic ode, *The Chase.*

One panel, on the front entrant gate pillar, contains *The Chase's* last lines:

> *Fields, woods and streams*
>
> *Each towering hill, each humble vale below,*
>
> *Shall hear my cheering voice, my hounds shall wake*
>
> *The lazy morn, and glad the horizon round.*

Another panel, at the entrance to the kennel, has these words:

> My hoarse-sounding horn
>
> Invites thee to the chase, the sport of kings;
>
> Image of war without its guilt.[210]

Joe later called the finished product "a very satisfactory ensemble, especially when in a few years ivy, trees and shrubbery judiciously planted completed the picture." The "general effect," he explained, "is that of a building in the eighteenth-century manner."[211]

It's quite a building. The northern side of what Joe called the "hollow square" contains a spacious, two-floor, six-room huntsman's apartment, along with two bedrooms above the kitchen for the kennel keeper and other staff. Joe added those living quarters because he strongly felt that his kennel staff should be close to the animals they worked with. "If men's quarters must be built," he wrote in *Hounds and Hunting*,[212] "it is well to incorporate them in the kennel rather than to have out-buildings scattered here and there, with the hunt staff consequently removed from their charges."

Also along the north side is a kitchen for the canine residents (Joe called it "the hound cook room") and a giant dog food pantry. Those "feed rooms," long-time Hunt Country observer Kitty Slater wrote, included chuted bins connected to the kitchen, in which "huge vats of oatmeal porridge continuously simmered over a slow fire."[213]

The cellar underneath contained coal bins and a coal-fired, hot-water furnace that heated the apartment, along with a laundry. Aside from the dog stalls (Joe called them "lodging rooms") and their enclosed outdoor runs on the east and west sides, Joe included a trophy room and office, two veterinarian's "hospital rooms," and a garage that he referred to as a "motor shed."

The square-shaped walled courtyard is divided into concrete paved areas. The paving, Joe noted, "is of a brick-color to obviate glare." The outdoor dog runs are divided by "stout wire panels and doors stretched on steel frames set in concrete." There are water hydrants throughout and drains "for quick sluicing-down with hose."

Joe Thomas spent lavishly on his new kennel. Loudoun County tax records valued the kennel at $3,000.[214] However, according to the architect Claude Haga, whom Joe hired to be his Superintendent of Buildings at Huntland, the total cost for the kennel added up to much, much more than that: $41,500—the equivalent of more than $1 million in 2023.[215]

Haga, a young, prominent Alexandria architect who specialized in concrete construction, had started his work at Huntland not long after Joe took possession early in January 1912. A graduate of the University of Virginia, Haga had designed buildings in Virginia and in Washington, D.C., and in 1912 patented a new type of concrete form.[216] Haga worked closely with Milton Dana Morrill, an architect who in 1908 began to specialize in designing concrete buildings. In 1911, Morrill co-owned Read & Morrill, Inc., which made steel forms for concrete construction projects in its Brooklyn factory. The firm used a streamlined process that he developed called "The Morrill System."[217]

The finished kennel, Haga later wrote, was based on Joe Thomas' "ideas," as well as designs "for various works" created by Joe's New York City architect friend and neighbor, Frederick Sterner.[218] In all likelihood, Haga took Joe's plans for the kennels (and later the Huntland stables and outbuildings), and prepared the drawings that were used in the construction. Haga had Read & Morrill make the steel forms, and he superintended the construction.

That team effort came up with—in Haga's words—a structure that "is considered the most modern and best kennel building in the world." Joe Thomas used similar words in 1920, describing the building as "unquestionably the most complete kennel in America and exceeded by nothing abroad."[219]

By the end of 1912, with the kennel complete, Joe Thomas turned his attention to designing and building a state-of-the-art stable complex next door to the kennels. Joe "did what any good houndsman would do," Betsee Parker said. "He built the kennels first, he built the stables second and he did the house third."[220]

Occasionally, a newspaper reporter or magazine writer described Joe Thomas as an architect. He was not professionally trained but read widely on the subject and had strong opinions about building design and decoration. And while he did not draw up any formal architectural plans himself, he employed and worked with accomplished architects in designing his kennel, stables, farm outbuildings, and the additions and renovations to the house William Benton built at New Lisbon.

As he did with the kennel, Joe shaped virtually every detail of the expansive, multi-stall stable, which he completed in 1913, that arose next door to the kennel at Huntland. Stables, he wrote, "should be planned so that there will be a place for everything; consequently there can be no excuse for things out of place."[221]

Never one to shy away from superlatives or hyperbole, Joe described the Huntland stables in 1920 as "the most complete in America. And while adapted to American conditions and strictly in accordance with the American architecture of the house, in practical details they are second to none of the best sporting stables of England."[222] Joe designed the stables to be "in a similar proportion and design" to the kennel, as he put it in his book.[223] In concert with his remodeled house, the three buildings, he said, make "a very efficient working establishment."

The stables resemble the kennels next door in that they are arrayed in a square building surrounding a courtyard with brick pilasters supporting arched entrances and cypress-shingled roofs. The horse stalls faced each other on either side of the courtyard. In addition to the stalls, a "cleaning room," a harness room, and a tack room, the complex also includes offices, a trophy room, and apartments for the grooms. Joe added several modern touches, including a lift to raise carriages to second-floor storage areas and a mechanical device that prepared oats for the horses' feed.

A visitor from New York described the kennel and stables in 1917 as "extensive English-looking buildings of brick and stucco." Viewed from a distance, he wrote, they "suggest a beautiful country house, and which, visited, teach one that certain favored hounds and horses in this world live much better than certain human beings. One building is given over to the kennels, the other the stables; each has a large sunlit court, and each is as beautiful and as clean as a fine house—a house full of trophies, hunting equipment, and the pleasant smell of well-cared-for saddlery. In a rolling meadow, not far distant, is the race course, all green turf...."[224]

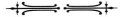

"Upon completion of the Huntland kennels," Kitty Slater wrote, "Mr. Thomas extended an invitation to Mr. [Daniel] Sands and the Board of Piedmont and Middleburg [Hunts] to kennel the pack here. This was readily and gratefully accepted."[225] With that accomplished—and with an ambitious foxhound breeding operation underway—Joseph B. Thomas established himself and Huntland as the nexus of foxhunting in Hunt Country.

Within two years, Joe moved up from honorary Whipper In to Master of the Piedmont Fox Hounds, taking over from his friend and neighbor Daniel Sands, who had held the position since 1909. Malbon Richardson, an old friend from Boston who had moved to Hunt Country about the same time Joe did, served as Joint Master. That same year (1915) Sands became Master of the Middleburg Hunt.

Both hunts operated out of Huntland, as did the Piedmont Beagles. Those operations, under the day-to-day management of Huntsman Charles W. Carver and Kennels Manager Frank D. Stuart, came with considerable cost. Joe Thomas picked up the lion's share of the expenses. He claimed that from 1912-1915 he spent the princely sum of $62,285 on buying and maintaining the Huntland "hounds and beagles, foxes, panelling [*sic*], damage, etc." That big number did not include, Joe said, "personal expenses" nor "the costs of the kennels."[226]

At the same time, Joe estimated that his foxhunting hub had added about a million dollars to the local economy in the form of "improvements subject to taxation" during those years. Plus, he said, local landowners received $443,000 from "people directly interested

In hunting who have come to the country for that purpose." That not-insignificant sum included—Joe figured—$350,000 for land; $25,000 for "hauling and motor hire;" $20,000 for "feed, food stuffs, lumber, etc.;" $15,000 for "subscriptions to schools, roads, churches, etc.;" and $12,000 for stable and house rentals and board."

What Joe Thomas did at Huntland in the four years after he purchased it—designing and building the kennels and stables; establishing a nationally renowned foxhound breeding operation; all but taking over the Piedmont and Middleburg Hunts; and more—was unparalleled in the history of foxhunting in the country.

"I think," Betsee Parker said, "you can say without dispute that Joseph B. Thomas was the greatest hound man or Master in American history."

For one thing, Parker said in 2016, "more packs are descended from the hounds he bred than any other." For another, Joe Thomas "was not your typical Master or owner of a pack. He approached it in a very academic way. He studied everything he could about his craft," and "spent hours and hours in the saddle and watching his hounds."

Joe is "probably the most unsung hero of American foxhunting," Parker said. "People in the South were very suspicious of carpetbaggers" when he arrived on the scene fifty years after the start of the Civil War. But Thomas and the other northerners who came to Hunt Country "helped to stabilize the economy, which was in really bad shape."

The upshot she said, "was to revitalize what is, to my mind, the most beautiful part of the United States."[227]

After completing the Huntland kennels and stables, Joe Thomas continued to revitalize William Benton's New Lisbon. He built a dairy barn and a string of agricultural outbuildings, a spring house, a large cistern, guest and workers' cottages, distinctive masonry walls and gateposts, and an extensive English garden—and repaired and preserved the old smokehouse.

Most significantly, Joe redesigned and enlarged the New Lisbon house, turning it into "a Colonial Revival-style masterpiece," as Maral S. Kalbian put it, and Huntland into "one of the premier country estates in the region."[228]

CHAPTER SIX
A Country House of Character

Huntland "typifies to an unusual degree what usually happens in American houses of early date where the taste of the owner was intelligently expressed in assembling beautiful things from various corners of the earth."

—Joseph B. Thomas, 1920

In his quest to turn Huntland into an ideal farm and residence, Joe Thomas first looked to the past. "I tried to place myself in the position of a planter-merchant of the American Atlantic coast living about the year 1800," he wrote in 1920. With that in mind, Joe said, he "spent five years developing the house, gardens, stabling and farm buildings, every detail being thought out... with utmost care to keep everything strictly in the atmosphere of the day."[229]

Joe decided to keep the original architectural scheme of the 1834 Federal-style brick house at Huntland, while updating it to a more modern dwelling. Its two-story, gable-roofed main block featured a center-passage, double-pile plan, and included a one-story service wing to the south. Joe examined East Coast "architecture of the day" looking for "various interesting details," especially for the interior. The idea for matching flanking wings was probably inspired by the existing Benton wing. Joe then turned to one of the East Coast's top architectural firms that specialized in designing and remodeling upper-crust residences—Peabody, Wilson & Brown in New York City—for technical advice and to draw up the plans.[230]

Beginning in 1915, Joe Thomas' vision (and those plans) transformed the 1834 house at Huntland into a stately Colonial Revival-style residence with 20th century conveniences. That accomplishment did not go unnoticed.

Country Life in America, the monthly magazine that focused on rural upper-class life, for example, choose the newly remodeled Huntland as one of seven American "country houses of character" that it highlighted in its November 1919 issue. The magazine was most impressed that "unlike so much of our modern architecture in America," Huntland derived "its precedent from the early architectural traditions of our own country."[231] The magazine pointed out that the remodeled house—as Joe said it would—"takes its fundamental qualities from the early days of pre-revolutionary Virginia."

Huntland was "modified to modern conditions of life," the article approvingly noted. In doing so, Joe Thomas created "the modern outgrowth" of a house that "would have been built a hundred years ago by any wealthy Virginia planter with an interest in his home surroundings and possessing the native taste which was, unfortunately, more common in those days than in the present." That sentiment uncannily echoes Joe's 1920 words about what he had intended to do with Huntland.

As did the article's concluding words: "It is not, however, modern civilization retreating to the shelter of old customs and conditions of living, not, in other words, a step backward; but rather a modernization of them, to bring them abreast of the modern standards of life and culture."

⊹⇥⇤⊹

Joe Thomas' exterior changes most significantly included remodeling the south wing and adding a matching wing on the north side of the house. He enlarged the windows on the three floors on the main block of the house and replaced the original double-hung sashes with multi-light casements. New louvered wooden shutters featured "a fox mask cutout near the top," as the Huntland National Register nomination notes, "alluding to the property's association with foxhunting."[232]

Joe also altered the front entrance. He replaced the original two-level porch with an imposing, two-story portico supported by monumental, white-painted brick columns. He added a double set of gently curving flagstone stairs with iron railings up to the portico's stone deck and the front door. He framed the paneled front door with fluted half columns and a fanlight. On the second floor, just above the first-floor entrance door, Joe added a set of French doors that open out onto a small semi-circular railing that acts as a balconet.

The one-story, gable-roofed, brick wings are fronted by porches with white-painted brick columns and wooden railings. Each side wing has a large brick chimney at the end and four sets of French doors topped by transoms and flanked by full-height louvered shutters with fox-head cutouts. Both porches have barrel-vaulted plastered ceilings. Every aspect of the new porches, Maral S. Kalbian noted, "is in keeping with the historic look of the original central" house.[233]

⊹⇥⇤⊹

Joe Thomas had part of the interior of the house gutted, removing the old stairway and much of the flooring, woodwork, and interior walls. He kept most of the original fireplaces. He had fine woodwork installed throughout the house, some of which includes, as the National Register nomination notes, symbols related to his "passion for foxhunting and his involvement with the Piedmont Hunt."[234]

Joe chose different designs for the cornices in each room and had them treated, he wrote in 1920, so "that they have every indication of age." He replaced some of the old floorboards with boards "of varied widths," and preserved others, primarily on the second and third floors. The "new wood-work has been hand planed to give the contemporary 'feeling,'" Joe said. For wallpaper, he went with those of "French, Chinese and American origin."

The front door opens into a modestly-sized center hall, the rear portion of which is

48

dominated by a dramatic, flying elliptical staircase with cantilevered steps and a mahogany handrail. The staircase prominently features a Waterford crystal pineapple finial—the traditional symbol of welcome—which Joe decided to top with his silver Piedmont Fox Hound insignia button, bearing the initials "P.H." for the Piedmont Hunt.

The most ornately decorated room in the house is the living room on the first floor, which the architects' plan refers to as a drawing room. Running the full depth of the house, the fully paneled room is divided into bays by fluted pilasters with detailed cornices. Motifs such as corn leaves and ears are carved into the woodwork and allude to the agricultural history of the property. The marble fireplace mantel features Tuscan columns.

A secondary parlor on the other side of the center hall is called the "boudoir" in the original architectural drawings. This elegant room has paneled walls and a molded cornice with trim that is simpler than what Joe put in the living room.

Joe added a bathroom in the existing room behind the secondary parlor and used the most modern fixtures of the time, including pink and black tiles for the flooring, sink, counter, tub, shower, and fireplace surround. The wall around the fireplace is fully mirrored, creating the illusion that the room is larger than it is.

Joe described the large main bedroom in the south wing and the north wing's dining room as "the most noteworthy rooms in the house." The bedroom—now used as a study—features a barrel-vaulted ceiling and original trim with a bamboo pattern. Joe decorated the room with Asian-inspired furniture and furnishings, including wallpaper that he said was painted by hand in China "probably around the year 1700," and "represents the most beautiful combination of birds, flowers and butter-flies in the most exquisitely decorated coloring on a grey back-ground."

All of those features made the room, Joe not-so-modestly wrote, "probably the most interesting Chinoiserie room in America."[235]

The new dining room (now used as a ballroom) in the north wing featured a wooden floor, French mural wallpaper, and full-height French doors leading to the porch.[236] The coved ceiling had two chandeliers imported from France. Today, a fireplace adorns the north end of the room with doors flanking it that lead into a pantry with a dumbwaiter and stairs up to a china-storage room and down to the basement kitchen.

"The mantle and doorway are authentic Adam [style] from the David Garrick house at Hampton Court" in England, Joe wrote.[237] The design, he said, "is made in imitation of the trunk and branches of the palm tree." The French chandeliers "strangely enough carry out the idea of branches from the palm tree."

He summarized the room—and, in essence, the entire house, including the old basement kitchen—by observing that it "typifies to an unusual degree what usually happens in American houses of early date where the taste of the owner was intelligently expressed in assembling beautiful things from various corners of the earth."

Joe had hand-painted murals depicting scenes of birds installed on the walls of the second-floor hallway landing. That floor contains three bedrooms and a study, all with original fireplaces, wood flooring, plastered walls, and wooden baseboards, chair rails, and cornices. The flying elliptical staircase continues to the attic where the four bedrooms and a bathroom likely were used by Thomas' household staff.

The basement level beneath the north wing includes the kitchen. A secondary staff dining room, complete with a bell box, a bathroom, and two dens (one of which was the original Benton kitchen), are located in the main block and south wing. The basement layout is well suited for accommodating the needs of foxhunters.

"At Huntland, everything was geared to the chase" when Joe Thomas owned the property, the journalist and author Jane McClary, who grew up in Middleburg, wrote in 1988. "After a long day in the hunting field, one entered the downstairs mud room, where a valet pulled off muddy boots, in order not to damage the fine carpets, and served a 'dressing' drink. Guests then changed in their rooms, in what was known as the bachelor's wing, before ascending to the main part of the house for apres-hunting tea or a formal dinner."[238]

Joe Thomas added much more to New Lisbon than the new kennels, barn, and expanded and remodeled house. He surrounded the grand house with English gardens and landscape features and built two garden cottages, a manager's house, a tenant house, and a dairy barn and other farm outbuildings. In that way, in addition to fashioning the "ideal residence" of an upper-crust Virginia planter-merchant, he also created an estate at a country crossroads that, as the National Register nomination puts it, "recalls small rural English hamlets."[239]

At Huntland's primary entrance off Pot House Road near the junction with Foxcroft Road, Joe installed double-leaf iron gates flanked by two large brick posts. The left post contains a tablet with a raised-lettered inscription of several lines in Latin from Book III of Virgil's first century B.C. epic agricultural poem, *The Georgics*. Roughly translated, this call to the hunt says:

"Come, then, break the sluggish bonds of delay. With mighty shout Mount Cithaeron calls the hounds of Taygetus and Epidaurus, tamer of horses, and their cry, echoed by the call of the woods, roars back."

Joe chose an inscription from William Somerville's 18th-century poem, *The Chase*, for the right post:

HUNTLAND

Fields Woods and Streams
Each Towering Hill
Each Humble Vale Below
Shall Hear My Cheering Voice
My Hounds Shall Wake
The Lazy Morn
And Glad the Horizon Round

Joe had Claude Haga build a tall, white-stuccoed masonry wall with brick-colored, rounded concrete along the top along a good stretch of the perimeter of the property, wrapping around the junction of Foxcroft and Pot House roads and extending west a short distance. Nearly all of the stones used in the concrete mix for the wall were "gathered from the fields of the estate."[240]

Haga also superintended the building of two, one-and-a-half story, seven-room cottages with porches near the main entrance that today are used as tenant houses. In 1915, one was a guest cottage and the other the gatekeeper's residence. Those buildings—one designed by Haga and the other by Frederick Sterner—are made of specially mixed, poured concrete with twelve-inch-thick walls in one and eight-inch-thick walls in the other. Both are stuccoed on the outside. Their front masonry walls are a seamless part of the wall that wraps around the perimeter of the property.[241]

Joe Thomas engaged local farmer Oscar Irvin Beavers, the son of Margaret Benton Beavers, to transport the materials to build the masonry walls that surround part of the Huntland property. According to his grandson, John D. Beavers, Thomas had the brick that tops the walls imported from England. The masonry was shipped to The Plains by train where O.I. Beavers loaded it into a wagon pulled by a four-horse team and delivered the load to Huntland. Lem Neal, a local African American, worked with Beavers throughout the process.[242]

Joe installed an extensive, three-level terraced English garden just below the south side of the main house. It was most likely designed by Peabody, Wilson, and Brown, with plenty of input from Joe. It includes two pergolas, two terraced lawns, and a cruciform-shaped serpentine-walled formal garden. Never one to shy away from extolling his own work, Joe described the garden in 1920 as "unquestionably the most interesting modern" one in Virginia, "there being a terraced garden, an Elizabethan garden with water flowing through it, and an old fashioned wall garden."[243]

Behind the house Joe had a man-made, stone-lined pond and watercourse installed. Nearby is an elaborate stuccoed-and-brick bridge that Claude Haga designed and built over the small waterway. It is similar in design to the walls at the front entry gates and along the perimeter.

Haga described the bridge as "all solid concrete work with brick veneered pillars and arch." He applied white stucco, Haga said, "so as to appear as if the bridge were originally of brick and stuccoed over, with some of the stucco falling off." The general appearance, he said, "is very interesting and quaint."[244]

The architect estimated that he used 750 barrels of cement to construct the bridge, not including what went into the stucco and the copings. The total cost was $3,700, Haga reported, "not including grading and filling."

That bridge—along with the kennels, stables, the remodeling and expanding of the main house, and everything else Joe Thomas did at Huntland from 1911-15—as Maral S. Kalbian aptly put it, "defined the stunning estate for the balance of the 20th century and to the present day."[245]

In 1913, 1914, and 1915 Joe Thomas, as Master of the Hounds of the Piedmont Hunt, took full advantage of his newly built kennels and stables at Huntland. He enthusiastically hosted fox hunts during the 1912, 1913, 1914, and 1915 hunting seasons. When Joe wasn't hunting, riding, socializing, and overseeing Claude Haga's work in Middleburg, he found time to involve himself in other sporting and business activities—and in the New York social scene.

Joe, for example, was among the "well-known sportsmen" on the planning committee for the big third annual American Sportsmen's dinner held April 2, 1913, at the famed Willard Hotel on Pennsylvania Avenue in Washington, D.C. The dinner attracted scores of sportsmen from across the country—representing "the professions, business life, the army, the navy, and other branches of the government," who were "united last night in paying tribute to the horse," *The Washington Post* reported the following day. Gen. Leonard Wood, then the U.S. Army's Chief of Staff, gave a spirited speech to the men on improving the quality of military cavalry horses.[247]

In August that year Joe joined the Executive Committee of a fledgling organization, the Foxhunters' Association, which set up its headquarters in New York. The association's purpose: "improving the condition of foxhunting in every part of the United States." The group also would "urge the adoption throughout the country of democratic principles of common responsibility and methods of thorough organization which will make foxhunting a permanent institution."[248]

Joe hosted an elaborate party at his house on East 19th Street on St. Patrick's Day, March 17, 1914. There was dancing in "the large Italian room," a *New York Times* society reporter wrote, and an "informal chafing dish supper" was served in the dining room, "which overhangs the Italian room like a wide balcony, to which one ascends by a narrow, winding stair." An orchestra serenaded Joe's guests during supper, which took place from 11:30-12:30. After that, a twenty-three-year-old New York socialite, Clara Fargo, performed several "exhibition dances."

Late in April, Joe booked passage on the RMS *Mauretania*, an enormous Cunard Line ocean liner, for a New York-to-Liverpool Atlantic crossing. Naturally, he choose the ship's royal suite. The night before the sold-out liner left New York for Liverpool, three thousand people showed up to see off relatives and friends. The Hotel Vanderbilt orchestra set up on board, *The New York Times* reported, to serenade the man who occupied the royal suite.[250] In mid-December, four months after the start of World War I in Europe, Joe sponsored a fundraising dance at his 19th Street New York townhouse to benefit the British War Relief Fund.

On New Year's Eve 1914, tragedy struck the small Thomas family. Joe's only sibling, Ralph Hill Thomas, died of pneumonia at his home in New York City. He was just thirty-two years old. Joe and his younger brother had inherited vast wealth, but Ralph accomplished very little during his relatively short life. The Thomas brothers both went to prep school in New York City and then to Yale. Joe graduated in 1903, and Ralph two years later. Ralph

Thomas went to work in an administrative capacity at American Sugar for a few years after college. But he had left the family business when he married Helen Margaret Kelly Gould in July of 1910, a little over a year after she and Frank Jay Gould—the son of the famed Gilded Age financier Jay Gould—divorced.[251]

When he died four-and-a-half years later, Ralph "had not been actively engaged in any business for some time," a Yale University publication reported in 1915, "although for four years he was connected with American Sugar Refining Company, where his father was a director."[252]

Six weeks after his brother's death, on February 12, 1915, Joe Thomas established the Ralph Hill Thomas Freshman Lectureship at Yale with a gift of $10,000. Beginning in 1918, that bequest paid for a required set of lectures for Yale freshman "given by men of public distinction," as the Yale course catalog put it, "on some subject elucidating the true purposes and value of a college course."[253]

It's difficult to envision a more eligible bachelor in New York or Virginia in 1910 than the wealthy, handsome, athletic, multi-talented Joe Thomas. We know that Joe socialized extensively wherever he went. That included in Middleburg where more than one observer of the social scene reported that he was romantically linked with one of Hunt Country's most eligible unmarried women, Charlotte Haxhall Noland, who in 1914 started a young women's boarding school, Foxcroft, a figurative stone's throw from Huntland.

It's likely that Joe Thomas and Charlotte Noland met in 1908 when he stayed at her mother's hunting inn, Burrland, in The Plains; it's all but certain that they spent time together in 1912 when Joe leased Burrland for a few months while Huntland was being remodeled.

Miss Charlotte—as she was widely known during and after her forty-two-year stint as the founder and head of Foxcroft—was born in 1883 at Burrland. An active, inquisitive, athletic girl and young woman, she took a strong interest in horses from an early age and in education beginning in her teens. Early in the 20th century, she and a cousin spent two summers studying at the Sargent School of Physical Education in Cambridge, Massachusetts—then affiliated with Harvard and now part of Boston University.[254] She also studied phys ed in the summers of 1906 and 1908 in Germany, and operated her own gymnasium in Baltimore.[255]

Around the time Joe Thomas bought New Lisbon, Miss Charlotte ran a rudimentary summer camp for boys and girls that she called a "Farmette" at Burrland. When she was twenty-nine years old, in the summer of 1914, Charlotte Noland started Foxcroft School from scratch by personally recruiting students (by mail) after taking a loan to purchase the property. She arranged with Joe to rent a building he owned known as the Pink House, which sits not far from Huntland's main entrance at the intersection of Foxcroft and Pot House roads. Miss Charlotte used that house as a dormitory that first term.

"I leased the Pink House from Joe Thomas," she said in a 1934 speech, "and had him build a sleeping porch on the second floor."[256]

Charlotte Noland "started Foxcroft with nothing and didn't know if she would make it," said Mary Lou Leipheimer, who began teaching there in 1967 and retired in 2014 after twenty-five years as Head of School. "But she had faith in her gut and made all the right decisions and never wavered from that."[257] The boarding high school was an immediate success when it opened with twenty-three students (including one boy) in September of 1914.

From its beginnings to today, Foxcroft has offered an equestrian program for its students who ride for pleasure and for those who are competitive riders. Foxcroft students, moreover, have the option of bringing their horses to the school, which has its own horse-boarding facility. Miss Charlotte, a serious equestrian, taught riding at Foxcroft (where students are members of one of two intramural sports teams, the Foxes and the Hounds), encouraged her students to fox hunt, and served as co-Master of the Middleburg Hunt (along with Daniel Sands) from 1932-46.

Joe Thomas and Charlotte Noland—foxhunting friends and neighbors—became an item during Foxcroft's first year, if the recollections of Nancy Perkins Lancaster (1897-1994), a member of that first graduating class, are accurate. Foxcroft students "were very impressed because Mr. Joe Thomas had just done up the house next door," she said in a 1975 oral history interview. "He wore very white, tight trousers and great, big white sombreros. And he was in love with Charlotte and he used to bring her a box of chocolates. Of course, we girls knew all that."[258]

But, Nancy Lancaster said, "he proceeded to fall in love with Miss Clara Fargo" who was staying with Daniel Sands and his wife Edith at Benton. Clara "was so beautiful and she had some accident, and we all went and serenaded her. She came to the window with long hair and two candles [on] each side and we serenaded her."

⊹⸺ ⸺⊹

Joseph Brown Thomas, 36, married Clara Fargo, 24, on February 15, 1915, at Saint Thomas Episcopal Church at 53rd Street and Fifth Avenue in Manhattan. The couple had announced their engagement just a few weeks earlier.

"Miss Fargo," an article in the Society Pages of *The New York Times* said, "is well known in society as an amateur dancer, having appeared with her brother, James C. Fargo, 2d, at charitable entertainments." It noted that Joe lived with his mother at 135 E. 19th Street, where he "has entertained society frequently at costume and musical affairs," and that because of the recent death of his brother Ralph, "the wedding is to be quiet."[259]

Town & Country magazine featured a full-page picture of Clara Fargo in silhouette with short hair and a long string of pearls in its engagement announcement. Joe "has a residence in New York," the picture caption noted, and then inaccurately reported that he "expects to build a house in Middleburg, Va., where his kennels are situated."[260]

Clara Fargo and Joe Thomas grew up in the same upper-income New York City milieu. She was born in 1871 in rural Bedford, New York, in Westchester County north of the city, and grew up in Manhattan. Her great-uncle William George Fargo (1818-1881) co-founded the American Express Company in 1850 in Buffalo, New York. Two years later he and Henry Wells formed Wells Fargo & Company in San Francisco. American Express started as a freight forwarding business and evolved into today's giant financial products and travel services company. Wells Fargo started in Gold Rush San Francisco as a banking company that specialized in transporting gold and other valuable commodities by stagecoach.[261]

Clara's grandfather, James Congdell Strong Fargo (1829-1915), took over as president of American Express after his older brother died in 1881. He held the position until 1914, the year before he died. He was instrumental in developing the concept of the traveler's check. Clara's father James Francis Fargo, a director of the Hanover National Bank in New York, served for many years as American Express vice president and treasurer.

Clara, as Joe did, went to private school, in her case, the all-girls Miss Spence's School in New York City, and also studied in Paris, where she lived on the Ile St.-Louis.[262] As a girl, she spent some summers with her family in a leased private cottage at The Loon Lake House in the Adirondacks—an expansive luxury hotel frequented by the nation's wealthiest early-twentieth-century families. As a young woman, she often made the society pages of the New York City newspapers attending cotillions, costume parties, receptions, theater parties, benefits, dinner dances, tea dances, and the like. Her parents formally introduced Clara to society on November 27, 1908, when she was seventeen at a reception, dinner, and "informal dancing party" at their five-story townhouse on East 37th Street just off Park Avenue.[263]

Clara acted, sang, and danced at some of those high-society events. Two months after she officially became a debutant, in February 1909, Clara appeared in a performance of the musical comedy "The Girl o' Mine" at a Junior League-sponsored benefit at the Plaza Hotel ballroom, during which she performed a "Spanish dance in a red and black costume."[264] In April that year, Clara acted in several performances of the comic opera "Kilts and Kelts" put on at the Berkeley Theatre by the Society of Miss Spence's School to benefit the Henrietta School for Crippled Children.

In 1913, she won first prize, a silver vase, at a holiday tea dance on Christmas Eve at the Plaza ballroom. The dance had a Japanese theme, in which "a Japanese girl in native costume was at the tea table, assisted by Japanese waiters," *The New York Times* dutifully reported.[265] In February 1914 she and her brother James contributed some exhibition dances to a benefit dance at a private home near Washington Square in Greenwich Village.[266]

In her early twenties, Clara Fargo took an interest in foxhunting. In the fall of 1914, she journeyed south to Hunt Country, and checked into Burrland Hall, the area's only country inn catering to fox hunters.[267] In all likelihood, she came to Burrland to be in Joe Thomas' orbit, as they had known each other for at least a year.

A few months later the handsome couple took their wedding vows at New York City's St. Thomas Episcopal Church, which had incorporated in 1824. Owing to the recent deaths of Joe's brother and Clara's grandfather, they had what the society pages described as a low-key ceremony in front of a small number of relatives and friends, followed by a modestly sized reception at her parent's townhouse.

The bride, the *New York Tribune* reported, wore "a gown of white chiffon and satin and a tulle veil held by a bandeau of diamonds, the gift of the bridegroom."[268] Clara's sister Grace served as matron of honor—Clara's only attendant. Walter L. Goodwin, a former Yale classmate from Hartford, Connecticut, stood as Joe's best man. "Mr. and Mrs. Thomas," the newspaper reported, "will go to Virginia on their wedding trip. Later they will go to California and return to New York about May 1."

Photographs of Clara—looking young, demure, and fetching—in her wedding gown appeared in *Vogue* and *Harper's Bazaar.* "The bride's gown was exceedingly lovely and simple," *Vogue* said; *Harper's* described it as "exquisite."[269]

Now "that he is married," *The Spur* magazine predicted in May—around the time Joe and Malbon Richardson took over as co-masters of the Piedmont and Middleburg Hunts—Joe Thomas "intends to have his home at Huntland, the Virginia estate which he has owned for several years. There he will be more prominent than ever, while he makes his house even more hospitable—if such a thing is possible."[270]

Joe and Clara certainly made their home at Huntland, but the newlyweds also spent considerable time at Joe's townhouse in New York and at the Thomas family farm in Simsbury, Connecticut—as well as doing a fair amount of traveling. Clara "cruised with her husband in their yacht all summer," of 1915, *Vogue* magazine reported, also noting that she was "a wonderful dancer, and her accomplishments in this art rank far above those of most amateurs."[271]

After their yacht-cruising summer, the couple returned to Huntland for the 1915-16 foxhunting season. Clara served as Huntland's hostess and joined in other Hunt Country social activities. She was, for example, among the fourteen women who met at Confederate Hall in Middleburg on November 23, 1915, and formed the Fauquier and Loudoun Garden Club. Charlotte Noland chaired the meeting, at which the club adopted a constitution and appointed officers and committee chairs. Edith Sands became Secretary and Treasurer and headed the Seedsmen Committee. Clara Thomas left the meeting as the chair of the club's Library Committee.[272]

In the middle of that hunting season, however, Clara took the train to the New York City, where as *Vogue* put it, she "now takes up her social duties." And after the season, Joe began spending more and more time in New York City tending to business matters, including his exporting firm, the France American Purchasing Company.

Back in Virginia, however, all was not serene on the social front. When Joe brought Clara to Huntland as his bride, Kitty Slater wrote, "several of the local ladies supposedly had a hand in helping to create a rather chilly atmosphere for the newlyweds. All in all, life became less than utopian for the Thomases."[273] That dystopian atmosphere very likely had to do with the fact that the "local ladies" believed that Joe had abandoned their friend Miss Charlotte for Clara Fargo.

"The people who lived in the area were so upset at him for not marrying [Miss Charlotte] that... from then on no one would have anything to do with him," Isabel Brown Wilson, whose father George Brown bought Huntland in 1954, said in 1988. Because of that social ostracism, she said, Joe Thomas "was never as happy in the house as he thought he was going to be."[274]

Kitty Slater and Isabel Wilson based their observations on decades-old local stories,[275] which probably contained at least a germ of truth. More likely, though, Joe Thomas' disenchantment with Middleburg stemmed from a bitter foxhunting dispute he had with his friend and neighbor Daniel Sands that bubbled up soon after Joe and Clara married. Adding to the equation: Miss Charlotte and Edith and Daniel Sands were close friends.

The territorial fight led to Dan Sands barring Joe Thomas from hunting on some of his land. More portentously, it set in motion Joe's decision to sell Huntland in 1918, just a few years after he had transformed the place into an ideal farm and residence, the aptly named center of foxhunting in Hunt Country and a true mecca for horsemen and huntsman.

CHAPTER SEVEN
An Ideal Sportsman's Estate

"This place posted against Jos. B. Thomas and any and all persons acting in a paid capacity about his hounds. Trespass of said persons will be prosecuted by law."

—Daniel C. Sands, Jr. broadside, 1915

Daniel Cox Sands, Jr. was born on November 22, 1875, in New York City. He grew up there and on his family's country place in Westchester County, New York. Soon after he married Edith M. Kennedy of Southampton, New York, on October 31, 1907, Sands bought William Benton's Spring Hill farm from the Benton descendants, renamed it "Benton," and the newlyweds moved to Middleburg.

Dan and Edith Sands presided over a large farming operation at Benton. In 1910, less than two years after they moved in, the Sands household, according to that year's U.S. Census, included an African-American couple, Middleton and Mary Moore, who served as butler and maid, and two young Black teenagers, Edward Evans, 13, a bootblack, and his brother Richard, 15, listed as a stable boy. Also in the Sands' employ: William Van Horn, 52, the family's "hired man" and coachman.[276]

D.C. Sands and J.B. Thomas shared many traits. Both grew up in extremely comfortable circumstances in New York. As young men, they both owned, trained, and showed dogs and horses. In 1905, they were among the twenty-six founders of the Dalmatian Club of America, and sat on that fledgling group's Board of Governors.[277] Within the span of four years they moved to neighboring farms in Middleburg that had been owned by William Benton. Soon after arriving in Hunt Country, they both plunged into the fox-hunting scene and traveled in the same social circles. In the summer of 1909 Dan Sands was elected Master of the Piedmont Fox Hounds. When he stepped down in 1915, Joe took over, and Sands became Master of the Middleburg Hunt.

Both were among the founders of the American Foxhound Club in 1911, with Daniel Sands becoming the organization's first president. His pack of five foxhound couples took first place in the club's first dog show in 1913.[278] Joe and Daniel Sands fox hunted side by side and soon after the Huntland kennel opened its doors, it became the home of the Piedmont and Middleburg Hunt's foxhounds. Sands' Piedmont Hunt Beagles—with his wife Edith serving as Master of the pack—boarded at a smaller kennel that Joe had built on the farm.

On February 22, 1913, a week after that first American Foxhound Club show, the

Middleburg Hunt's fox hounds caused a sensation at the big Westminster Kennel Club show in New York City. Things started out well for the Middleburg and Piedmont Hunt hounds. A newspaper reporter described their entrance onto the floor at the Grand Central Palace exhibition hall as "the most picturesque scene of the show." The foxhounds were shown "by huntsmen and whip in hunting costume. The scarlet coats, the blasts of the hunter's horn, and the crack of the whips, together with the incessant activity of the packs of barking dogs, made a very animated scene."

The scene soon turned a bit too animated, though, when the Middleburg Hunt hounds broke away and "scattered pell-mell through the big crowd which was jammed about the ring." Dan Sands and Malbon Richardson, the whipper-in, could not control the dogs and a "revolt of the hounds" ensued. As the hounds bolted into the crowd, "women screamed and tried in vain to get out of the way." The Piedmont Hounds reacted to the chaos by running "all over the ring among the spectators." Things didn't calm down until after the judges "dragged two of the hounds from under the chairs." Oddly enough, after the hound revolt, the show ended well for the Piedmont Hunt canines. They took first place in the foxhound category.[279]

Joe Thomas left Middleburg less than ten years after he bought Huntland. D.C. Sands, on the other hand, stayed, and for decades stood among the leading members of the fox-hunting community. "One can certainly say that Mr. Sands has done more for fox hunting and sport than anyone in the country around Middleburg," his friend and fellow fox hunter Thomas Atkinson wrote in 1954."[280] Sands, in fact, became such a prominent member of the community that for many years he was known as "Mr. Middleburg."[281]

In addition to his long-standing involvement in foxhunting, Dan Sands raised Guernsey cattle and Thoroughbred horses on his farm. He founded the Middleburg National Bank in 1924, and served as its first president for many years. He also was president of the Loudoun County Health Association for fifteen years in the 1920s and thirties, and served as president of the Middleburg Community Center, which opened its doors in 1948. He won a seat on the Loudoun County Board of Supervisors representing the Mercer District of Western Loudoun in 1935 as a Democrat, and served on the Board for eighteen years.

In 1911, Dan Sands organized the first Middelburg Hunt Race meeting at Mount Defiance just west of town. In 1932, Sands laid out the Glenwood Race Course on property he owned north of the town of Middleburg; since then, the Middleburg Spring Races at Glenwood has been among the premier steeplechase events in the world. Dan Sands subsequently donated Glenwood and its 112 acres to a nonprofit to preserve open space for races and other events. When he donated the land for what would become Glenwood Park, Sands stipulated that part of proceeds from events held there would go to local charities, including Loudoun Hospital in Leesburg. The Glenwood Park Trust continues to honor that stipulation today.

Edith Sands—a leading member of the Fauquier and Loudoun Garden Club who served as president of the Garden Club of Virginia from 1936-38—died in a car accident in 1948 in Middleburg when she was 73. Dan Sands resigned as Master of the Middleburg Hunt in 1954, forty-four years after he started. He died at Benton on May 10, 1963, at age 87.

When Daniel Sands stepped down as Master of the Piedmont Fox Hounds in the spring of 1915 and Joe Thomas became co-Master, their close relationship began to sour.[282] Sometime in late 1915 or early 1916, Dan Sands posted a quite un-neighborly sign on his property:

THIS PLACE POSTED AGAINST JOS. B. THOMAS

And any and all persons acting in a paid capacity about his hounds.
Trespass of said persons will be prosecuted by law.

D.C. SANDS, Jr.[283]

It's not clear why Sands took such a drastic step. However, it's likely that the Sands-Thomas rift had to do with money. On April 3, 1916, Dan Sands sent a strongly worded telegram to A.C. Reid, who owned a country general store in Upperville, in which he insinuated that Joe Thomas was being dishonest about hunt money matters. Sands alleged that two local horse breeders—John McKenzie Tabb and Fred C. McElhone—had fraudulently authorized Reid to "reimburse J.B. Thomas for the money spent in keeping the Hunt Horses," as well as the salaries of the huntsman and the whip. Tabb and McElhone, Sands said, were dropped members of the Piedmont Hunt and had no authority to direct Reid to do any reimbursing— presumably from Hunt funds.[284]

Two days later, on April 5, 1916, Joe wrote a long letter that appears to be a riposte to Sands' telegram. He sent it to fellow foxhunter Henry T. Oxnard, who lived in New York and Upperville, where he raced and bred Thoroughbred horses.[285] In the letter, Joe laid out details (for the first time in "public," he wrote) about the amounts of money he had spent on foxhunting "for the benefit of the Piedmont District." He indicated one reason he went public had to do with Dan Sands.

"While Mr. Sands remained Master of the [Piedmont] Hounds and Mrs. Sands Master of the Beagles," he wrote, "I remained particularly secretive as to expenses on my part as I had a theory that a Master should receive all the credit possible for the work for which he was nominally responsible," Joe wrote, "and I did not care to receive thanks as long as the game went on successfully."

He went on to say that he didn't consider that "one cent has been foolishly spent if the Piedmont District is to be placed on a par" with the best hunts in the country. From 1912 to 1915, he said, he had "borne almost the entire expenses of hunting in our vicinity...."

Joe then said he'd be "very glad" to sell his foxhounds to the Piedmont Hunt "for what they cost me" if the hunt would keep them "in their present standard for a term of years." Alternatively, he said he would lend the pack without cost to three or more "responsible gentlemen" if they maintained them in their "present state of efficiency."

There's no evidence that the Piedmont Hunt took Joe up on any of those offers. And the Sands-Thomas schism situation continued to fester. Late in April, Henry Oxnard wrote a scathing letter to F.J. Bryan, the National Steeplechase and Hunt Association's Hunts Committee secretary, complaining about the "deplorable condition that exists in re the Middleburg Hunt." Dan Sands had recently taken over as Master of the Middleburg Hunt, and although Oxnard did not mention Sands by name in the letter, he had little good to say about that Hunt and he staunchly defended Joe Thomas' role in foxhunting in "the Middleburg country."[286]

Joe, Oxnard said, "has financed and hunted... with utmost efficiency, providing it with hounds, kennels, horses, panels, foxes, etc., etc." and "has the unqualified support of the land owners."

Oxnard then said that because of unspecified "selfish" and troubling actions of local horse dealers Johnson Russell and Louis C. Leith (a close friend of Dan Sands who served as the Middleburg Hunt's Huntsman at the time) along with two other Middleburg Hunt members (W. Silcott and Joseph M. Martin), Joe "has been obliged to withdraw all connection with the Middleburg Hunt, which, therefore, exists now only on paper, having no hounds or equipment."

What's more, Oxnard said, "the farmers of the country are up in arms against the schemes of Messers. Leith and Russell, and have... petitioned your Committee to suspend the Middleburg Recognition until such time as the situation can be adjusted." He urged the committee not to recognize the Middleburg Hunt; if it did, he said, "the trouble will go on indefinitely."

According to one account, when Joe had asked Dan Sands in 1915 to step down as the Master of the Piedmont Hunt, Sands was so offended that he resigned from both hunts. That same account says that Joe served as Master of both hunts during the 1915-16 hunting season; that there was no Master of the Middleburg Hunt the following season; that Dan Sands was Acting Master of Middleburg for the 1917-18 season; and that he then returned as elected Master of the Middleburg Hunt in 1919.[287]

During the turmoil, and despite the harsh words from Oxnard and Joe Thomas, the Hunt Association's Hunts Committee continued to recognize the Middleburg Hunt. However, the Thomas-Sands schism over money and hunting territory continued for the next four years.

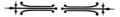

Even as the rift widened, Joe and Clara went on with their very busy non-foxhunting lives. In July 1916, for example, they journeyed north and spent a few days hobnobbing with the high society social set in Newport, Rhode Island. In May 1917, Joe judged five classes of dogs—Russian and Irish wolfhounds, American and English foxhounds, and Scottish deerhounds—at the annual Nassau County (N.Y.) dog show. In October that year, Clara gave birth to their first child at the 19th Street townhouse in New York City. They named the boy Joseph B. Thomas IV, following family tradition. Six years later, in 1923, Clara gave birth to her second child and—again going with Thomas family tradition—named her Clara Jane Diana Thomas. Family and friends called her Jane.

Joe and Clara entertained a college classmate of Joe's, Harry Wilford DuPuy, and his wife Lily at Huntland during the summer of 1918. DuPuy had joined the Army the summer before, a few months after the United States had entered World War I. After training and serving in the Quartermaster Corps in Chicago, Washington, D.C., and at Camp Holabird in Baltimore, DuPuy had resigned his commission on July 13, 1918, and the couple spent the rest of the summer as guests at Huntland.[288]

With World War I still raging across Europe, Joe Thomas joined the Army in the summer of 1918, receiving his commission as a major in the Quartermaster Corps on August 27. He immediately went to work in the Office of the Construction Division of the Army in Washington, and stayed there until his discharge on January 6, 1919, two months after what was then known as the Great War ended.[289] During his military service Joe turned over the operation of the Piedmont Fox Hounds to Walter L. Goodwin, a polo-playing banker friend and foxhunter who lived in Hartford, Connecticut. Goodwin put together a committee of Piedmont Hunt members to help run things. The group included Eugene Gatewood of Upperville.

"So much has been done to make this a good Pack and a good [foxhunting] country, that it seems a great pity to let it die out," Goodwin wrote to Gatewood on August 30, 1918, soon after Joe Thomas went into the Army. "My only idea in this effort is to keep up the sport which we have all so much enjoyed, so that it may not absolutely vanish during these trying times." Joe Thomas, Goodwin said, "has assured me that the financial support of the Pack would be continued by him as in the past."[290]

It appears that Goodwin and Gatewood, with Joe Thomas' consent, suspended the Piedmont Hounds' official 1918-19 season. However, Joe allowed his Huntsman, Charles Carver, to lead informal, unaffiliated fox hunts.[291]

By the spring of 1919, Joe Thomas had decided that he no longer wanted to be involved with either the Piedmont Fox Hounds or the Middleburg Hunt—and that he had had enough of Middleburg altogether. He resigned as Master of the Piedmont Hounds, offering to let the Hunt use his hounds, kennel, and Huntsman for the following foxhunting season, with the proviso that the hounds be returned to him "in as reasonably good condition as when given to" the Hunt.[292]

Joe claimed that he stepped away from hunt matters that year because he would be "busy in the interest of the French Government in this country."[293] In fact, Joe did get involved with France, which was trying to recover from the catastrophic devastation in the French countryside during World War I. In the fall of 1919 he started a business, the French-American Purchasing Company, to sell cattle to the French government. The French agreed to buy 60,000 head of American Holsteins from Joe; the first shipment of 10,000 cows and registered bulls arrived in France in October 1919.[294]

Joe made two trips to France to put the deal together, in the spring of 1919, and a year later. His cattle business, Joe's friend and lawyer Alan Fox wrote in May 1920, was "of great importance both to France and to this country."[295]

For her part, Clara Fargo became a staunch supporter of the "Free Milk for France" campaign as a member of the New York Committee for Free Milk for France. On July 14, 1918, at a big Bastille Day mass meeting at Madison Square Garden, Clara purchased a box that she decorated with a French and an American flag and a banner that read, "Give of the Milk of Human Kindness, for Little Children, Wounded Soldiers and Tubercular Patients."[296] One of the committee's goals was to ship a ton of dry milk every day to France.[297]

But this time, Joe and Clara had all but left Huntland. After his Army discharge they spent most of their time in New York City and at the farm in Simsbury, Connecticut. In addition to his cattle-shipping business, Joe served on the boards of several companies, and as president of Cornucopia Mines Co. in New York, which he had started in 1915 and operated out of his office on Wall Street.[298] The company had a handful of mining operations going in 1919 in and around the town of Cornucopia in the rugged mountains of Eastern Oregon where gold had been discovered in 1880. That included two gold mines and a processing facility called an amalgamation mill that employed a hundred workers.[299]

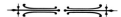

By the time he made that second trip to France, Joe Thomas was finished with fox hunting in Middleburg. "I will never again take up the matter of running a hunt unless absolutely perfect arrangements can be made in relation to the good will and thorough backing of all landowners," Joe wrote from his office in New York to Eugene Gatewood in January of 1920.[300]

When Joe resigned as Master of the Piedmont Hounds in 1919, the club merged with the Middleburg Hunt and became the Piedmont-Middleburg Foxhounds. Dr. A.C. Randolph served as the new club's Master of Foxhounds. "A $10,000 kitty was raised through sale of stock" to form the new club, Kitty Slater wrote, "a pack was rounded up, and Walter Goodwin, formerly of Hartford, Connecticut, donated kennels and stables on his farm near Middleburg."[301] That arrangement, however, lasted for just the 1919-20 fox-hunting season.

By the end of 1919, Joe decided to put Huntland on the market. Sometime early the next year he drew up an eight-page, heavily illustrated marketing brochure offering Huntland for sale. In 1915, he had started a real estate company called Samoth Realty Co., in New York. In 1919, he served as president of the company with his friend Alan Fox as vice president and Mary R. Pugh as treasurer. The office was on the first floor of 132 E. 19th Street, the apartment building Joe owned across the street from the five-story townhouse where he, Clara, and their children lived.

Samoth took out real estate ads for Huntland in several publications, including *Country Life*. One advertisement described the house as an "18th Century Virginia Mansion," although William Benton built the house in 1834. It went on to describe the property as "an ideal sportsman's estate... in highest state of cultivation—48 miles from Washington, D.C.—in the finest agricultural and sporting district of Virginia; modernized..., 20 rooms, 6 baths, wonderful old wall papers, old-fashioned wall gardens; most complete hunter stables (30 boxes) and kennels in America—the whole laid out in symmetrical 18th Century style. Best dairy and farm barns in the country."

The estate, the ad noted, included a garage, manager's cottage (with seven rooms and two baths), a gate lodge, and nine tenant houses, "all in perfect order and repair." The estate was suited for fox hunting, the ad proclaimed, as well as beagling, shooting, fishing, racing and horse shows."[302] The asking price: $350,000.

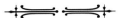

Despite cutting ties with the local hunts in Middleburg, Joe Thomas held on to his foxhounds. He took them out of the Huntland kennel, though, and set up a breeding operation not far away at Ashby Gap west of Upperville in the Blue Ridge Mountains. "He began a program of hound breeding on a prodigious scale" at Ashby Gap, the foxhunting author and editor Norman Fine wrote in 2003, and provided "entire packs of entered hounds to newly formed hunts. His influence on the American foxhound was enormous and his bloodlines still thrive" in many packs "across the country."[303]

In 1929, after selling Huntland, Joe moved his hounds to the Southern Grasslands Hunt and Racing Club at Fairvue Plantation in the Nashville suburb of Gallatin, Tennessee. While at Grasslands, Joe had a hand in founding the first international steeplechase race on American soil, which the Grassland Club ran on December 6, 1930. He and Clara were on hand for the ball the night before at the forty-room Fairvue mansion and for the races the next day.[304]

From 1919 to 1929, when he wasn't tending to business matters in New York City or making the occasional visit to Huntland or overseeing the hound breeding at Ashby Gap, Joe accepted invitations to take his foxhounds, known as "Mr. Thomas's Hounds," and his accomplished huntsman Charles Carver on hunts in Virginia, New York, Georgia, and North Carolina.[305] That included two-month stints for several hunting seasons beginning in 1920 at Overhills, the 11,000-acre sporting estate near Pinehurst, North Carolina, owned by Joe's close friend Percy A. Rockefeller (1878-1934), a fox-hunting nephew of John D. Rockefeller.

Joe, not surprisingly, did more than hunt at Overhills. He designed the kennels there for Percy along the lines of the one he had built at Huntland. He also laid out the fox-hunting routes on the property. In his 1928 book *Hounds and Hunting through the Ages* Joe described the "hunting establishment" at Overhills as "perhaps the prettiest one to look at that I ever saw." The entrance gate posts, he wrote, "are surmounted by figures of a fox and a hound originally brought from Huntland."[306] He also sang the praises of the Overhills landscape, especially along the hunting routes he created.

"These rides," he wrote, "radiating from a given point, give delightful vistas through the woodland remindful of... rides in French forests...."[307]

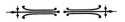

A snapshot of Joe Thomas' somewhat precarious financial situation came to public light in May of 1921. That's when Joe, the co-executor of his mother's estate, asked a New York City Surrogate Court judge for permission to set up a plan to pay $210,000 that he owed to the estate, according to an article in *The New York Times*. It seems that Joe had received the bulk of the $333,000 estate in the form of a trust fund following his mother Annie Thomas' death at age 69 on July 28, 1916. He evidently had borrowed a large chunk of that money from the trust fund and less than five years later didn't have the cash to pay it back. His lawyer told the court that in order "to make payments of his debt to the estate" Joe had "mortgaged a $215,000 stock farm in Loudoun County"—Huntland—and also "pledged insurance policies of $150,000."[308]

The next year Joe faced more adversity, this time in the form of an official reprimand from the Executive Committee of the Masters of Foxhounds Association. His misdeeds: taking actions "prejudicial to the interest of fox hunting" and "unbecoming of a Master or an owner of Foxhounds." To wit, Joe had shipped a "considerable number" of foxes from the territory of the Loudoun Hunt and in "close proximity of the territories of" the Orange County and Middleburg Hunts out of the State of Virginia. What's more he compounded that unethical practice by advertising "for the purchase of foxes" in a publication that was "issued and circulating in a fox-hunting state."[309]

After looking into the matter, the committee sternly reprimanded Joe. But because he made a "full and ample apology to all concerned," and offered to make "proper amends," the body took no further action.

Mortgaging Huntland and the lack of interest among potential buyers for the property seems not to have put a damper on Joe and Clara's lifestyle. They spent the winter of 1921-22 in Florida, for one thing.[310] They also continued to take part in the New York City social scene. The young couple regularly hosted events at the East 19th Street townhouse, where they employed five women: a nurse, cook, and maid, and two other "servants," according to the 1920 Census.[311] Little wonder that *The Spur* magazine characterized the townhouse that year as "singularly well adapted to entertaining."[312]

Among other events, Joe and Clara hosted two benefits for "needy artists" in 1924 and 1925. Following a dinner at the second event in January 1925, the entertainment consisted of musical performances by a soprano, a baritone, an English cellist, a Russian quintet, and a group of fifteen singers, along with a mock lecture on "civic economy." When guests entered the house, they were greeted by wax figures representing Joe and Clara.

"The figures, with outstretched hands," the *New York Tribune* reported, "greeted the guests as they arrived, and appropriate salutations were given by means of a microphone hook-up."[313]

In Virginia, farming operations continued at Huntland after Joe put the place on the market and he and Clara began spending the bulk of their time in New York City. At the eighth annual Loudoun County Fair and Horse Show in September 1926, Huntland horses and cattle took home a healthy stack of ribbons. Among them: a Holstein bull won first place in the "any age" category; "Milkmaid," won a first-place ribbon for best grade Jersey cow;

and the farm manager, W.L. Simpson, received a slew of first, second, and third places for the farm's Percheron draft horses.[314]

Joe Thomas made his second significant foray into New York City real estate in 1927 when he built an up-scale, fifteen-story co-op apartment building at 450 East 52nd Street facing the East River, which—among other unique features—had its own boat landing. Joe's plan allowed for just one apartment on each floor, although six floors had triplex apartments and two had duplexes. He named it the Campanile, "bell tower" in Italian, although the relatively narrow brick building with stone trim did not have a bell or a tower. The floor-through apartments sold for $50,000 to $65,000.[315]

From 1924-28, Joe found the time to research and write his second book, *Hounds and Hunting through the Ages*, a detailed history of foxhunting. The recently founded Derrydale Press, which specialized in sporting books, published the book in August 1928. The endeavor started as a "simple series of letters" to his son, Joe wrote in the preface, which "would impart something of the romance and practice of hunting" to "spare him some of the mistakes I have made." But, "urged by friends who felt that a book of broader scope addressed to hunting men, and to laymen as well, was much needed," he said, Joe "enlarged the work to its present form."[316]

Critics and fox-hunters lavishly praised *Hounds and Hunting*. S.W. Cousans, writing in *The Spur*, called it "one of the most wonderful books in the magnificent library of fox hunting... truly an epoch-making volume."[317] *Hounds and Hunting*, a Chicago *Daily Tribune* reviewer wrote, "a volume of hunting lore and practice," is "a record of incomparable experiences... Mr. Thomas not only tells of the history of the hunt, but imparts the secrets of a lifetime devoted to a love of the sport and an active participation in it."[318] *The Wall Street Journal* characterized it as "the most constructive book upon [foxhunting] within the century," and went on to praise Clara Fargo's illustrations in the second edition for their "originality and execution."[319]

Around the time that Joe started the book, Clara announced that she had tired of the "placid rounds of social life" and decided "to adopt a career." She "has elected," a New York newspaper society column writer reported, to become "a painter of theatrical scenery, and has already completed sets for a play which will be produced on Broadway."[320] Clara began designing and creating sets that spring; a photograph of her at work painting a set for "Grounds for Divorce," a three-act, Broadway-bound comedy starring the stage actress Ina Claire, appeared in the March 15, 1924, issue of *Town & Country*.

Clara soon made good on her promise to leave the high-society social scene behind. By 1929, she had moved on from scenery painting and embarked on a successful painting career, specializing in creating murals. An exhibition of her murals attracted attention in May that year at the Wanamaker Auditorium on Broadway and 9th Street. As did another exhibit of her murals at the Leicester Galleries in London.

In 1933 Clara painted murals "all over the walls" as *The New Yorker* put it, of the New York City offices in the Daily News Building of Col. Robert R. McCormick, the famed publisher of the Chicago *Tribune*.[321] Three years later, she completed an eighteen-by-twenty-three foot mural called "The Freedom of the Press" for McCormick in the lobby of the Tribune's tower in Chicago.

Clara joined the National Society of Mural Painters, and created murals for the Fairvue Plantation house at Grasslands and the Royal Suite of the Grosvenor House in London's Mayfair district, among other upper-crust places, and for such luminaries as Vincent Astor and Joe's old friend Percy Rockefeller.[322] In August 1935, during a three-month visit to London, she painted an eleven-foot high, sixty-five-foot long mural celebrating the history of feminine beauty called "A Pageant of Beauty," which had a three-week run at a West End London gallery.[323] In October that year, Saks Fifth Avenue in New York exhibited the mural.[324] Clara painted another highly praised mural, "The World of Steel," for the U.S. Steel Corporation's pavilion at the 1939 New York World's Fair.

Clara and Joe sold 135 East 19th Street in March 1945 to Alfred Lyon, the president of Philip Morris & Co. When they did, Joe and Clara decided to live apart. She moved full time to her summer house called Fortune Rock on Mount Desert Island in Maine. He relocated to a house on Gloucester Street in Back Bay neighborhood of Boston that came to him through his grandfather's trust.

Fortune Rock, a dramatic, cliff-side cantilevered house, overlooks Somes Sound, about forty-five miles south of Bangor. Clara had commissioned the famed modernist architect George Howe to design the house in 1937. She adorned Fortune Rock with, among other things, a mural she painted depicting the 1913 wreck of the three-masted wooden schooner *Joseph B. Thomas* (named after Joe's grandfather, the 19th century shipping and sugar baron) in the house's dining room and entrance hall. Joe and Clara's daughter Clara Jane married Peter Bulkeley Greenough at Fortune Rock on August 12, 1944.

Clara Thomas spent most of the rest of her days at Fortune Rock in Maine. In 1963, she founded the Mount Desert Festival of Chamber Music in Northeast Harbor, Maine, which continues today. She died at Fortune Rock, succumbing to cancer on April 26, 1970, at age 79.

+≡·≡+

For his part, after selling Huntland, Joe Thomas kept up his membership in the Masters of Foxhounds Association of America and paid regular visits to friends in Hunt Country through the late 1930s. In the early 1940s he was active in the Gramercy Park Association, serving several terms as the neighborhood association's president. He sold his Boston house in 1950 and rented a place in Southern California. Joe Thomas died on July 14, 1955, at age 75 in Pacific Palisades where his son Joseph and his family lived.[325]

Nineteen years earlier Nina Carter Tabb of Middleburg provided a eulogy of sorts for Joseph B. Thomas in her Washington, D.C., *Evening Star* newspaper column, "The Hunting Log." In reporting on Joe's visit to Middleburg in March 1936 to take in the Piedmont Fox Hounds' hunter trials, Tabb said she'd overheard "two well-known Virginians" say this about Huntland's former owner:

"We should build a monument to Joe Thomas here, for he is not only one of the best sportsmen in America, but he did more for the sport of fox-hunting in Virginia than any one man. Coming here years ago, he was one of the original boosters of fox-hunting, bringing people to Virginia who were interested in the sport and putting up the land value in this part of Virginia. We old Virginia boys know what he did for our country and we thank him. And there are many of his friends who wish he would come back and buy Huntlands [*sic*] again, for we feel that he would be more appreciated than years gone by."

Tabb very likely creatively re-created those words. But it's also likely that more than one person in Virginia's Hunt Country who knew Joe Thomas had spoken words to that effect.

What is accurate is Tabb's description of Joe Thomas in 1936 at age 57:

"He is even better looking now with his gray hair and brilliant coloring than he was as the dashing, black-haired young man we used to know."[326]

CHAPTER EIGHT
A Gem of Americana

"Well, this house is an inspiration, for in addition to being a truly livable home, the neighborhood in which it is located is rich in natural beauty."

—Works Progress Administration Historical Inventory of Huntland, 1936

In 1918, two years before Joe Thomas put Huntland on the market, he and Clara formed a business entity, the Thomas Holding Company. The Company immediately took out a deed of trust giving Huntland's legal title to Joe's lawyer friend Alan Fox of New York as security for three notes totaling $257,442 that Joe had borrowed from his mother's estate.[327] In June 1927, presumably after the deed of trust had been terminated, the Thomas Holding Company agreed to sell Huntland and its surrounding 411 acres (along with all the estate's furnishings, livestock, and equipment) to Gwendolyn D. and William A. Robinson, who lived in Washington, D.C. The total selling price: $200,000.[238]

Joe said the reason he sold Huntland for $100,000 less than the asking price had to do with the fact that the Robinsons were not particularly enamored of the way he decorated the house. "When I sold the place," Joe later wrote, "Mr. Robinson was not interested in what I considered to be the essence of the cachet of the house; i.e., the wall papers and many items of furniture, which took years to collect. When setting the price for the property, I took off a large sum, and removed many of the treasures. However, they have but one proper home, and that is Huntland."[329]

The parties completed the sale in May 1927. H.W. Hilleary, a big Realtor in Washington, D.C., who had branch offices in Charlottesville, Leesburg, and Warrenton, Virginia, helped arrange the settlement. Calling Huntland "a gem of Americana," Hilleary announced that the Robinsons would take possession of the place in June.[330]

William Anderson Robinson, who lived in Louisville, married Gwendolyn Denys in 1921. Although identified as "Dr. William A. Robinson" in Loudoun County deed books, it appears that he was not a physician. Gwendolyn Denys was born on August 25, 1892, in Piermont, New York, and raised in Washington, D.C., and at her family's winter home in Aiken, South Carolina. Her parents—the prominent Washington, D.C., Episcopal clergyman, the Rev. Dr. F. Ward Denys (1854-1941), and his wife Mabel Eaton Denys (1863-1924)—had three other daughters, Dorothea, Margaret, and Rosalynd. The sisters grew up in extremely comfortable circumstances, principally because Mable Denys had received a large inheritance from her father, John Eaton, the founder and president of The Oil Well Supply Company in Western Pennsylvania.

The Denys daughters took part in many social events in Washington, D.C., in the nineteen teens. That changed abruptly for Gwendolyn and Dorothea in the summer of 1918, however, when they left the Washington social scene behind and sailed to France to work as Red Cross volunteer interpreters and nurses aides during the last months of World War I. The sisters remained in France after hostilities ended and returned to Washington the following year.

On April 11, 1921, Gwendolyn Denys married William Alexander Robinson at her family's Aiken, S.C., home. This "wedding of wide interest in Washington," as the Washington *Evening Star* characterized it, was "witnessed by only a small company of relatives and friends" due to the recent death of the groom's mother.[331] After the wedding, the new bride resigned as vice-president of the Washington Junior League, and the couple moved to Louisville, and later to Tulsa, Oklahoma, before returning to the Nation's Capital early in 1927.[232]

Gwendolyn Robinson appears to have been the driving force behind buying Huntland as she was very interested in horses and dogs from an early age. "She was a great sporting gentlewoman and took keen pleasure in a day at the races," a friend wrote after her death.[333]

As for dogs, in 1936, two decades after Joe Thomas had convinced the American Kennel Club to officially recognize the Russian Wolfhound, Gwendolyn (and her second husband, Gordon Massey) registered the first Norwich Terrier with the AKC. As Joe did with Borzois, in the thirties Gwendolyn and Gordon Massey made several transatlantic crossings to England, returning to their home in Maryland with several terriers. For decades, Gwendolyn regularly attended the annual Westminster Kennel Club Dog Show in New York City, almost always staying in her favorite hotel, the St. Regis.

While her fondness for horses and dog breeding likely attracted Gwendolyn Robinson to Huntland, she and William Robinson spent very little time in Middleburg. What's more, not long after taking possession, Gwendolyn Denys Robinson divorced her husband and sold the place. Soon after, in February of 1930, she married Gordon Massey in New York City. She died at age 86 in Easton, Maryland, in 1979.

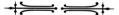

In November 1929, shortly before she remarried—and just two-and-a-half years after the Robinsons bought Huntland—Gwendolyn Robinson (under the corporate name, Huntland Plantation, Inc.) agreed to sell the property to Thomas H. Talmage and Mildred D. Talmage. The Talmages, who lived in New York City and had recently bought a horse farm near Warrenton, took out a $200,000 mortgage on the Huntland property. That was the same amount the Robinsons had paid Joe Thomas.[334] The sale closed on March 1, 1930.[335]

Thomas Hunt Talmage (1894-1972) had a few things in common Joseph Brown Thomas. Both were New Yorkers named after their fathers; both were interested in horses[336]; graduated from Ivy League schools—in Hunt Talmage's case, Princeton, class of 1917—served in the U.S. military during World War I; traveled widely; and inherited vast amounts of money. Hunt Talmage's inheritance came to him when he was just a year old following his father's death at age twenty-nine in 1895.[337]

72

On July 30, 1918, about a year after he graduated from Princeton, Hunt Talmage joined the U.S. Army, enlisting in the Coast Artillery as a private. He served at Fort Hamilton, New York, for three months, then finished his enlistment at Fort Monroe in Virginia until his honorable discharge on November 21, 1918, ten days after World War I had ended.[338]

On June 15, 1919, Hunt Talmage married twenty-four-year-old Mildred Mary Donnell at her family home in St. Louis. Sometime in the 1920s the couple moved to Paris, where Hunt practiced law at the French branch of Munroe & Co., an American investment bank. The couple's third daughter, Jacqueline, was born at the American Hospital at Neuilly-sur-Seine on December 15, 1927, just about a year before the Talmages purchased Huntland from Gwendolyn Robinson.[339]

There is no evidence that the Talmages lived at Huntland. In 1933, four years into the Great Depression, they forfeited on several bond and note payments, and relinquished the property to the Bank of New York and Trust Company.[340] On January 15, 1935, the bank officially purchased the property for $80,000 at a public auction on the courthouse steps in Leesburg.[341] The bank held the property until 1938.

During the years that the Robinsons and Talmages owned Huntland, farming operations continued. That included a thriving dairy. In the summer of 1931, for example, the Loudoun Dairy Herd Improvement Association announced that a Guernsey owned by "Huntland Plantation" was among the top milk producers in the county. The prolific dairy cow produced 891 pounds of milk in the month of June, along with 63.3 pounds of butterfat.[342] The Piedmont Fox Hounds also held occasional meets at Huntland. And Taylor Scott Hardin, who rented one of the cottages on the property from 1935-37, was known to take guests on rides around the property and surrounding area in his four-horse coach.[343]

On December 31, 1935, Elizabeth F. Morgan, a writer who lived in nearby Bluemont, paid a visit to Huntland in the employ of the federal government's famed New Deal jobs program, the Works Progress Administration.[344] Her report on Huntland, published in 1936, provides a rare, detailed, post-Joe-Thomas look at the house, inside and out.

Morgan opened her report with this enthusiastic, un-bureaucratic sentence about Huntland and the surrounding countryside: "Well, this house is an inspiration, for in addition to being a truly livable home, the neighborhood in which it is located is rich in natural beauty."[345]

She went on to cite the "perfectly lovely designs of English box bush, roses and evergreen trees" on the property, and the stunning view of the "beauty and surrounding country" to be had from the roof of the house—a flat roof, she reported, complete with five skylights.

Inside, Morgan found "many features to delight the eye." They included log-burning fireplaces, "colored tile bathrooms with sunken bath pools, and large magnificent glass chandeliers with prisms," along with "concealed radiators with rectangular openings in the side walls (to let in heat)." She wrote that some walls were "covered with bamboo... resembling cane used for reseating chairs."

The wallpaper in the large main bedroom in the south wing and the north wing's dining room was covered with "tropical scenes, oriental scenes, huntsmen scenes, beautiful water scenes with rock bridges, large and small size and shape, sea gulls, icebergs, etc., [as well as] Florida scenes with palms, swans and lakes." Other wallpaper in the house, she wrote, had images of "herds of deer, peacocks, birds of paradise, parrots and even a picture of a snake...." Some of the walls in the house were adorned with "hand painted tapestry just as gay and bright as the scenes on the wall paper."

It "is said," Morgan reported, "that the Thomas' had the wall paper of the oriental scenes in this house made to resemble an old royal residence in Japan." Actually, Joe Thomas, as we have seen, described the wallpaper designs he chose as of "French, Chinese and American origin."

As far as Huntland's exterior, Morgan noted that on the front porch all the legs and planks were hand hewn, and "came out of an old cabin in the yard that was once used for slave quarters." She went on to describe the front entrance, and the portico and steps. She then provided a generally accurate condensed history of the place. She based that portion of the report on searching Loudoun County land records and interviewing four of James Monroe Benton's children. Morgan described them as "old ladies" who "lived their entire lives in this community... Mrs. Elizabeth Baldwin, Mrs. Nannie Monroe, Mrs. Maggie Beavers and Mrs. Webb Monroe."

Morgan also noted that there was "no occupant" in the house in December 1935 when she visited Huntland for the WPA during the depths of the Great Depression. That situation changed in March of 1937, when Raymond F. Tartiere and his wife Gladys Rosenthal Tartiere rented the main house from the Bank of New York and moved in with their young daughter Elaine.[346] The Tartieres oversaw the continuing farming operations at Huntland until the property sold a little over a year later, in May 1938.[347]

Gladys Tartiere (1892-1993) was born in Chicago. In 1929 she married her second husband, Raymond Tartiere (1881-1950), a banker who was born in Lyon, France. The couple lived in Paris and Washington, D.C., but left France in late 1936 or early 1937, about two years before the outbreak of World War II in Europe.[348] The Tartieres rented Huntland until 1938. In 1940, they bought Glen Ora, a 400-acre farm in Hunt Country south of the town of Middleburg.[349]

On July 30, 1938, the Bank of New York agreed to sell Huntland to Colin MacLeod, who had recently moved from Boston to Hunt Country, for $75,000.[350] The transaction settled on July 27, 1939, after MacLeod and his wife Katharine Wright MacLeod formed a business, Huntlands, Incorporated, and took title to the property.[351] The Washington *Evening Star* real estate section, in announcing the sale, called Huntland "one of the show places of the Virginia horse country."

The *Loudoun Times-Mirror* in Leesburg announced the sale by reporting that "Mr. McLeod [*sic*], well known horseman," is "a poloist interested in agriculture and horse breeding."[353] The newspaper article went on to extoll the beauty of Middleburg for its readers. To wit: "The vicinity in which Huntland is located is notable for its fox hunting, shooting, fishing, racing, and horse shows. It is a rolling agricultural country, dotted with small coverts of oak trees. It lies between the Blue Ridge Mountains on the west and the Bull Run Mountains on the east."

Colin MacLeod was born on July 13, 1881, in Buffalo, New York. He worked as an IRS agent and then as a tax judge in Boston, according to his *Washington Post* obituary.[354] After retiring in 1936, MacLeod moved to Hunt Country, where he became a prominent racehorse breeder and trainer. Colin and Katharine MacLeod lived most of the year at Huntland, regularly spent the month of August at Saratoga Springs in New York, and "went to Florida every winter, Palm Beach," said Ann MacLeod, who married Colin "Sandy" MacLeod, Jr. in 1946. The MacLeods, she said, "were very interested in racing. They had a box at the Hialeah racetrack in Miami."[355]

Soon after moving to Huntland, Colin and Katharine MacLeod hired a cook, Isabelle Grant, and a butler, John Chinn, both of whom were African American. The MacLeod family quickly became part of the Hunt Country social scene, and with the help of their household staff did much entertaining at Huntland.[356] In June 1939, for example, they hosted a dance at Huntland for "young people" following the wedding of Bettina Belmont and Newell Ward.[357] In May 1940 the MacLeods threw a big pre-wedding party at Huntland for Lucy Bayne Proctor and Aldridge Dudley, Jr., a friend of Sandy's.

"Cocktails, preceding the buffet supper, were served on the lawn in the rear, which slopes down to the swimming pool," Nina Carter Tabb, who covered the Hunt Country social scene for *The Washington Post*, wrote of that event. "White flowers adorned the long tables in the dining room where supper was served. Guests were seated at small tables arranged over the lower floor of the house and on the lawn. Attractive bridal favors were given the guests. Musicians played for the dancing which followed."[358]

The MacLeods bought Huntland, one 1938 newspaper report had it, for their son Sandy, 23, a recent "graduate of Dartmouth and a polo player, who is interested in agriculture and horse breeding."[359] Sandy MacLeod did live at Huntland with his parents, and did get involved in horse breeding and training. But the coming of World War II changed that. Sandy MacLeod registered for the draft with the Loudoun County Draft Board on October 16, 1940, two months before the U.S. entered World War II. On May 21, 1942, he enlisted in the U.S. Navy Air Corps.[360] With the war raging in the Pacific, Sandy left Virginia and trained to be a pilot at the Naval Air Training Center in Pensacola, Florida.[361]

Sandy MacLeod came home to Huntland for a visit in June 1944. After he had gone back on duty, in late December 1944, a young woman stopped by the house. Twenty-one-year-old Jane Thomas Greenough, who lived in New York, came to Middleburg to meet family friends during a visit to her husband, U.S. Army Air Corps Capt. Peter Bulkeley Greenough, who was stationed in Washington, D.C. While she was in Middleburg, Jane, Joe and Clara Thomas' daughter, dropped in on the MacLeods.[362]

On December 9, 1945, the MacLeods sold Huntland to Fred B. Prophet and Vera S. Prophet of Detroit and Palm Beach. According to Ann MacLeod, her in-laws had decided to part with the place earlier that year. "Sandy was in the Navy Air Corps," she said, "and it looked like the war was going to go on in the Pacific after V.E. Day [May 8, 1945, when Germany surrendered]." So the MacLeods put Huntland on the market, and bought a 150-acre property in Upperville. They renamed it Dunvegan Farm, and started a horse breeding and training operation there. While building Dunvegan, the MacLeods rented Burrland, where Charlotte Noland grew up, outside Middleburg.

After Colin MacLeod died on January 13, 1948, his son Sandy took over the big equine operation at Dunvegan. "He bred and trained racehorses," Ann MacLeod said of her husband. They sold yearlings at first at Saratoga and then race horses. "We'd go to Belmont and Saratoga every summer."[363]

The new owner of Huntland, Frederick Butler Prophet, was born on November 9, 1884, in Hastings, Nebraska. In 1946, when he purchased Huntland, he owned and operated one of the largest and most successful industrial catering firms in the country, the Fred B. Prophet Company, with headquarters in the Fisher Building, the iconic downtown Detroit skyscraper.

Fred Prophet started in the food business in 1918, "first as an individual, but since 1924 as a company," *Nation's Business* magazine reported in 1944.[364] "He inaugurated the practice of bringing hot dishes to workers at their benches with rolling food wagons at the Curtiss aircraft plants in Buffalo and Hammondsport, N.Y." during World War I. In 1944, the Fred B. Prophet Co. had 3,800 employees, according to *Nation's Business*, operating seventy-two food processing plants in fifty cities in seventeen states.

"Each day," the magazine said, "this organization, through 90 cafeterias and 308 rolling wagons, serves an average of 250,000 workers in one way or another."

The Prophets arrived in Middleburg in the spring of 1946 and stayed at the Middleburg Inn—now the Red Fox Inn—in town while they were "seeing about opening Huntland," as Nina Carter Tabb put it in her Hunt Country column in *The Washington Post.*[365] The "opening" came soon thereafter and the Prophets spent most of that summer there.

But the new owners held on to Huntland for only a little more than two years. They agreed to sell the place on February 6, 1948, to Priscilla Dickerson Gillson de la Fregonniere and her husband Count Guy de la Fregonniere.[366]

"Mrs. Priscilla de la Fregonniere of Nassau, Bahamas," bought "historic Huntland Farm near Middleburg," *The Washington Post* announced on January 29, 1948, saying that "the new owner plans to make the estate her permanent residence, and to devote the farmland to cattle raising."[367] The New York *Herald Tribune* also took note of the sale, adding that Mrs. de la Fregonniere "has been living in England and France for several years and is now in Nassau Bahamas...."[368]

Priscilla Ogden Dickerson was born in 1905 in New York City. Her great grandfather, Philemon Dickerson (1788-1862), was a well-known New Jersey lawyer, judge, U.S. congressman, and one-term governor. Her father, Edward Nicoll Dickerson, Jr. (1852-1938), moved from New York to Miami, became a prominent man about town there, and was a founder of the famed Miami private beach club, The Surf Club.[369]

Priscilla—known as "Dickie"—Dickerson married Godfrey Anthony Gillson in England in 1934 and the following year renounced her American citizenship.[370] Following her divorce from Gillson, she married Guy de la Fregonniere, a French count, in 1947 in Horsham in West Sussex, England. The Count and Countess moved among the (pre-jet) jet set—and came to the U.S. soon after they married, although they spent considerable amounts of time at his home in Nassau, including much of the winter of 1947-48. Among their friends and neighbors in Nassau: Prince Stanisław Radziwiłł and his wife Princess Lee Bouvier Canfield Radziwill, Jackie Kennedy's younger sister.

The Fregonnieres bred and raced horses and did their share of entertaining at Huntland during the six years they owned the place. They threw a reception, for example, in November 1950 at Huntland following the wedding of Genevieve Cambon and Alain deBrell (a young French couple living in New York) at St. John the Apostle Catholic Church in Leesburg.[371] The Fregonnieres also kept the farming operations going at Huntland and hosted foxhunting meets.[372] Their horses raced at, among other venues, Belmont Park in New York and the Atlantic City Race Track in New Jersey.

In 1951, Priscilla de la Fregonniere had second thoughts about having renounced her American citizenship sixteen years earlier in England. She took her case to her Congressman, Democratic Rep. Howard Worth Smith of Virginia, saying that she renounced her citizenship "under duress and at the urging" of her father.[373] In June 1952, the U.S. House of Representatives and Senate approved Private Law 713. That measure granted Priscilla Ogden Dickerson Gillson de la Fregonniere the right to apply for naturalized American citizenship and to obtain "the same citizenship status as that which existed immediately prior to its loss."[374]

Trowbridge Littleton, who grew up in Middleburg near Huntland, spent time there and at nearby Farmer's Delight in the early 1950s when he was a child. "I was there often," he said, visiting a friend whose parents lived in one of the Huntland cottages. "I can remember a monstrously big house and everything looked manicured." Priscilla de la Fregonniere, he said, was "very tall and very polite and I remember that she had a very strong French accent."[375]

In 1953 or 1954 the de la Fregonnieres put Huntland on the market, listing it with Grasty & Co., one of the four real estate firms in Middleburg. On December 3, 1954, Priscilla de la Fregonniere "in her own right and Guy de la Fregonniere, her husband" (as the official warranty deed put it) agreed to sell Huntland to George R. Brown. The de la Fregonnieres left Virginia to live at their houses in Paris and in the Bahamas. When the sale to Brown closed on December 13, another important chapter opened in the history of Huntland.[376]

That sale marked the fifth time the property had changed hands since Joe Thomas bought Huntland in 1912. "Huntland, tossed aside like an old boot, became a stepchild that nobody seemed to want," Kitty Slater aptly put in her book, *The Hunt Country of America*.

With that sale, she wrote, "Joe Thomas, the contributor of a colorful chapter not only to the Piedmont Hunt but to the Hunt Country as a whole, soon was the Forgotten Man."[377]

Huntland, then known as New Lisbon, in the late 1800s with its original two-story porch and side one-story service wing. The child on the porch is Inez Harrison Beavers (1883-1977), a great granddaughter of William Benton, Sr. (Janet Hitchen from original photo of John D. Beavers).

New Lisbon Female Seminary.

THE commodious and pleasantly-located buildings, formerly occupied as a Boarding House for the Male Academy, 4 miles North of Middleburg, Loudoun Co., Va., have been secured and furnished for a Female Boarding School. Conveniences for Bathing are also furnished.

Mrs. E. H. GREER, Principal Preceptress.
Miss HELLEN S. BENEDICT, Teacher of French, Music on Piano and Organ, Drawing and Painting.

The scholastic year will embrace 10 months, divided into two terms of 21 weeks each. The sessions will commence on the 1st *Monday in February* and the 1st *Monday in September*

TERMS PER SESSION:
Board and Tuition. including Lights and Washing, $75
Latin, French, Music, Drawing and Painting (extra) each 10

Bills payable quarterly in advance.
For particulars, address   E. H. GREER,
March 8, 1854—1y   Middleburg, Loudoun Co., Va.

An 1854 advertisement for the New Lisbon Female Seminary, a boarding school at New Lisbon/Huntland, one of many ads that appeared in local mid-19th-century newspapers (*Winchester Virginian*, September 13, 1854).

A 19th-century oil portrait believed to be of William Benton, Sr., builder of New Lisbon/Huntland (Betsy Leith Kelly).

Sketch of Hannah Benton, who was born at New Lisbon/Huntland in 1853. She was one of five children of Margaret and James Monroe Benton, son of William Benton, Sr., who built the house in 1834 (Betsee Parker).

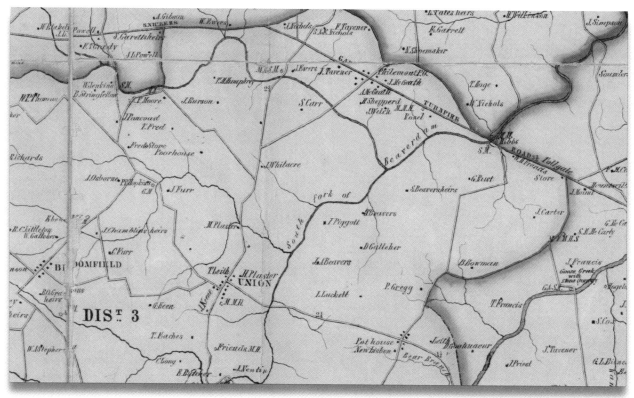

New Lisbon/Huntland at the bottom right-hand corner of the 1850s Yardley Taylor Map of Loudoun County (Library of Congress Geography and Map Division).

Joseph B. Thomas in 1914 at his newly constructed kennel at Huntland (Library of Congress).

Circa 1914 image of Daniel C. Sands, Jr., a long-time leader of the foxhunting community in Middleburg (Library of Congress).

VIRGINIA
MIDDLEBURG   LOUDOUN COUNTY

"HUNTLAND"
In the Centre of the Famous Hunting Country

18th CENTURY VIRGINIA MANSION—an ideal sportman's estate of 408 acres in highest state of cultivation—48 miles from Washington, D. C.—in finest agricultural and sporting district of Virginia; modernized Colonial Mansion, 20 rooms, 6 baths, wonderful old wall papers, old-fashioned wall gardens; most complete hunter stables (30 boxes) and kennels in America —the whole laid out in symmetrical 18th Century style. Best dairy and farm barns in the county.

Garage—manager's cottage, 7 rooms, 2 baths—gate lodge—9 tenant houses. All in perfect order and repair. Fox Hunting—Beagling—Shooting—Fishing—Racing—Horse Shows.

For particulars apply to
SAMOTH REALTY CO.
132 East 19th Street   New York City

Samoth Realty Co., owned by Joseph B. Thomas, ran this ad in *Country Life* magazine in 1920.

Late-1940s image of Charlotte Haxall Noland, the founder of Foxcroft School in Middleburg, Virginia, located near Huntland (Nancy Bedford).

Circa 1914 image of an elaborate tent at the Loudoun Camp Meeting at Benton's Woods at Huntland (Thomas Balch Library).

Circa 1912 image of Clara Fargo, who married Joe Thomas in New York City in 1915 (Genthe photograph collection, Library of Congress).

The front of Huntland from Joe Thomas' ca. 1920 marketing brochure (Betsee Parker).

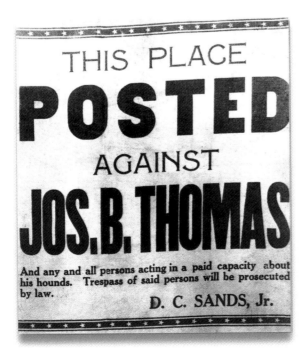

1915 broadside posted by
Daniel Sands
(Thomas Balch Library).

Huntland dining room ca. 1920
(Betsee Parker).

Huntland master bedroom
ca. 1920 (Betsee Parker).

Tenant houses at Huntland ca. 1920 (Betsee Parker).

Huntland's front entrance gateposts ca. 1915 with a fox and hound that Joe Thomas removed before selling the property in 1920. Betsee Parker installed replicas of the two statues in 2023 (Liederbach & Graham Architects LLP collection).

Mid-20th-century image of the back of Huntland after Joe Thomas completed renovations (John D. Beavers).

Thomas Hunt Talmage and his wife Mildred purchased Huntland in November 1929. They sold it four years later (U.S., Passport Applications, 1795-1925).

Circa 1942 photograph in front of Huntland of Colin MacLeod, who purchased the property in 1938, and his son Colin "Sandy" MacLeod, Jr. (Ann MacLeod).

Huntland ca. 1950, during the ownership of Count Guy de la Fregonniere and his wife Priscilla, who purchased the property in 1948 from the MacLeods (Thomas Balch Library).

George R. Brown with Lyndon B. Johnson in the White House in 1968. George and his brother Herman, who ran the giant government contracting firm of Brown & Root, bought Huntland in 1954. Their heirs sold it to Roy Ash in 1990 (LBJ Presidential Library).

George C. McGhee, then U.S. Ambassador to Germany, with President Johnson at the White House in 1967. Texas-born McGhee purchased a historic farm near Huntland known as Farmer's Delight in 1948. Betsee Parker acquired Farmer's Delight in 2013 and has meticulously restored the house and outbuildings (LBJ Presidential Library).

United States Senate
Office of the Democratic Leader
Washington, D. C.
August 11, 1955

Dear Dr. Gibson:

This is the first opportunity I have had to write to you and express the deep gratitude of myself and my family. Without your prompt and decisive action, I would not be here and I feel that I owe you as much -- if not more -- as I do to any other man.

I will never forget those hours of turmoil in which everyone around me appeared harassed and flustered and inadequate to the situation. Your calm, efficient manner and your obvious capability had all the effect upon me that a sudden rain storm would have on a man dying of thirst in the desert.

You brought me hope at a very crucial time.

I have always had a deep respect and admiration for men who could come directly to the point without waste motion. I will always be grateful to the good Lord that such a man appeared in a time of crisis and if there is anything on this earth that I or my family can ever do for you, you will find us ready to pay one of the greatest debts that I owe to anyone.

Sincerely yours,

Lyndon B. Johnson

Dr. James W. Gibson
Middleburg
Virginia

August 1955 letter from Lyndon B. Johnson to Dr. James W. Gibson of Middleburg expressing his deep appreciation for saving his life (James W. Gibson, Jr.).

Vice President Lyndon B. Johnson, at the White House with President John F. Kennedy in 1963, was a frequent visitor to Huntland during the ownership of the Brown brothers when he was Senate Majority Leader (1955-61) and Vice President (1961-63). On at least one occasion, Kennedy and his wife Jackie–who rented a country estate nearby—came to Huntland where Johnson gave them a tour of the house and property (LBJ Presidential Library).

Lady Bird Johnson, in her White House office in 1963, was a regular visitor to Huntland. In May 1964, she wrote a nine-page memo at Huntland in which she made a case for her husband not to seek re-election in 1968 because of his heart condition (LBJ Presidential Library).

Middleburg Hunt at the front gates of Huntland on December 18, 2010 (Janet Hitchen).

Huntland, 2017 (Maral S. Kalbian).

(Above) West parlor (Janet Hitchen).

(Right) Main staircase (Maral S. Kalbian).

(Below) East Parlor (Joanne Maisano).

Huntland stable and kennels (Janet Hitchen).

Huntland stable, 2023 (Maral S. Kalbian).

Huntland kennels, 1914 (Library of Congress).

(Above) Huntland kennels (Joanne Maisano). *(Below left)* Middleburg Hunt foxhounds at the Huntland kennel in 2018, led by Huntsman Barry Magner (Joanne Maisano). *(Below right)*

In December 2022, Betsee Parker welcomed the Middleburg-Orange County Beagles, founded by noted horsewoman Eve Fout, when MOC moved its pack into the restored

Huntland kennel. The occasion marked the first time since 1918 that a pack of beagles or hounds took up residence in the kennel (Joanne Maisano).

(Above left) Betsee Parker spent nearly two years as a Team Lead for the Office of the Chief Medical Examiner of New York City working in pathology at Ground Zero at the former World Trade Center following the 9/11 attacks. This photo was taken on 9/11 after the first tower fell (Betsee Parker). *(Above right)* Betsee Parker signed on to a climate change statement issued by Pope Francis in the Vatican on July 21, 2015 (Betsee Parker).

(Left) Betsee Parker in May 2022 at Saint Paul's Cathedral (1851) in St. Helena, South Africa, when she was installed as Canon Emeritus of the Anglican Church of Southern Africa. She became the first woman to hold that title (Leah Coxsey). *(Above)* Betsee Parker and her horse trainer Scott Stewart at the National Horse Show in Lexington, Kentucky (Shawn McMillen, photographer, Betsee Parker).

CHAPTER NINE
Hope at a Very Crucial Time

"I have found the most marvelous place."

—Frank "Posh" Oltorf to George Brown, 1954

Frank Calvert Oltorf—the man who engineered the Brown Brothers' purchase of Huntland—graduated from high school in 1940, started college at Rice University, and then enlisted in the U.S. Army after the United States entered World War II. He served as a lieutenant in India. In 1954, Oltorf was one of George Brown's top lieutenants, managing Brown & Root's Washington, D.C., office.

After his military service, Oltorf, who grew up in the small city of Marlin, Texas, and whom everyone called "Posh," embarked on a political career. In 1946, at age twenty three, he won a seat in the Texas Legislature. He served for two terms, earned a law degree from the University of Texas, and enmeshed himself in Democratic Party politics in the Lone Star state. In the next few years Posh Oltorf worked for—among others—Rep. Lyndon Johnson and John Connally, who in 1963 would be elected governor of Texas. In 1948, he joined Harry S Truman's presidential campaign. A few years later Posh Oltorf took a job as an executive with Brown & Root in Texas.

When he arrived in the Nation's Capital, Oltorf lived up to his nickname by moving into the city's most exclusive hotel, the Hay-Adams, a block from the White House. He stayed there for four years. Although many believed that Posh Oltorf worked for Brown & Root in Washington as a lobbyist, he publicly insisted that he did not directly lobby members of Congress on the company's behalf.[378] Instead, Oltorf said, he performed myriad other tasks for the huge construction company that specialized in large-scale government contracts.

Mainly, he worked with high-ranking U.S. government officials and foreign embassies, he said, and as "a solver of political problems," as one observer put it.[379]

In 1954, Posh Oltorf solved a quasi-political problem for George Brown: finding him a place to live in the D.C. area. Brown spent a good deal of time in Washington, but was tired of doing his lobbying out of a suite at the old Carlton Hotel.[380] He also wanted to cut down on travel time to and from his home in Houston. This was "before we had jet airplanes," Brown said in 1968. He and his brother would "get caught in New York or Washington on the weekend and have to be [in Houston] on Monday, so we thought we ought to have some place to go without having to fly all the way, ten hours back to Texas and ten hours back."[381]

That's why George Brown decided to buy a place in the D.C. area, Posh Oltorf said in a 1971 interview.[382]

"I'm here so much," Brown explained to Oltorf. "I'd like to have a place that's not over an hour from" Washington "where he could "have some pleasure and go when I'm here." That was the start of the unlikely tale of how the Brown Brothers came to buy Huntland.

Posh Oltorf followed orders and began searching for the right place. After about eighteen months of looking, he came upon Huntland not long after the de la Fregonnieres had put it the property on the market.

He drove out to Middleburg, toured the house, and was shocked that it was listed for about a third "of what places not nearly as grand were selling for," he said. So Posh Oltorf immediately called George Brown in Houston.

⊣⊨ ⊨⊢

Oltorf remembered the conversation going something like this:

"George, I have found the most beautiful place. It's the greatest buy. It has to be bought right now."

"I'm not going to be able to get up there" to see it, George Brown replied.

"If you don't buy it, I'll buy it," Posh said, only slightly tongue in cheek, "because I can borrow the money and then I'll sell it to somebody at a profit."

To which George Brown replied: "I'll buy it."

"So," Posh said, "we got it, and it is a beautiful place."

George Brown's daughter, Isabel Brown Wilson, confirmed the gist of Oltorf's account—and added several details—in a 1988 interview. Posh Oltorf "spent several months" looking for the right property, she said, "when he telephoned my father with great excitement one day and said, 'I have found the most marvelous place.'"[383]

When her father asked how far Huntland was from Washington, Posh Oltorf, she said, replied that it was an hour's drive.

"Well, in truth," Isabel Wilson pointed out, "it was more like an hour and a half, especially in those days. But [my father] was very excited about it and he thought it was a rare buy." A rare buy, she said, because the family had heard that the de la Fregonnieres "needed some ready money" and that's why they put Huntland on the market "at a very good price."

Isabel Wilson then told a slightly different version of how the conversation went when her father told Posh Oltorf that he wouldn't be able to come to Virginia to see Huntland for at least a month.

"You've got to act on this right away," she said Posh said. "We need to do it in the next two or three days because otherwise it'll be gone. Somebody else is going to buy it."

Isabel Wilson said that her father then told Posh to call a mutual friend, Oveta Culp Hobby, whom President Eisenhower had appointed the first U.S. Secretary of Health, Education, and Welfare the year before. George Brown told Posh to "get her to go out there with you. If she says she likes it, we'll buy it."

Posh did as he was told. Oveta Culp Hobby came out to Huntland, then immediately called George Brown in Texas. She extolled Huntland's virtues and convinced Brown to buy it, Isabel Wilson said, adding that her "mother and father and aunt and uncle never saw it until several months after" the purchase.

Isabel's parents, George Rufus Brown and Alice Nelson Pratt Brown, and her aunt and uncle, Margarett Root Brown and Herman Brown, and their descendants would own Huntland for the next thirty-six years.[384]

The Brown Brothers were born in Belton, Texas, five-and-a-half years apart—Herman on November 10, 1892, and George on May 12, 1898. Herman Brown left the University of Texas after a year to go to work for a contractor in his hometown, which today is a suburb of Killeen. In 1914, he started his own construction business.

After high school, George enrolled at Rice University intending to be a doctor, but withdrew and joined the Marine Corps in the waning months of World War I. After the war, he later said, he "decided [he] didn't want to be a doctor" and "went to Colorado School of Mines to become a mining engineer."[385] When he graduated in 1922, George Brown went to work as a mining engineer for Anaconda Copper in Butte, Montana. He left Montana shortly thereafter, however, after being seriously injured in a mining accident in which he suffered a fractured skull, a broken arm, and broken ribs.[386] George came home to Texas, recuperated, and then joined his brother's small road-paving business.[387]

Herman Brown, twenty-four, married twenty-two-year-old Margarett Root—who was teaching school in Belton—on September 9, 1917. In 1919, Margarett's brother Dan Root, a prosperous cotton farmer in Granger, Texas, a small town not far from Belton, invested $20,000 in the business, which from then on operated under the name Brown & Root, Inc. The company expanded rapidly, mainly with lucrative road-paving and bridge-building contracts from central Texas counties. From Brown & Root's beginnings, Herman Brown concentrated on the construction details and his brother George on contracts and other business matters.

George Brown met Alice Nelson Pratt in 1924 when she was a student at Southwestern University in Georgetown, Texas, soon after he had come back to Texas to work with his brother. On November 25, 1925, after Alice had graduated from Southwestern, she and George were married in Lometa, Texas. They moved to Houston in 1926.

In the mid-thirties, thanks in large part to George Brown's salesmanship and the brothers' contacts, the firm began winning large contracts in Texas. First came a huge 1936 contract to build the mammoth Marshall Ford Dam for the U.S. Department of the Interior and the Lower Colorado River Authority on the Colorado River near Austin. Then, in 1940, Brown & Root won an even bigger government job, building a $90-million Naval Air Station at Corpus Christi.

In 1942, during the darkest days of World War II, Brown & Root expanded into shipbuilding. By the time the war ended, the Brown & Root Shipbuilding Company had built 359 Navy vessels (primarily submarine chasers, landing craft, and destroyer escorts) valued at some $500 million at their Green's Bayou Fabrication Yard in the Houston Ship Channel. That shipyard employed some 25,000 workers.

After the war, the company expanded into building natural gas pipelines and offshore drilling platforms, and won a $100-million contract to design and build a Union Carbide polyethylene (plastics) plant in Seadrift, Texas, along the Gulf of Mexico near Corpus Christi. Meanwhile, the company continued to get large federal government contracts to construct air and navy bases overseas. In 1962, Brown & Root reeled in a $1.5-million contract to do the architectural design work for the Manned Spacecraft Center (since renamed the Johnson Space Center) in Houston.

Not long after Herman Brown's death on November 15, 1962, Brown & Root was sold to Halliburton Company. George Brown died on January 22, 1983.

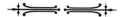

In 1954, the de le Fregonnieres conveyed virtually all the furniture and furnishings at Huntland to the Brown brothers. The house was "almost wholly furnished, not entirely," George Brown's youngest daughter Isabel (who had graduated from Smith College the year before and was working as a newspaper reporter for the *Houston* Press), said in 1988.[388] There were "no paintings and no silverware and no china or any of that," she remembered, "but much of the furniture was there. There were certain pieces that had to be added later, occasional tables and some chairs and things." Her mother Alice, she said, went to New York and bought those items, and also did some furniture shopping in Hunt Country "because she wanted antiques. They were not fine antiques, but things that would look right in the house."

George and Alice Brown and their three daughters spent more time at Huntland than Herman and Margarett Brown did—mainly because Herman and Margarett did not travel as much as his younger brother and his wife. Huntland "served as a sort of home away from home for George Brown," his biographers noted, especially as he became "more deeply involved in national economic and political affairs."[389]

George Brown served on more than a few corporate boards (including Armco Steel, IT&T, TWA, Southland Paper, and First City Bancorp) and on federal and Texas state government commissions (including President Truman's Materials Commission). When he purchased Huntland in 1954, George chaired the Rice University Board of Trustees. He traveled widely for Brown & Root and in conjunction with his work on the corporate boards and governmental commissions. As he did, Huntland became "a convenient place to stop over and rest on weekends stranded away from home."

George and Alice Brown also used Huntland "as a sort of guest house for their Washington friends," as Kitty Slater put it.[390] The Browns spent "as much time as they could" at Huntland, Isabel Brown said, "but unfortunately they never seemed to have enough time to spend." Plus, she said, Huntland "was not air conditioned, and in the summer it was quite warm. A swimming pool and air conditioning were added later." The latter was installed, she said, "primarily for Aunt Margarett, who had quite bad asthma. She needed the air conditioning to be able to visit at all in the summer."

Soon after buying Huntland the Browns hired Teresa "Tessie" Anderson to be their cook and house manager, and her husband William (Bill) Anderson as the stable manager. The couple wound up working for the Browns at Huntland for twenty-eight years.[391] "Miss Tessie," as the Browns referred to her, "was the most beautiful cook," Isabel Wilson said. "She was Virginian and spoke with the wonderful, broad Virginia 'a.' She had been trained by the French count [Guy de la Fregonniere] and was also naturally a very good cook. It was nothing fancy, but it was the best food I think I've ever eaten in my life. I can still remember it with happiness. Her vegetable soup was the best vegetable soup I've ever put in my mouth."

George Brown had Posh Oltorf oversee the agricultural operations at Huntland. "They had a dairy on it," Oltorf said in 1971, "and I was in charge of seeing to it that the farm tried to pay for itself. I don't think it ever did."[392] The Browns later ended the dairy operation and began raising cattle on the property.[393]

They leased the horse stable to local equestrians including Bobby Burke and legendary horseman Morton "Cappy" Smith. The Browns also occasionally allowed the Piedmont Fox Hounds to meet at Huntland. As for Joe Thomas' world-class kennel—which hadn't housed foxhounds for more than twenty-five years in 1954—the Browns used it "chiefly for storage," Kitty Slater wrote in 1956, "with one section having been converted into stalls for horses."[394]

Aside from air conditioning the place, the Browns also put their mark on Huntland by building a swimming pool near the house and dredging an old fishing pond on the property and stocking it. Speaker of the House Sam Rayburn—a friend of the Browns—often gravitated to the pond during his not-infrequent visits to Huntland.

"He loved to fish," Isabel Wilson said of Rayburn, who grew up on a farm near Window, Texas, and loved the Huntland pond so much that "we used to call it Lake Rayburn."

Lyndon Johnson had an extremely close relationship with the Brown Brothers. They were "devoted friends," Posh Oltorf said, "like brothers."[395] The Brown Brothers had lavishly supported LBJ since he first ran for Congress in 1937 with significant campaign contributions, personal gifts, introductions to other wealthy Texas businessmen, and other favors, including hosting him and his family at their residences in Texas—and at Huntland.

LBJ reciprocated by using his growing influence in Washington to help Brown & Root.[396] The Brown Brothers' relationship with Lyndon Johnson, journalist and author Dan Briody wrote, was "an unprecedented business and political association that propelled both the Browns and Johnson to the top of their respective professions."[397]

The Brown Brothers and Lyndon Johnson's lives were "entwined" for thirty years, LBJ biographer Robert Caro wrote. As Brown & Root became, "thanks to Johnson, an industrial colossus, one of the largest construction companies—and shipbuilding companies and oil-pipeline companies—in the world, holder of Johnson-arranged government contracts and receiver of Johnson-arranged government favors amounting to tens of billions of dollars, suave George Brown and his fierce brother Herman became, in return, the principal financiers of Johnson's rise to national power."[398]

The presidential historian Robert Dallek agreed with that assessment, adding that the Brown Brothers were "indebted" to LBJ for World War II wartime ship-building contracts and "for two post-war deals that opened new opportunities for growth and profit." In 1946, when Johnson was a member of a House subcommittee on U.S. governance of former Japanese-controlled islands, Dallek said, "the Browns won part of a $21 million Defense Department contract to build navy and air force bases on Guam. The Browns profited even more from the acquisition of oil and natural gas pipelines built during World War II, which Johnson helped them buy from the government."[399]

Lyndon Johnson used Huntland "like it was his own," LBJ's long-time aide Walter Jenkins said in 1982.[400] LBJ began using it not long after the Browns took possession early in 1955. Johnson would visit Huntland more than sixty times when he was the Senate Majority Leader (1955-61) and Vice President (1961-63). Most of the time the jaunts from Washington to Middleburg (mainly by car, but occasionally by helicopter) amounted to R&R for LBJ: He came to Huntland to get away from the stresses of Washington and relax, primarily in the company of George Brown and a cast of Texas Democratic members of Congress.

In addition to Speaker of the House Rayburn, that cast included Homer Thornberry, who had succeeded Johnson in 1948 as the Texas 10th congressional district congressman, and served for seven terms before LBJ appointed him to a federal judgeship in Texas in 1963 and to a seat on the Fifth U.S. Court of Appeals in 1965. Frank Ikard, a five-term Texas Congressman (1951-61) who went on to serve as president of the American Petroleum Institute from 1963-80, was another regular Huntland/LBJ visitor. So was Jack Brooks, who represented Texas' 2nd congressional district in Congress for forty-four years (1953-95). Brooks, a close ally of Speaker Rayburn and LBJ, fought at Guadalcanal as a U.S. Marine during World War II.

LBJ protégé Albert Richard Thomas, who put in twenty-nine years (1937-66) as a U.S. Congressman from Texas' eighth congressional district in Houston, was also a regular guest of LBJ at Huntland. Albert Thomas and George Brown became friends as students at Rice University in the early 1920s. Thomas helped pave the way for Brown & Root's move into shipbuilding at the Houston Ship Channel in 1941 and 1942, and also played an important role in steering the Manned Spacecraft Center to Houston.[401] George Brown endowed the Albert Thomas Professor of Political Science at Rice University in honor of his old friend, who died in office in 1966 at age sixty-seven.

These men were all friends of Lyndon Johnson, Isabel Wilson said. He could relax with them, she said, and "felt at ease" with them. The weekends with friends at Huntland "were very easy [and], informal, with good food and conversation."

Visiting Huntland "was a chance to spend, say, two or two-and-a-half days of total relaxation where [LBJ] was out of the turmoil of the capital and the phones bothering him," Johnson's secretary Bob Waldron said. He'd "just be among the people he enjoyed being with."[402]

The conversations, naturally, tended to deal with politics. "I don't remember any intellectual conversations," Isabel Wilson said. "They were political because that's what they were interested in." LBJ "always talked politics," Waldron said. His conversations at Huntland "were politically motivated or at least slanted, because that was his life.... I just always enjoyed him kind of summarizing what had happened that week in the Senate."

LBJ "loved Tessie's cooking," and "I think he relaxed there as well as almost anywhere. He felt at ease and comfortable among friends. These were brief weekends. Many times they would be there just one night."

Most of the time Lady Bird Johnson joined her husband on the weekend jaunts. "We adored going to Huntland," Lady Bird said in a 1994 interview. "It was an old pre-Civil War brick house way out in the country. The Browns lived there for a few weekends, days—maybe at the utmost for a week." They "used it as a retreat for themselves and their friends, and made it available to us at times."

Huntland, Lady Bird added, was "well-staffed, casual nevertheless, had a swimming pool [and] beautiful gardens. Lyndon went down there with George and a bunch of their special friends."[403]

A typical LBJ Huntland weekend visit would start either on Friday afternoon or Saturday morning or afternoon. The entourage usually included Lady Bird Johnson and a few members of LBJ's staff. Early on Saturday afternoon, February 20, 1961, for example, Johnson and his chauffeur Norman Edwards picked up Homer Thornberry and his wife Eloise in the Majority Leader's big limo, and then collected LBJ's personal secretaries Bob Waldron and Mary Margaret Wiley. They arrived at Huntland in time for a late lunch.[404] Lady Bird Johnson and the Johnsons' younger daughter Luci joined the group at Huntland later that afternoon, along with Walter Jenkins.

After a dinner that began at 9:00, the relaxation turned to dancing. LBJ "tried to learn to cha-cha," according to his staff diary, "and seemed to enjoy himself. He stayed up until quite late—4:00 or so."[405]

Even though Jack and Jackie Kennedy regularly visited Glen Ora, the Middleburg estate they began renting from the Tartieres soon after he became president in January 1961, it appears that the first couple visited Vice President Johnson only once at Huntland. It happened on Sunday morning, March 12, 1961, when the Kennedys were spending the weekend at Glen Ora. They were driven to Huntland at around 11:30, along with Jackie's sister, Princess Lee Radziwell, where Vice President Johnson gave them a tour of the house and the property.[406]

The only recorded visit of the Johnsons to the Kennedys at Glen Ora came on Sunday, April 23, 1961—just two days after the CIA-sponsored Bay of Pigs invasion of Cuba had ended disastrously. "We were all out around the pool" at Huntland, Mary Margaret Wiley said in a 1988 interview, and LBJ "said something about maybe wanting to call the President and see if we could all drop over."[407]

Bob Waldron remembered the circumstances of the visit somewhat differently. He said that LBJ had a saddle made for four-year-old Caroline Kennedy as a gift and wanted to present it to her. Johnson "called and invited President and Mrs. Kennedy to come over to Huntlands [sic] for lunch," Waldron said in 1976, but "President Kennedy said that they had house guests and they couldn't come, but why didn't Vice President Johnson and Mrs. Johnson come over there to visit."[408]

Johnson accepted and asked Waldron, Mary Margaret, Lady Bird, and the journalist and presidential historian William S. White to come along.[409] At around 5:00 that afternoon[410] the party drove up to Glen Ora, Glen Waldron remembered, and LBJ and Jackie Kennedy "came out to meet us. It was the dearest memory in that Caroline greeted [LBJ] like a long-lost friend, very warmly. He presented her with the saddle, and she wanted him to go with her to the stable... to see her pony."[411]

Later at Glen Ora, LBJ and JFK "visited very quietly," Waldron said, discussing the Bay of Pigs "fiasco." Then the two men and William White "went down to the far end of the terrace near the swimming pool and talked for a while and came back." It was "a very solemn, quiet visit and the three men spent most of the time alone." JFK, Waldron said, was "very, very vividly agonized over that part in history."

The Johnson entourage stayed at Glen Ora that afternoon "for forty-five minutes or so, something like that," Mary Margaret Wiley remembered. After that, they returned to what she called "George Brown's house."

The weekend of June 18-19, 1955, at Huntland had been anything but relaxing for Lyndon Johnson and his friends and family. He set out for Middleburg on Saturday afternoon, June 18, after having lunch with Florida Sen. George Smathers in the private Senate Dining Room where Johnson "ate his usual double meal, and gulped the food," Smathers later said.[412]

On the ride to Middleburg LBJ "kept complaining about his pain," Smathers said in 1982. So Norman Edwards stopped in "a little old grocery store," went in, and bought some baking soda (Smathers called it "bicarbonate of soda") as they all believed LBJ had indigestion. Edwards mixed the baking soda with water, LBJ drank it down, "belched a little bit," had a second glass, and the party drove off to Huntland.[413]

When the men showed up at Huntland, Lady Bird already had arrived. That evening LBJ played dominoes, saying he felt better but still had some chest pains. The following morning LBJ insisted he was fine, although Smathers thought he looked sick and suggested he see a doctor. Johnson and company returned to Washington Sunday evening and the next day LBJ paid a visit to the Capitol physician, Dr. George Calver.

But "this wasn't a real exam," Smathers said, and Dr. Calver told him he was okay.[414]

Johnson—who was overweight and chain smoking three packs of cigarettes a day— continued his frenetic Majority Leader pace for the next two weeks.[415] He planned to get away from the stresses of working eighteen hours a day in Washington by spending a quiet Fourth of July weekend with friends and family at Huntland. He would drive out on Saturday, July 2, and Lady Bird and Luci would join him on Sunday because Saturday was Luci's eighth birthday.

But that's not what happened—by a long shot. Instead, Saturday, July 2, 1955, ended with a helter-skelter late-night ambulance ride from Middleburg to Bethesda Naval Hospital after LBJ suffered what one observer called "the most serious health crisis of his life"—a severe, life-threatening heart attack.[416]

Johnson had kept up his busy pace on Saturday morning and afternoon. He had intended to drive out to Huntland early in the day with Posh Oltorf and George and Alice Brown. But Johnson scuttled that plan because he had too much Senate work to do. That morning he left his Washington house on 30th Place N.W., off upper Connecticut Avenue near Rock Creek Park to put in a day's work at his Capitol Hill office—Room G-14, the Senate Majority Leader's office. He held four separate meetings with Republican Sen. Francis H. Case of South Dakota, made seven phone calls dealing with senatorial matters in between those meetings, and paid a visit to his tailor to get measured for two new suits as he'd gained nearly forty pounds in the previous five months.

After returning to his office on the Senate side of the Capitol building, LBJ got into a shouting match with a newspaper reporter over a seemingly trivial matter during a 3:00 briefing. He stormed out of his office after that and ate a late lunch—wolfing down a plate of hot dogs and beans and half a cantaloupe in the Senate Dining Room. LBJ then paid a visit to a friend and colleague, seventy-seven-year-old Georgia Sen. Walter George, who was recovering from an illness in his apartment at the Mayflower Hotel in downtown Washington.

Johnson left the Mayflower in his limo with Norman Edwards at the wheel at around 4:45. Not long after they left Washington, Johnson started feeling unwell. "I remember it suddenly began to seem terribly close" in the car, he wrote in a 1956 magazine article, "and I told Norman to turn on the air conditioner. He said it was already on, and I said to turn it on full steam, and he said it was already on full steam.... There was this sense of pressure on my chest. My chest hurt...." It felt "like there were two hundred pounds on it."[417]

When the Senator's limo pulled up to Huntland at around 6:00, George Brown was taking a nap and Posh Oltorf and Alice Brown were about to go for a swim at a neighbor's pool. LBJ "came to the door," Oltorf said, "and we said George was taking a nap and would he like to come swimming with us." LBJ declined, saying "he felt badly, and that he had to stop on the way down; he had terrible indigestion."

Alice Brown offered to wake her husband; LBJ declined and said he also wanted to rest. He went to the basement library to do so. Alice and Posh left to go swimming. When they came back, George Brown met them at the front door, Posh said, with "a rather worried look on his face. He said, 'Lyndon is sick. He's downstairs on the couch. I'm trying to make him lie down and rest but he says he's got these pains, and I'm worried about him. Do you know a doctor around here? It might be his heart.'"

Posh called a local friend who recommended Middleburg's only doctor, James W. (Jimmy) Gibson. Posh managed to locate Dr. Gibson, and asked him to come to Huntland.[418] While he was en route, New Mexico Sen. Clinton Anderson knocked on the door. "Evidently," Posh said, "Lyndon had told him that he was going to be" at Huntland, and Anderson "was passing through... and wanted to talk to him very briefly about something."

Johnson sat down with Anderson, who had had a heart attack. He described the symptoms to LBJ, which didn't help the situation, Oltorf said. It just made LBJ "more frantic."

Clint Anderson and Johnson began arguing, with Johnson insisting that he had indigestion, even though his father had had two heart attacks and died at age sixty and two of his uncles also had heart issues and died in their early sixties. George Brown, who had given LBJ an antacid (Amphojel) and some baking soda—and then "a good, strong drink" of whiskey—backed him up.[419] It's likely Johnson was in denial about his heart attack because media pundits had started mentioning him as a possible 1956 presidential candidate and he feared the political repercussions of news media reports of him being rushed to a hospital with a serious heart problem.

Then Dr. Gibson arrived, told Johnson he had every symptom of a serious heart attack, and that the local hospital didn't have the best equipment to treat him. He strongly recommended they get to a hospital in Washington right away.

"You'll probably go into deep shock in about an hour and a half," Gibson told Johnson, "which just gives us time to get you back into town... if you feel like you can do it." At that point, Johnson stopped arguing and agreed to leave for the National Naval Medical Center in Bethesda, Maryland, about fifty miles away—at least a ninety-minute drive in 1955.

"So they got the ambulance," Posh Oltorf said, "which was not only an ambulance but what they used for a hearse in Middleburg." LBJ asked Oltorf to ride with him and the ambulance/hearse took off for Bethesda. Norris Royston, Sr., who ran Royston's Funeral Home in Middleburg, drove and Dr. Gibson sat in the front passenger seat. Johnson "stretched out it the back" of the hearse and Posh Oltorf sat on a chair next to him.

It was, Oltorf said, "a very hectic ride."

LBJ was in pain and asked Gibson for something to relieve it. The doctor said they'd have to stop in order to do so, but time was critical. He told Johnson that if he could stand the pain, they would keep going as it was vital to get to the hospital as soon as possible. Johnson agreed.

Through the pain, LBJ kept up a steady stream of conversation with Posh Oltorf. "I think he definitely felt there was a possibility that he'd die before he got there," Posh said. LBJ spoke of his will, how he wanted to leave everything he had to Lady Bird, and about his ranch in Texas.[420]

When Johnson arrived at Bethesda Naval, the hospital's 34-year-old head of cardiology, Dr. J. Willis Hurst, took charge. LBJ's blood pressure was zero over forty and he was placed in an oxygen tent. Lady Bird, who had arrived at the hospital after George Brown called her at home from Middleburg, said LBJ "looked just like himself" as he was brought in on a stretcher. But he soon "became as gray as the cement sidewalk.... I was horrified. He was no longer Lyndon.... [he] was a totally different person."[421]

Lyndon Johnson began improving after his condition stabilized the following day, July 3. But it was "a very close call," George Brown said.

Johnson spent more than a month at Bethesda Naval Hospital. Dr. James Cain, a Mayo Clinic staff physician and Johnson family friend who flew in from Texas the day after the heart attack to oversee LBJ's care, said he had suffered a myocardial infarction and had "narrowly escaped death." LBJ "went into shock" at Huntland, Dr. Cain, an internist and gastroenterologist, told newspaper reporters at Bethesda Naval on July 6, and "only through the efforts of some very fine doctors is he here with us."[422]

The doctors released LBJ from the hospital on August 7. He recuperated at home in Washington, and then flew to his ranch in Texas on August 27, his 47th birthday. He didn't return to the Senate until December.

Four days after he'd left the hospital, on August 11, Johnson dictated a letter to Dr. Jimmy Gibson. The letter, typed on U.S. Senate Office of the Democratic Leader stationery, reads in its entirety:

"This is the first opportunity I have had to write to you and express the deep gratitude of myself and my family. Without your prompt and decisive action, I would not be here and I feel that I owe you as much—if not more—as I do to any other man.

"I will never forget those hours of turmoil in which everyone around me appeared harassed and flustered and inadequate to the situation. Your calm, efficient manner and your obvious capability had all the effect upon me that a sudden rain storm would have on a man dying of thirst in the desert. You brought me hope at a very crucial time.

"I have always had a deep respect and admiration for men who could come directly to the point without waste[d] motion. I will always thank the good Lord that such a man appeared in a time of crisis and if there is anything on this earth that I or my family can ever do for you, you will find us ready to pay one of the greatest debts I owe to anyone."

On August 29, Virginia Sen. Harry F. Byrd wrote to Dr. Gibson, saying that Johnson told him while he was recuperating in the hospital that "he believed he owed more to you than anyone else the fact that he is living today." LBJ and Lady Bird, Sen. Byrd said, "are full of gratitude to you for all that you did, and he especially commented on the fact that you had the training and capacity to know the right thing to do in a time of minutes."[423]

Dr. Gibson rarely spoke of his actions that night. His son, James W. Gibson, Jr., who was born in 1956, said that he never heard his father talk about it—except on one occasion. It had to do with LBJ's offer "to pay one of the greatest debts I owe to anyone."

"When I saw the letter on my Dad's office wall," he said, "I remember asking could we ask Mr. Johnson for a pony.

Of course my Dad said, "'No; that is not going to happen.'"[424]

CHAPTER TEN
The Huntland Agreement

"The world's man of the hour, the 36ᵗʰ President of the United States, would be at ease at Huntland and it with him."

—Kitty Slater, *Loudoun Times-Mirror*, Dec. 5, 1963

In March of 1962, seven years into the Browns' ownership of Huntland, the Kennedy Administration was looking for a place to hold secret negotiations on a delicate foreign policy matter that had significant geopolitical ramifications: a tense dispute between the Netherlands and Indonesia over the last remaining Dutch colony on the Indonesian Archipelago—Netherlands New Guinea, also known as West New Guinea and West Papua.

The Netherlands, through its Dutch East India Company, had colonized all of what today is the sprawling South Pacific island nation of Indonesia early in the 17ᵗʰ century. Indonesia wrested its independence from the Dutch in 1949 after four years of armed rebellion following the end of the Japanese occupation during World War II—except for the western half of the large island of New Guinea, which became known as Netherlands New Guinea.[425]

After thirteen years of intermittent negotiations—and periodic armed conflict—and with another violent Dutch-Indonesian confrontation on the horizon, the U.S. State Department tried to bring the two sides together. The goal: to hammer out an agreement to avert all-out war and pave the way for the independence of Netherlands New Guinea.

The stakes were high. If large-scale fighting broke out on the island, President Kennedy told Dutch Prime Minister Jan de Quay, it would be "a war in which neither The Netherlands nor the West could win in any real sense. Whatever the outcome of particular military encounters, the entire free world position in Asia would be seriously damaged. Only the communists would benefit from such a conflict. If the Indonesian Army were committed to an all-out war against The Netherlands, the moderate elements within the army and the country would be quickly eliminated, leaving a clear field for communist intervention."

If that happened, JFK warned, "the whole non-communist position in Viet-Nam, Thailand, and Malaya would be in grave peril and... those are areas in which we in the United States have heavy commitments."[426]

The task of arranging the talks fell to the Kennedy's National Security Council Adviser McGeorge Bundy and one of his top aides, the former CIA intelligence analyst W. Robert "Blowtorch Bob" Komer—both of whom would go on to play crucial roles in formulating

Kennedy (and Johnson) Vietnam War policies. Working in conjunction with Secretary of State Dean Rusk, the administration chose Ellsworth Bunker, the former U.S. ambassador to Argentina, Italy, and India, to moderate the talks.[427]

The Kennedy Administration made it clear that its sole goal was to help the parties achieve "a peaceful solution," according to a March 2, 1962, State Department "Talking Points Paper." In doing so, the State Department said that Indonesia requested a third-party moderator, but preferred "someone other than [UN Secretary General] U Thant or his UN representative and have suggested the US."

Which is why the State Department said that the United States was "prepared to undertake the third party role." The expectation was that the Dutch and Indonesians "would give assurances that they would not undertake any military action while the talks are under way."[428]

When it came time to find a venue, it's very likely that Vice President Johnson suggested Huntland as the ideal place for the hush-hush talks between Jan H. van Roijen, the Dutch Ambassador to the United States, and Adam Malik, the Indonesian ambassador to the Soviet Union, and their staffs. Newspaper accounts speculated that the talks would be held in New York or Washington, D.C.[429] They began on Tuesday, March 20, at Huntland—although the State Department announcement that day did not disclose the site.[430]

Nor did the Dutch government a day earlier when it announced the talks would begin. One reporter speculated that the parties would be meeting "at a private house within thirty miles of the capital."[431]

That house was Huntland, about fifty miles from Washington. Holland's UN delegate, C.W.A. Schurmann, accompanied Ambassador van Roijen to Huntland. Sudjarwo Tjondronagoro, who headed the European section of the Indonesia Foreign Ministry, joined Ambassador Malik. The four men and Bunker held a total of three days of formal discussions, taking a break on March 23 when the diplomats returned to New York to consult with their governments. Bunker brought along Michael Newlin, a State Department political officer in charge of the office of Dependent Area Affairs, and another Foreign Service Officer.

Huntland proved to be an "ideal setting" for the talks, Bunker's biographer Howard B. Schaffer later wrote. "Secluded and comfortable, it was an easy drive to Washington, where Bunker consulted government colleagues and the Dutch and Indonesians used their D.C. embassies "to communicate" with their governments. What was "even more important," Schaffer noted, was the fact that Huntland offered "informal, relaxed exchanges" as the conferees "chatted over cocktails and fine dinners, swam in the pool, and strolled the estate's handsome gardens."[432]

"International pressure," as one observer put it, brought the diplomats back to Huntland in mid-July for more talks (and socializing).[433] On July 30, the parties announced that they had agreed on the proposal that the Indonesians and Americans had been pushing for: The Dutch would give up Netherlands New Guinea, its last Asian colony, and the Indonesians would hold a plebiscite to allow the 700,000 Papuan people who lived there to decide whether to remain part of Indonesia or become an independent nation. The parties signed the agreement at the United Nations at 6:30 p.m. on August 15.

The agreement, Michael Newlin later said, "provided a face-saving solution to the Dutch for a problem that was left over from Indonesian Independence [in 1949]. It required a great deal of jawboning, including the intervention of the President."[434]

On August 16, President Kennedy wrote to Queen Juliana of the Netherlands, telling her of his "personal satisfaction" that the "long and difficult negotiations over West New Guinea have at last been successfully concluded." He told the Queen that the U.S. knew "how deeply your Government has been concerned to insure an honorable future for the Papuan people," and assured her "of the continuing concern of the United States for this same objective."[435]

Some observers called the pact The Huntlands [sic] Agreement since it was negotiated "shielded from prying eyes by a high, cream-colored brick wall" at Huntland, as *Time* magazine reported at the time. After "4 ½ weary months," *Time* said, "the negotiators shook hands on a deal."[436]

Howard Schaffer wrote that Bunker "promoted and greatly valued" Huntland as "a pleasant and isolated rural venue" that was conducive to productive negotiations. Bunker used Huntland "first as a useful setting for an informal exchange of views," Schaffer said, and then zeroed in on getting the parties to agree on the concrete details of a resolution they both supported."[437]

Michael Newlin provided a picture of the scene at Huntland in a 2002 letter. "We had morning and afternoon negotiating sessions," he wrote. "Cocktails around six, followed by dinner and then digestifs after dinner." The social parts of the time at Huntland, Newlin said, were "relaxed, non-protocolaire affairs where all members could establish personal links. There was a tacit agreement that the social occasions would not be used for negotiations."

However, he added, "from time to time after dinner when the Dutch or Indonesians wished to discuss a matter bilaterally," the heads of their delegations "would sit in a corner and converse in Dutch."[438]

Lyndon Johnson regularly used Huntland as his Virginia country retreat, spending scores of weekends there during his vice presidency—although not when the New Guinea negotiations were going on.

LBJ and Lady Bird, for example, took off for Middleburg at 9:00 on Saturday evening, April 7, 1962, from their Washington house on 52nd Street in upper Northwest (where they had moved after he became Vice President) following a reception there. They brought along Bob Waldron, Mary Margaret Wiley, and another Johnson staffer, Geraldine Williams, as well as Lyndon Johnson's close friend and business lawyer Don Thomas and his wife Jane, who were visiting from Austin.[439] The party had a late dinner at 10:30 at Huntland with two other guests, LBJ's journalist friend Bill White and his wife June.

Everyone slept in on Sunday morning, April 8, and then had a late breakfast at 11:00. At 1:00, three additional guests arrived: the famed FDR aide, lawyer, and lobbyist Thomas G. Corcoran, and his adult children David and Cecily. "Tommy the Cork" Corcoran—dubbed by *The New York Times* the "personification of the Washington insider"—had helped George and Herman Brown win their giant shipbuilding contract during World War II and had a close social and professional relationship with Lyndon Johnson since he first ran for the Senate in 1941.[440] After the three Corcorans arrived at Huntland, everyone adjourned for a 3:00 lunch.

The Whites left after lunch and the Corcorans before dinner. The Johnsons dined at Huntland that night at 9:30 with Don and Jane Thomas, Bob Waldron, Mary Margaret Wiley, and Geraldine Williams.[441]

At 7:30 Monday morning, April 9, Norman Edwards drove everyone back to Washington. LBJ's official duties that day included opening the Senate at noon and joining President Kennedy for opening day of the 1962 Major League Baseball season at the brand-new, federally owned D.C. Stadium. Kennedy and Johnson and an entourage of cabinet members, senators, and congressmen were among the crowd of more than 44,000 people on hand to watch the Washington Senators play the first ever regular-season baseball game at the stadium. President Kennedy threw out the first ball. The Senators defeated the Detroit Tigers, 4-1.

Another typical LBJ Huntland weekend began on Saturday, January 19, 1963, when the Johnsons left for Middleburg at 7:20 p.m. from Washington with Nancy Brown Negley (one of George and Alice Brown's daughters) and Eugene and Adele Locke. They arrived at Huntland at 9:00. Gene Locke, a close friend and political ally of LBJ's, was born in Dallas and served in the Navy in World War II after graduating from Yale Law School. At the time of his visit to Huntland, Locke chaired the Texas State Democratic Executive Committee. LBJ appointed him Ambassador to Pakistan in 1966 and Deputy Ambassador to South Vietnam during the height of the Vietnam War in 1967.[442]

Everyone spent the night at Huntland. The main activity the following day—Sunday, January 20, 1963—for Vice President Johnson and his guests consisted of "driving around the estate" in the late afternoon.[443] Homer and Eloise Thornberry joined the group after the drive. Norman Edwards drove the Johnsons and the Thornberrys back to Washington at 10:10 on Monday morning.

At 1:10 on Saturday afternoon, March 16, 1963, the Thornberrys took off for Huntland with LBJ and Lady Bird from the Pentagon helicopter pad, touching down in Middleburg about twenty minutes later. Also on board: Leonard and Dorothy Marks.

Leonard Marks, a prominent Washington communications lawyer, began serving as legal counsel for Lady Bird and Lyndon Johnson's television and radio stations in Texas soon after he met LBJ in 1948. By the early sixties Marks had become "a trusted figure" in LBJ's "inner circle," one observer wrote, "and a top fundraising adviser."[444] Johnson appointed Marks—one of his few advisers who was not from Texas (he was born and raised in Pittsburgh)—director of the U.S. Information Agency in 1965. At the same time that he ran the USIA, Marks also sat on LBJ's National Security Council, where he advised Johnson primarily on Vietnam War policy.[445]

On St. Patrick's Day, Sunday, March 17, 1963, Dorothy and Leonard Marks joined LBJ, Congressman Jack Brooks and his wife Charlotte, and the Thornberrys for an afternoon walk around the 415-acre Huntland property. After that jaunt, LBJ and Homer Thornberry were driven to Farmer's Delight, a neighboring historic property that George C. McGhee, then serving as the Kennedy Administration's Under Secretary of State for Political Affairs, had purchased in 1948 and extensively renovated. They spent about an hour with the Texas-born McGhee, and then walked back to Huntland. Leonard and Dorothy Marks were driven back to Washington that afternoon; the Johnsons and Thornberrys took a helicopter to the Pentagon at 8:40 on Monday morning.

The transportation situation differed slightly on the next Johnson visit to Huntland on Sunday, June 23, 1963. This time Homer Thornberry drove to the Johnson's residence in Washington at 7:30 a.m. with Eloise and took LBJ and Lady Bird in his car to Huntland. That evening Lady Bird drove around the property with the Thornberrys and Lera Thomas, the wife of Congressman Albert Thomas. At 9:25, Lera Thomas drove Lady Bird back to Washington.

It appears that the last visit Lyndon Johnson made to Huntland came on Sunday, October 6, 1963. LBJ, Lady Bird, and his executive assistant Liz Carpenter and her husband Les made the drive from the Johnsons' upper Northwest Washington house to Huntland at around 2:30 in the afternoon. After arriving, they all took a walk around the property. The group headed back to D.C. at 5:00. LBJ had hired Liz Carpenter, who came to Washington in 1942 to cover the White House and Congress for the *Austin* (Texas) *American-Statesman*, to his staff as his executive assistant when he became Vice President in January 1961. She was the first woman to hold that position.

Not long after Lyndon Johnson became President following the November 22, 1963, Kennedy assassination, people in Middleburg began speculating that LBJ would use Huntland as his presidential weekend retreat. The "conjecture" in Hunt Country, Kitty Slater wrote in the *Loudoun Times-Mirror* early in December, is that "we may have the opportunity to welcome President Lyndon B. Johnson as a sometime neighbor just as we had the late President Kennedy."[446]

Slater based that conjecture on the fact that the Browns had used "the beautiful and historic estate" as a "sort of guest house for their Washington friends" and that they had been "seldom in prolonged residence" in the eight years they'd owned Huntland. Perhaps, she wrote, the Brown Brothers already were considering using Huntland as "a country retreat" for LBJ, whom she described as their "friend of long acquaintance." Middleburg, she noted, was "convenient to Washington" and "acclimated" to dealing with a President and his family in its midst. Locals, she pointed out, respected the Kennedy's privacy "in moments of relaxation," and that LBJ and his family could expect "the same cordial welcome and quiet acceptance."

For supporting evidence, Kitty Slater pointed to a rumor that began circulating in Middleburg that the "telephone company" was about to install "additional communication devices" at Huntland and that she herself had spotted cars "that appeared to be workmen rather than the usual limousines" in the circular front driveway on Thanksgiving Day, November 28, six days after LBJ had taken the presidential oath of office. She also saw significance in the wooden eagle that Joe Thomas had mounted on the façade at the top of the front portico. As in the Great Seal of the United States, the Huntland eagle is clutching arrows in one claw and an olive branch in the other

"Is not the eagle the emblem on the United States?" a friend of Slater's had asked rhetorically. "Maybe [Lyndon Johnson] will return to this house as President."

Slater and others also pointed out that Huntland offered security features fit for a president. They included the iron front gates, the gate house (which could be manned by guards), the wall surrounding the front of the property, and the house sitting back from the road. Plus, there would be plenty of room for a helicopter landing pad. The stables and kennel, Kitty Slater suggested, "both commodious buildings" not far from the house, "could be converted to whatever purpose needed for [the] Presidential entourage."

She ended her article with these words: "The world's man of the hour, the 36th President of the United States, would be at ease at Huntland and it with him."

Kitty Slater was an astute observer of the Hunt Country social scene. However, in this case, her words turned out not to be prophetic. It appears that Lyndon Johnson did not set foot in Huntland during his presidency, which began when he took the oath of office in Dallas on November 22, 1963, and ended on January 20, 1969, with the inauguration of President Richard Nixon in Washington. Nor did LBJ visit Huntland from the time he flew home to his ranch in Texas following the Nixon inauguration until January 22, 1973, the day he died at age sixty four.

Lady Bird Johnson, on the other hand, did come to Huntland more than a few times after she became First Lady, sometimes with one of her daughters Lynda Bird and Luci. Occasionally, Luci Johnson would spend a day at Huntland by herself.

Lady Bird Johnson spent a good part of Monday, August 8, 1966, for example, at Huntland visiting George and Alice Brown and their Middleburg neighbors and friends George and Cecilia McGhee. She arrived at Huntland early that afternoon and, with the temperature in the upper eighties, sat around the pool with the Browns. After a nap, she returned to the pool where the McGhees and their daughters joined her. After that, everyone drove to nearby Farmer's Delight in Ambassador McGhee's pick-up truck, where the adults had cocktails and then "drove all over the McGhee estate," according to Lady Bird's official Daily Diary. The Browns and McGhees joined Lady Bird for dinner at Huntland. After dinner, at around 10:00 p.m., she returned to the White House.[447]

On Friday, September 1, 1967, Lady Bird managed a short visit to Huntland, leaving the White House just before 1:00 in the afternoon, and returning at 5:00. She spent those few hours at Huntland with her daughter Lynda and her fiancée, U.S. Marine Corps Captain Chuck Robb, whom she would marry on December 9 at the White House.

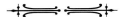

The most memorable moments Lady Bird spent at Huntland came during a three-and-a-half day "vacation with Luci" in May 1964. That was also when Lady Bird created an extensive record of Huntland and its environs for the first and only time in the form of a recording with a portable tape recorder she called "my machine." The result is the most-detailed description on record of the house and grounds during the Browns' long ownership (1954-1990).

On Wednesday, May 13, after a day of work in Washington, she left the White House in a limo along with her Secret Service agent Jerry Kivett and Luci's sixteen-year-old friend Beth Jenkins, the daughter of LBJ's aide Walter Jenkins. Luci Johnson had been driven to Huntland earlier in the day.[448]

On that unseasonably cool May day, Lady Bird said, it rained steadily all the way out to Middleburg. But the rain stopped as they drove through Huntland's main gate. Bill Anderson, the stable manager, came out to greet the First Lady, she said, "grinning from ear to ear, with word that 'Miss Luci' had taken a nap."

When Lady Bird stepped into the house, she found the hall "fragrant with lilacs and the peace of Huntland enveloped me." She had dinner with Beth and Luci "in the cozy little downstairs room [the former William Benton kitchen] that is like what an English pub may have been in the 18th century, paneled oak walls, a fireplace, windows with small, wavy panels with glass, pewter on the shelves."

After dinner, Lady Bird sat in front of a fireplace and started reading Bill White's just-published book, *The Professional: Lyndon B. Johnson*.[449] She went to bed at midnight after taking a call from LBJ, who, she said, sounded "lonesome." She awoke the next morning at 9:00, had breakfast in bed, and read the morning newspapers. Luci and Beth Jenkins later joined her for lunch. The "girls," she said, had stayed up very late the night before, "talking about whatever it is sixteen-year-olds have on their minds—and playing cards."

After lunch, Lady Bird took a walk with Jerry Kivett. "Virginia in mid-May is balm for any trouble," she said. "No silent spring here. The green arch of fresh spring leaves almost met over the rugged country road, brown thrush flashed through the underbrush; occasionally you would see a little chipmunk perched on a rail fence. A flock of crows cawed in the distance, across the lush green meadow, over which the dairy cows—Holsteins, I think they were—placidly ambled. And every time you came to a rise, [there] it was: the lovely blue outline of the [Blue Ridge] mountains in the distance."

The First Lady and her bodyguard walked for nearly two hours. At one point they saw a "handsome country home, behind a fieldstone fence.... And in the distance, a ring around which six horses, with riders, were going round and round and in the center of the ring, I suppose he must be the teacher. What a beautiful way to live! The melancholy call of mourning doves announced that it was spring. There were plenty of robins hopping about and once a cardinal flashed across the road."

They strolled past "a lot of blackberries growing beside the fence," she said. "The blossoms had already fallen and the little berries were beginning. Along the way, we saw several holes, burrows in the bank, and we wondered what sort of an animal—rabbit, fox—whose home [that was]. I peered down one, and it was a duplex!"

On the last morning of the visit, a "bright, beautiful" Saturday, Lady Bird took another long walk along "the country lane that turns right when you go out of the gate [Pott House Road], where the trees meet overhead." At "the top of the hill, [we] cut across through the pasture, knee deep in clover, past rail fences, with a lush view of the stables and the dairy barn, and the Huntland manor house in the distance. And finally across to the pond—the one where Sam Rayburn used to fish. There is a little boat there, and Luci had gone out and had such fun with Beth and her agents."

Lady Bird and company continued walking through the Huntland fields, "hip high and very thick, and red-winged blackbirds swaying on the top of stern, and then circling off in to the blue sky. There couldn't have been a more perfect day!"

The party "walked across [to] the next fence line and then down the field past the dairy barn and the dairyman's house, and the elegantly built old stable where" Joe Thomas "came to teach this countryside how to hunt fox properly, clad in red coats and with the correct English etiquette. He must have had so much pleasure with the perfection of the bucolic scene that he had achieved."

She later walked "all over the garden." The watercress and forget-me-nots "are thick on the little stream that bubbles out from the lake surrounded by pine trees," Lady Bird said. "The alley of boxwood is very dark and deep with dreams, rather foreboding. But the bridal wreath and columbine and the lilacs are lovely. And the loveliest thing of all is the utter stillness, except for the song of the birds."

⁍══ ══⁌

The other remarkable thing about those four days at Huntland was what took place the second evening—Thursday, May 14, 1964—when Lady Bird met with LBJ's doctors J. Willis Hurst and Jim Cain to discuss "in detail," as Hurst later put it, "the wisdom of [Lyndon Johnson] running for the presidency" that year.[450]

The two physicians drove to Middleburg after Lady Bird had called Hurst at the

White House in the afternoon asking them to come out. While waiting for them, Lady Bird wrote out a long "analysis" containing her thoughts about the big question they would be discussing. She considered her husband's health, but also how running for president (and winning) would affect her and their children. She particularly worried about how they would be "criticized and slandered for things we have done; that we maybe in part have done; and things we never did at all." That, she said, would be "painful."

Lady Bird concluded that her husband had sufficiently recovered from his heart attack and had the physical strength to run for president that year. But she wanted him to do so only if he paced himself "as well as his personality will permit" by not working on Sundays and taking occasional vacations. Then, after winning the 1964 race, she said, she wanted LBJ to make an announcement in "February or March of 1968, if the Lord lets him live that long" that "he won't be a candidate for re-election...."

Drs. Cain and Hurst arrived at Huntland at around 8:00 p.m. When they walked in the front door, Lady Bird handed them an envelope containing the nine-page analysis she'd written. She asked them to give it to the President when they met with him the next morning. She wrote LBJ's name on the outside of the envelope, along with the words "personal please." A 2021 biography of Lady Bird refers to the analysis as the "Huntland Strategy Memo."[451]

The three sat down in the "small sitting room," she said, but soon adjourned to the dining room, "candle-lit, fire going, a bowl of lilacs on the table, steaks and wine for dinner." Luci and her friend Beth joined them. "It was wonderful," Lady Bird said, "to see how joyously [Luci] and Jim [Cain] greet each other." Luci, she said, usually was restrained in front of her parents' friends. However, for a few people, including Tommy Corcoran, "the Cains and Dr. Hurst," she "is the most articulate, outspoken little girl—a rebel, but delightful... We had a really gay time."

The teen-agers played cards (crazy eights) after dinner. Lady Bird and her husband's two doctors had coffee around the fire where they discussed "the possibilities for Lyndon."

Lyndon Johnson did choose to run in 1964, and he did win, decisively defeating his Republican challenger, Sen. Barry Goldwater of Arizona. Johnson was eligible to run for a second full term four years later. But on March 21, 1968, at the height of the increasingly unpopular and divisive Vietnam War—and almost exactly when Lady Bird had predicted—the President stunned the nation when he announced he would end his 1968 presidential campaign.

LBJ made that surprise announcement near the end of a nationally televised speech to the nation. He started the speech with another unexpected, shocking piece of news: He was ordering a bombing halt in the Vietnam War and would be asking the North Vietnamese to begin peace talks. Near the end of the forty-minute, solemn speech Lyndon Johnson delivered the second thunderbolt, fulfilling Lady Bird's wish from four years earlier:

"I have concluded that I should not permit the Presidency to become involved in the partisan divisions that are developing in this political year. With America's sons in the fields far away, with America's future under challenge right here at home, with our hopes and the world's hopes for peace in the balance every day, I do not believe that I should devote an hour or a day of my time to any personal partisan causes or to any duties other than the awesome duties of this office—the Presidency of your country.

"Accordingly, I shall not seek—and I will not accept—the nomination of my party for another term as your President."

CHAPTER ELEVEN
A Beautiful, Well-Kept Country Estate

"As a historic preservationist, I saw all the purist possibilities in Huntland."
—Betsee Parker, March 26, 2019

George and Alice Brown took sole title to Huntland following the deaths of Herman Brown in November of 1962 and Margarett Root Brown in January 1963. In 1975, George and Alice turned the title over to a holding company they owned called Highland Management.[452] The property consisted of some 580 acres: the original 413 acres George Brown bought from the de la Fregonnieres in 1954, along with 91 acres he purchased in 1957, 53 in 1958, and 22.6 (from Charlotte Noland) in 1960.

George Brown retired in 1975, two years after Lyndon Johnson's death, and rarely visited Huntland from then until his death in 1983. He and his wife Alice (who died in 1984) devoted much of their post-retirement time to the Brown Foundation, a Houston philanthropic organization the brothers and their wives formed in 1951. Herman Brown had left the bulk of his estate to the foundation. The Brown Foundation, which remains in existence in 2023, has donated hundreds of millions of dollars mostly to educational and cultural institutions in Texas, primarily in Houston.[453]

George and Alice Brown's daughters Isabel Brown Wilson, Alice Maconda Brown O'Connor, and Nancy Brown Negley inherited Huntland, along with their cousins Louisa Stude Sarofim and Mike Stude (Herman and Margarett Brown's adopted children). All of the Brown children and their husbands became generous philanthropists following their parents' deaths.

The eldest of George and Alice Brown's daughters, Nancy Nelson Brown, spent significantly more time at Huntland than any other member of the family in the 1970s and 1980s. Nancy, who was born on October 3, 1927, married Alfred Walter Negley around 1950. They had three children, Leslie, Alice, and William. Alfred Negley died at age sixty-four in 1980. In addition to chairing the Brown Foundation Board of Directors, Nancy became the driving financial force behind the founding of the San Antonio Museum of Art.

Nancy Brown Negley rented Huntland from her family beginning in the mid-seventies, according to Jimmy Hatcher, who worked for a Middleburg neighbor, the socialite and Democratic Party activist Pamela Harriman, at the time, and knew Nancy Negley well. Soon after she rented the property, Hatcher said, Nancy decided that Joe Thomas' house needed some remodeling. At first, she focused on the upstairs bathrooms.

"She said the bathrooms made too much noise," Hatcher said, "and there were bedrooms on each side of the bathroom, so she had those walls padded." Nancy spent "a lot of money," he said, on that, as well as on redecorating and remodeling other parts of the house.[454]

Part of the redecorating effort involved a week-long trip to Paris hunting for antiques. Nancy invited Jimmy Hatcher to come along and advise her. "She had an antiques expert and we shared an apartment on one side of the [Seine] river and she had [a rented] apartment on the other," he said. "She took her grandchildren to a cooking school at the Ritz, and at night entertained her lady friends from all over the country. The decorator and I [were] the males at dinner with the older women."

When her granddaughters weren't in cooking school, Hatcher said, "we'd have lunch with them and Nancy and the antiques expert, who helped furnish the house. He was an American and an expert on French furniture"

Nancy Negley divided her time between Huntland and Houston following the death of her first husband in 1980. Rev. Martin K. Spilman, Jr., a Methodist minister, officiated at her second marriage, which took place in Middleburg on August 2, 1985, to Keith Sears Wellin, who lived in New York City.[455] She boarded her horses at Huntland, and hired a professional horse trainer, Mike Elmore, who lived on the property. Nancy also took part in fox hunts on occasion, Jimmy Hatcher said.

"She wasn't really that horsey, though. She did it because she was [living in Hunt Country] and wanted to be part of everything."

In 1985, Nancy Negley opened Huntland to the public as part of the annual Hunt Country Stable Tour, a fundraising event run by Trinity Episcopal Church in Upperville during the Memorial Day Weekend that began in 1959. It marked the first time that Huntland had been included on the tour, although soon after the Brown Brothers bought Huntland, in April 1956, they participated in Virginia's Historic Garden Week, the Garden Club of Virginia's statewide event that draws thousands of visitors to gardens across the state.[456] The 1985 Stable Tour visitors took in Joe Thomas' stables, but not the kennels, which the Browns never used, Jimmy Hatcher said.

Nancy regularly entertained family and friends at Huntland, and Lady Bird Johnson visited on occasion. Once, in the early seventies, Hatcher remembered, Nancy Negley threw a memorable black-tie party at Huntland in which scores of guests, including Lady Bird, showed up in limousines. Nancy "had the porches decorated and there were tables set up outside," for "a fancy, sit-down dinner," he said.

The tenant houses at Huntland regularly were rented out in the 1980s. One long-standing, tenant, Margaret van Schaack, signed a ten-year lease in October of 1973, and lived at Huntland through the 1980s. Margaret Caldwell Donald van Schaack was a researcher, writer, and curator who worked with many museums in the United States and Europe. While living in Middleburg she served on the advisory board of the Museum of Hounds and Hunting in Leesburg.

Also during Nancy Negley's tenure at Huntland—in 1976—LBJ's son-in-law Chuck Robb—who had visited the house several times with his fiancé Lynda Bird Johnson when her father was Vice President—held a private meeting in the house to discuss his political future. Robb had left the Marines Corps in 1970 after serving for nine years, including a tour of duty in the Vietnam War. After coming home from the war, he graduated from the University of Virginia Law School in 1973, and had taken a job at the big Washington law firm, Williams & Connolly.

In 1976, Robb, "an ambitious newcomer to Virginia politics at the time," a newspaper reporter later wrote, "summoned some fellow Democrats" to Huntland "to discuss a long-shot bid to win the party's nomination for lieutenant governor."[457] That longshot paid off as Robb won that nomination and then was elected Virginia's lieutenant governor in 1977. Two years later he ran for governor and won. He went on to serve two terms (from 1989-2001) in the U.S. Senate.

Many years later Robb had fond memories of Huntland. "I remember it as a beautiful, well-kept country estate," he said in 2019.[458]

The Brown Brothers and their heirs' ownership of Huntland ended in June of 1990 when Highland Management sold Huntland to Roy Ash, the co-founder of Litton Industries in California, and his wife Lila. According to an article in *The Wall Street Journal*, the Ashes paid $7.6 million for Huntland, the "highest price ever for a Middleburg property."[459]

Roy and Lila Ash had purchased another Hunt Country property, Ardarra, on Zulla Road between Middleburg and Rectortown, in 1982. The manor house on that 236-acre estate, designed by Alabama-born New York architect Penrose V. Stout, was constructed by master builder W.J. Hanback in 1931-32. The property includes a stable, a farmer's cottage, garage, chicken house, and cow barn. In addition to remodeling Ardarra's second-floor bedrooms, the Ashes put in a new, paved entrance road to the house, planted a peach orchard, and added four run-in sheds for horses.[460]

The Ashes lived part of the year at Ardarra, as well as in their house in the exclusive Bel Air section of Los Angeles in the foothills of the Santa Monica Mountains. In 1989, they added another Hunt Country property to their real-estate portfolio, Llangollen Farm, one of the area's largest and best-known estates. The 1,000-acre property reportedly had been listed for $10 million by its owner, Col. Cloyce J. Tippett, a retired U.S. Air Force officer and the widower of Mary Elizabeth "Liz" Whitney Tippett.[461] She had received the estate as a wedding present from her first husband, John Hay "Jock" Whitney in 1930. They divorced in 1940. Jock Whitney was a grandson of John Hay, President Abraham Lincoln's secretary who later served as U.S. Ambassador to the U.K. and as Secretary of State under Presidents McKinley and Theodore Roosevelt. Jock Whitney, who inherited an enormous family fortune, also served as U.S. Ambassador to Britain.

Roy Lawrence Ash was born in Los Angeles on October 20, 1918, the son of Charles K. Ash, a hay and grain dealer, and his wife Fay Dickinson Ash. Roy graduated from Manual Arts High School at sixteen in 1935 during the height of the Great Depression. The forbidding economic climate was one reason he skipped college and went to work for his father after high school. Soon thereafter, the young man took a job as a $65-dollar-a-week cash collections messenger for a Bank of America branch in downtown Los Angeles.[462] He stayed with the bank for more than six years, moving up to become a bookkeeper, teller, and operations officer of a branch in El Monte in the San Gabriel Valley. Not long after the U.S. entered World War II in December 1941, twenty-three-year-old Roy Ash quit his job and joined the Army Air Forces, the recently formed U.S. Army aviation branch (and predecessor of the U.S. Air Force).

He started as a private, but soon was chosen to join a new unit, the Army Air Forces Statistical Control Division. Army Chief of Staff Gen. George C. Marshall created it as part of his massive 1942 reorganization of the Army. Ash quickly was promoted to captain and spent the rest of his time in the Army as a member of a Statistical Control Division team working at the Harvard Business School.

Under the command of Col. Charles "Tex" Thornton—with whom Ash later would co-found Litton Industries—the statistical division overhauled all of the Army Air Force's reporting systems and implemented new management procedures. That statistical-heavy work insured—as one observer put it—"that there were enough planes where needed, with enough pilots and enough working parts to keep them airborne" throughout World War II.[463]

Thornton half-jokingly later explained that "statistical control" was simply "a fancy name for finding out what the hell we had by way of resources and when and where it was going to be required."[464] Joking or not, by the end of the war, Thornton's new statistical controls were "the most sophisticated and effective of all the armed forces," the U.S. Army reported in a 1975 study, and had played an important role in the planning and execution of the American victories over Japan and Germany.[465]

After the war, Tex Thornton left the military and joined the Ford Motor Company, along with ten of his Statistical Control Division men. The group soon became known as the Ford "Whiz Kids." It included Robert Strange McNamara, who later would become Ford's president and go on to serve as Secretary of Defense under Presidents Kennedy and Johnson from 1961-68.[466]

Roy Ash, who married Lila Marie Hornbek in 1943, did not join the Ford Whiz Kids after his discharge. Instead—without an undergraduate degree—he was accepted at Harvard Business School. Ash completed the two-year graduate business course in a year and a half, finishing first in his class. He took his MBA and went back to Los Angles to work for Bank of America in 1947.

Two years later Roy Ash rejoined Tex Thornton, who had left Ford to become vice president and general manager at Hughes Aircraft Company in Culver City, California. Thornton hired Ash to be the company's chief financial officer. Business at Hughes Aircraft boomed under Thornton and Ash's leadership, but both men left the company after a dispute with the eccentric Howard Hughes in 1953.

They decided to go into business together. Thornton and Ash convinced Lehman Brothers, the then-big Wall Street investment company, to lend them $1.5 million. They used the money to buy a small northern California electronics firm that produced microwave electron tubes owned by an engineer named Charles Litton. They promptly named the venture Litton Industries, and began acquiring a wide range of companies in the United States and around the world.

Ash and Thornton pioneered the concept of the conglomerate—the ownership of dozens of different companies "whose products ranged from manufacturing electronic typewriters and industrial microwave ovens to producing electronic guidance systems for aircraft and building ships," as his *Los Angeles Times* obituary put it.[467] At its peak, Litton owned more than a hundred corporations and operated seventy-one factories around the globe.[468] Revenues topped $1 billion by the early sixties. In 1961, Ash took over as Litton's president from Thornton, who then served as CEO and Board Chair.

Following the election of fellow Southern California Richard Nixon to the presidency in 1968, Roy Ash moved to Washington to head a high-level project, the President's Advisory Council on Executive Organization, which began its work on April 15, 1969. The council's mission: to do a thorough review of the executive branch's operating procedures and to recommend changes to streamline the many and varied (and sometimes overlapping) federal departments and agencies.

Ash's council met in formal sessions one or two days a month from April 1969 until it disbanded in April 1971. The staff conducted some 1,500 interviews during that time, met with Nixon five times, and produced fourteen memoranda. That included recommendations on how to reorganize the Executive Office of the President as well as to establish a federal environmental protection organization and a new government office that consolidated agencies dealing with the oceans, large waterways, and the atmosphere. The Nixon Administration adopted all the recommendations. That included, in 1970, creating the Environmental Protection Agency (EPA), headed by an administrator nominated by the President and approved by Congress, and the National Oceanic and Atmospheric Administration (NOAA) within the Department of Commerce.

After the Council on Executive Organization disbanded Roy Ash stayed in Washington. In 1972, he became the director of the Office of Management and Budget—an entity that he had advocated for as chair of the Council on Executive Organization—in the White House. He also resigned as president of Litton Industries, which had become one of the nation's biggest military contractors.

Roy Ash remained the head of OMB when Gerald Ford became president after Nixon's resignation in August 1974. Ash stepped down in February 1975, and in 1976 moved back into private industry, becoming chairman and CEO of AM International, a large Cleveland-based company that made duplication machines and other office equipment. He retired from business in 1981, although he served on several large companies' boards of directors, including Bank of America.

After buying Ardarra Farm in 1982, the Ashes—who had five children—split their time living in Bel Air and in Hunt Country. Roy Ash died on December 14, 2012, at his home in California at age 93. Lila Ash died at age 94 in Culver City, California, on November 17, 2017.

+≒= ≒+

In March 1998, *The Wall Street Journal* reported that the Ashes—the largest landowners in Loudoun County—had put Huntland and 47 acres of the property on the market. The asking price was $4.475 million.[469] It's likely they decided to try to sell because they did not live there, and didn't want to continue maintaining the property.

"He and Lila lived at Ardarra," Betsee Parker said. "Then they bought Llangollen and [Huntland]. Mr. Ash, I'm told, liked Huntland, but Lila liked Llangollen and they hoped that their kids would want" to live in Huntland and Ardarra.[470]

With no takers for Huntland and with none of their children interested in living in Hunt Country, the Ashes sold Ardarra in 2000. For the next seven years they stayed at Llangollen when they were in Virginia and continued to rent out the main house and cottages at Huntland. Roy Ash made a stab at breeding Thoroughbreds at Llangollen, but gave that up in 2001.

"We've sold our last horse," Ash told *The Washington Post* that summer. "We got in when the market was up, and we got out when the market was low."

Horse breeding, he said, was a risky and challenging business. But, he wryly noted, the "people who are in get a lot of psychic satisfaction out of it."[471]

On March 5, 2005, four months after Roy and Lila Ash had set up a family trust, they transferred the ownership of Huntland to that entity. The couple then decided to sell Huntland and Llangollen, their last two Hunt Country properties, and live full time in Bel Air. In October 2005, the Ashes listed Huntland for sale again—this time for around $17.8 million. Once again, there were no takers.[472]

Two years later, the Ashes sold Llangollen to Donald Brennan, a former Morgan Stanley executive, and his wife Patricia for $22 million, the highest price ever paid for a Hunt Country property.

+≒= ≒+

On May 8, 2007, the Ash Family Trust sold Huntland and 129.2 acres containing the house, kennel, stables, and barns to a family partnership for $7.3 million. Although not made public at the time, the Aix-La-Chapelle Limited Partnership was an entity formed by two members of the DeMoss Family, the sisters Elisabeth J. and Charlotte A. DeMoss, the daughters of the Christian televangelist and author Nancy DeMoss.[473]

"They bought Huntland the first time they looked at it," Betsee Parker said. "They only saw it once and bought it from Mr. Ash. I was told that they did not know what to do with it," except that they were about to "tear down the [kennel and stables] and were going to make them into dormitories" for "a fundamentalist, Christian organization. They were going to do camp meetings and change the name of this farm."

But the DeMoss sisters, Parker said, soon decided not to go through with that plan, "even though a wrecking ball was already in the stable courtyard," according to their interim manager. "It was very eleventh-hour," she said. They "gave up on Huntland about five months after they had bought it and put it on the market."

When Betsee Parker learned that Huntland was once again for sale, she quickly made an offer to Elisabeth and Charlotte DeMoss. "I found them very easy to deal with. I offered them cash, no contingencies, no changes in zoning—nothing. Take it or leave it. Ten days to closing with possession, and no negotiating. I gave them a real carrot on a stick and they took it. So I did manage to get it."

On November 2, 2007, Dr. Betsee Parker purchased the initial parcel of Huntland and its surrounding 129.2 acres from Aix-La-Chapelle Limited Partnership.

CHAPTER TWELVE
From Ground Zero to Hunt Country

"I knew at some point I was going to get" to Virginia.

—Betsee Parker

"I had wanted to live here since I was ten years old," Betsee Parker said in 2019 about her home in Middleburg.[474] She grew up near Minneapolis, graduating from that city's Southwest High School in 1969. Betsee received the school's Distinguished Alumni Award and was inducted into the school's Athletic Hall of Fame in 2019. She was just the second alumnus to receive both awards since the school opened in 1940.

Before that, as a horse-loving ten-year-old, Betsee had taken riding lessons at a stable near Wayzata, Minnesota, "a big bastion," she said, of "hunters and jumpers and English riding." That's when she first became aware of the Northern Virginia Hunt Country.

While sitting in the stable's lounge looking out into the indoor riding ring, Betsee said, she saw a copy of *The Chronicle of the Horse*—the weekly equestrian magazine published in Middleburg—on a coffee table. "I was fascinated by it," she said. "I took the magazine and paged through it and saw this wonderful section called 'Virginia Race Season' with articles about steeplechases and flat races and pictures of race season in Virginia. I became completely enthralled by Middleburg, Virginia, because of this magazine. Before long, I was starting to show ponies at Upperville."

The next year, when she was eleven, Betsee asked her parents to send her to Foxcroft, the all-female boarding high school a stone's throw from Huntland outside the town of Middleburg. Her parents were not enthusiastic. Even though Betsee continued to lobby them to send her there, they didn't budge. "So I never did get to go to Foxcroft," she said. "I fought with them about it till I was fifteen years old."

When her parents gave her the final no on Foxcroft, Betsee said, "I said to my father, 'That's okay, because I'm going to live there one day.' And he said, 'Yeah, sure, you are.' And the rest is history."

That history includes Betsee moving to Middleburg in 1993, purchasing Huntland in 2007, and enrolling her daughter Rosie at Foxcroft in 2017.[475]

Betsee Parker describes Southwest High School in Minneapolis as "a very big, inner-city high school with hundreds of kids in each of the grades. It was nothing like [in rural areas] where the whole school has as many as we had in one grade at my school." In that environment, she said, "I was just a number, just a statistic."

What's more, during Betsee's high school days, before Title IX—the federal statute that prohibits sex discrimination in educational programs—was enacted in 1972, she said, "there was very little for girl students in the way of athletics. There were a few activities that you could get into, but nothing was paid for like the boys' activities. If you wanted to do a sport, you had to do it outside of the school."

In 2018 Betsee went a long way toward remedying that situation when she donated $250,000 to the Southwest High School Foundation, requesting that those funds be used to "emphasize and support Southwest Women's Athletics and teacher innovation and development."

Southwest High School, she said, "is an important asset to our community. I am proud to contribute to the Southwest Foundation as it maximizes the potential of our school and city with equitable distribution of financial resources within the high school, encourages innovation, and establishes valuable community partnerships. I hope my contribution inspires others to give... and strengthens an already magnificent school."[475]

Southwest's women's basketball coach Dan Froehlich said that the donation would have wide-ranging benefits for the school and its students. "When we can demonstrate through equal opportunities to participate beyond the classroom and with financial support that the success of our young women matters," he said, "their entire high school experience builds confidence and purpose. Dr. Parker's gift will not only lift our financial wherewithal but the spirits of everyone involved with Southwest."[477]

When she was a student at Southwest High, Betsee said, "a lot of girls were doing things," and Betsee Parker was one of them. "There weren't many riders at my school," she said. "I had to travel twenty or thirty miles to a stable to ride. I had to get out of Minneapolis to do it, and go to Lake Minnetonka," west of the city. "That was what started the whole thing, and it just took off one year because I had such a strong interest in riding and training and jumping. You couldn't keep me away from the barn."

Betsee's love of horses led her to Wellesley College in Massachusetts, where she was co-founder and co-captain of the equestrian team. "I really wanted to be out East because I had shown ponies and horses out here," she said, knowing that at some point she would move to Virginia. Also during that time, she was the horse show trainer for the private Dana Hall School in Wellesley, Massachusetts, helping younger women move into the sport.

She graduated from Wellesley with honors in 1982, then moved to Boston to attend Harvard Divinity School.[478] Betsee received her Master's in Divinity in 1985, graduating at the top of her class, and went to England to start her ecclesiastical career.

She lived there for a few years, at a time, Betsee said, "before they ordained women to the [Anglican] priesthood. I was kind of a guinea pig there. I had a team parish with a colleague, but they also sent me around to a lot of parishes so people could see a woman preach and settle down with [the idea of seeing] a woman in a collar." She spent the late eighties and early nineties in England, and moved to Hunt Country in January 1993.

The impetus was an offer from a friend, John Smith, an Episcopal minister in Leesburg, Virginia, who asked her to join him as his "right-hand colleague," Betsee said. Smith was "a very wonderful liberal minister in Leesburg who had a big congregation. There were five priests serving in the parish." But when Betsee arrived in Leesburg, she said, the priest she was scheduled to replace "had a glitch in going to his next job and had to stay a little longer than he had planned." That's when Neale Morgan, the rector at Emmanuel Episcopal Church in Middleburg, offered her a job.

Neale Morgan "knew me," Betsee said, "and he said, 'Would you please help me because I need some help in this parish?' I had no idea that he was going to ask me. I was here only two days when he asked. So I got the job."

Betsee Parker moved into a rental cottage at historic Welbourne west of the town of Middleburg, the home of Col. Richard Henry Dulany, who founded the Piedmont Fox Hounds in 1840. In 1993, Nat Morison, a descendant of Col. Dulany, and his wife Sherry had been running that 520-acre property as a bed and breakfast for many years.

"I was friends with Nat and Sherry," Betsee said in 2019. "When I came over from England they asked me if I wanted to live there. And I did." Betsee rented a Welbourne cottage and also helped the Morisons operate the B&B.

"If they wanted to go to New York, I could run the inn, take the money, help with the guests, run the drinks hour, be at the breakfast table, and that sort of thing," she said. "In return, they charged me a very low price for the cottage. We were like a big family at Welbourne. Those were wonderful, magical years."

While living at Welbourne and working with Neale Morgan at Emmanuel Church in Middleburg, Betsee was active in equine activities, including training horses, entering them in shows, and giving riding lessons. Her interest in horses directly let to Betsee meeting Irwin Uran, the man who would become her husband.

"Irwin and I met at the Upperville Horse Show at Ring One on the Saturday of the [annual] horse show" in June, she said. "No one introduced us. We were standing by Ring One, the main ring, and got talking like you do with people, about horses. I had a pony going in the other ring and he had a couple of horses in the main ring. One thing led to another, and that was it." Betsee Parker and Irwin Uran married in 1998.[479]

Irwin Uran was born in 1926 in New York City. He joined the U.S. Army a month after his 18th birthday on May 8, 1944, during World War II.[480] He served with K Company of the 264th Infantry Regiment in the 66th Infantry Division. Known as the Black Panther Division, the 66th Infantry had been formed eleven months earlier, in April 1943.

After training in the U.S., the men of the 66th boarded troop ships and crossed the

Atlantic, landing in England in November 1944.[481] On Christmas Eve 1944, the 66th Division shipped out to join the fight against the German army in France. PFC Irwin Uran was among the 66th Division troops crammed into two Belgian passenger liners leased by the British government and converted to transport vessels that departed from Southampton to cross the English Channel on Christmas Eve.

He was one of some 2,200 Black Panther Division men aboard the S.S. *Leopoldville* when a German U-Boat torpedoed the ship just five miles from the port city of Cherbourg, France. Fourteen officers, 748 enlisted men, and some forty crew members went down with the ship or died trying to escape on lifeboats following the explosion. The American death toll was the second-largest from the sinking of a troop transport in the European Theater during the war.

"From the moment the torpedo hit," Irwin Uran wrote in 2002, "all I saw and observed was total and complete panic and chaos." On "the numerous decks, I saw many, many fistfights between officers and enlisted men. I saw—and I heard—people shouting, screaming, crying... I heard more wretched cries than I can remember."

Fifty-eight years later, he wrote: "There are still people alive like myself who can attest to the fact that there was total chaos and panic.... I saw soldiers jump and get crushed; others just jumping helter-skelter and drowning. They were horrific sights that will last in my mind as long as I live."[482]

Irwin Uran survived the horrific sinking of the *Leopoldville*. He went on to serve in France and Germany with the 66th Infantry through the end of the war. Along with the rest of the surviving Black Panther Division men, he saw combat during daily reconnaissance patrols and helped repulse enemy attacks in St. Nazaire and Lorient in Brittany, where tens of thousands of German troops remained surrounded by Allied forces following D-Day and the Battle of the Bulge. He was wounded in one engagement near Lorient when grenade fragments peppered the back of his hand.

In late May, following the German surrender, the 66th undertook occupation duty in and around the city of Koblenz. Among other things, they confiscated weapons and ammunition and worked with refugees and former POWs. On April 29, 1945, Irwin Uran later wrote, he was with the 42nd Infantry Division (the Rainbow Division) that liberated the infamous Dachau concentration camp near Munich.

"I helped open the gates" of Dachau, he wrote in 2000. "I was stationed near the entrance. The horrors I saw, on entering the camp, I will not describe." As was the case with the sinking of the *Leopoldville*, Irwin Uran's experience at Dachau haunted him for decades. Irwin then was stationed at a Displaced Persons Camp, where he helped find homes for many refugees.

The 66th Division sailed for home on October 27, 1945. Irwin Uran arrived in Fort Dix, New Jersey, early in November, expecting to be discharged, but his enlistment wasn't up. The Army then sent him to the maximum-security Green Haven federal prison in Stormville, New York, to work as an MP prison guard, then on to his final military assignment: serving in an MP unit at Fort Wadsworth on Staten Island, New York.

For his courage under fire in World War II, Irwin Uran received a total of seventeen military decorations, including the Silver Star (the third-highest Army award for valor), two Bronze Stars, and a Purple Heart.

After his discharge, he earned a B.A. from Hofstra University on Long Island, N.Y. He then moved to California where he became an extremely successful stock market investor and owned many corporations. Irwin Uran relocated to Leesburg, Virginia, in 1994, rented a horse farm in Upperville, and became well known in the community several years later when he began donating large sums of money to the Town of Leesburg, to Loudoun County, and to several local nonprofits. In 1997, Irwin Uran made national headlines when he donated $1.25 million to the Town of Leesburg with the only restriction that it be used to help children.

"I've given all my life," he told a reporter, "and now I want to come out and take credit for it. I like living here. That's why I gave."[483]

The following year, Betsee Parker suggested to Irwin that they provide the funds to build the first synagogue in Loudoun County. "Irwin loved the idea," Betsee said, and soon thereafter presented a check for $2 million to the small, fledgling Loudoun Jewish Congregation. "Every congregation wants a permanent home. He's given us a future," said Margie Oliver, the president of the congregation that had held its services in congregants' living rooms, community centers, schools, a storefront, and a local Episcopal church.[484] The renamed Congregation Sha'are Shalom opened its doors in September 2004 on Evergreen Mills Road in Leesburg.

In 1999, Irwin Uran donated $1 million to the Loudoun County Library system to underwrite the study of the Holocaust. Since then, the library has sponsored scores of events dealing with the Holocaust, including talks by William Styron (the author of, among other books, the Holocaust-themed novel, *Sophie's Choice*) and Elie Wiesel, the Nobel Peace Prize recipient and Holocaust survivor. That's in addition to Holocaust-related art exhibits, documentary films, musical performances—and the addition of some 3,000 items to the library's collection.

"We're stunned at what an amazingly generous opportunity this is," then Loudoun County Library Board of Trustees Chair John Czaplewski said when the gift was made public."[485]

Irwin and Betsee's other large charitable gifts in the late 1990s and early 2000s went to Leesburg Christian Academy to help rebuild its campus after a disastrous fire; the Afro-American Historical Association of Fauquier County in The Plains; the Loudoun County Animal Shelter; and the Loudoun Museum. They also donated vast sums to the Marion DuPont Scott Equine Medical Center at Morven Park in Leesburg, which had treated several of their horses.[486] There also were significant contributions to Virginia Tech, the Episcopal Divinity School in New York City, Wellesley College, and Harvard University, where Betsee established the Rare Books Room at the Harvard Divinity School.

After their 1998 wedding, the couple lived in Southern California. "We were there for a few months," Betsee said. "He liked to go to Southern California because his sister lived there. He also liked Martha's Vineyard a lot [and] he had a place in New York." They were in New York City on the morning of September 11, 2001. They had just met a locksmith in the lobby of their Upper East Side apartment building when he told them that a plane crashed into one of the World Trade Center towers.

When they heard the news, Betsee Parker later said, Irwin "looked at me and I looked at him, and the first thing he said was, 'You're going to have to put your collar on, aren't you?' I kind of stammered and I said, 'Maybe, yeah.' And he said, 'And it's going to be for a long time.'"

After she learned that the second World Trade Center tower fell, Betsee said, "I went down to the site. I took the No. 4 train.... I didn't know what to do except to put my collar on." When the subway arrived, she said, the doors opened, and "a whoosh of air sucked into the train full of plaster, dust, smoke, toxins, and the smell of jet fuel and steel burning. [It] hit me like two fists in the face. I inhaled and I suddenly couldn't breathe." Betsee "stepped off the train," she said, and walked out of the station and into "a panic and rush of people in tears, running, crying covering their faces. It was utter chaos."

Betsee Parker immediately decided to volunteer to help. She wound up working for more than two years—from September 11, 2001, to November 3, 2003—as a team lead for the Office of the Chief Medical Examiner's World Trade Disaster Team in New York City, helping locate and identify the remains of those who perished in the attacks. "It was something I was able to do," she said. "My service at Ground Zero was not really as a chaplain so much as it was doing pathology. That was what was needed. I felt that it was a way to truly honor the lives that were lost there."[488]

Niagara University and the State University of New York Morrisville honored Betsee Parker's voluntary service with the Medical Examiner's office by presenting her with Doctor of Humane Letters degrees in May of 2003. She also received a First Responder Award from the American Red Cross. Soon thereafter, Betsee and Irwin moved to Hunt Country. They bought a property, Delaplane Manor, west of Upperville, in 2006.

She and Irwin were well aware of Huntland, Betsee said, and would have purchased the place, but it was not available. "Even when Irwin and I lived in New York City we were looking at farms [in Hunt Country] to buy because we were always going to come back," she said. "His favorite was Huntland." Betsee had visited Huntland in "the early nineties," she said, when she arrived in Middleburg from England to work at the Middleburg Episcopal Church. "It was quite woefully rundown. At that time they were between renters so no one was in here."

In 2006, Betsee and Irwin contacted Roy and Lily Ash to see if Huntland was for sale, but were told that the tenants who were renting the house had an option to buy it, Betsee said. During the next four years, Betsee tried to rent one of the Huntland cottages, "but they were full of people and there was always somebody leasing the house who had first dibs on buying it."

Huntland remained unavailable until several months after Irwin Uran's death on June 23, 2007. That's when Betsee learned that the renters could not agree with the Ashes on terms for purchasing Huntland and the property would be put on the market.

CHAPTER THIRTEEN
Like Living in a Museum

Huntland "was completely derelict and not livable.
There wasn't any [working] plumbing—no heat, no electricity.
It was time to roll up my sleeves."

—Betsee Parker

When she heard that news, Betsee said, "I got very hopeful. I came out [to Huntland] the next day. There was no one on the land and I drove all over. The downstairs door was wide open and a raccoon was in there. I walked all over the house because it was not secured. People were driving in and out of here every day when I first bought it."

Huntland "was completely run down and not livable. There was no [working] plumbing, no heat, no electricity. All the systems were run down. Everything had to be revamped."

Within days after putting Huntland on the market, Betsee said, the listing agent had ten interested parties and one offer. One of the interested parties, a couple, later told her that they decided not to buy Huntland because they "didn't even know where to begin [repairing] that derelict house." They "said it was a big white elephant that looked like it was a teardown," and were "surprised that I was willing to take it on."

When Betsee told a friend who owned a nearby large farm that she was considering buying Huntland, "the first thing he said to me is, 'What are you crazy?'"

"I told him, 'No, you really don't know me,' and he said, 'That is just insane to buy that old, run-down place.' Years later, he actually apologized to me for [saying] that."

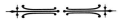

When Betsee Parker purchased Huntland in late 2007, no one had lived full-time in the house for several years. And it showed.

"The downstairs basement/chauffeur's room was underwater," Betsee said. "There were mushrooms and spores on the floor. It took us three and a half years to get to the point where we could even live in the house it was so severely run down. There was mud in the toilets. You had to scoop the mud out and get the entire system flushed out and started again."

From the outset, Betsee Parker's goal at Huntland was to repair, restore, and preserve the house to the period when Joe Thomas finished the additions and renovation on the house and built the kennel and the stables almost a century before—and to keep as much of the original Benton house as possible in working order. "I didn't want any commercial enterprises here, no bed and breakfasts, nothing," she said. "I wanted it to revert to the wonderful old, historic home it had once been. It is the favorite of all the places I've lived."

Betsee said that she had had a very strong interest in historic preservation from an early age. "I had studied it since I was a teenager," she said. "I have a private passion for it. I wanted to try my hand on [Huntland] because I had seen this farm years earlier and I knew that it had a lot of potential. I always liked the stable very much, even though it was horribly run down—the stalls were under mud and water and they weren't properly footed. It was a nightmare. And the kennel was beyond the pale."

The dilapidated condition of the structures on the property, she said, "didn't deter me because I knew that I could pay attention to detail and get most of it as right as possible." Betsee said her philosophy in preserving the house at Huntland has been "to let the walls interpret and then pay attention and learn from it. I was not trying to make some brash statement about this house. I wanted it to speak so I had to take the walls back to the layer that we wanted them to be. We agreed that it would be Mr. Thomas' layer because we think he may have gutted the original house and then put this interior in, which is really quite remarkable."

Her intent from the start, she said, was to "rescue" Huntland "for the community for posterity. I thought it was worthy of being rescued and I thought I would enjoy all the work getting it restored because [historic preservation] is one of the things I've done. It was something I knew I could do."

What's more, she said, "I wanted to have my project, like anybody does, and this farm was that for me. I knew I could bring it back so it would have this wonderful feel that it originally had and it would be like living in a museum."

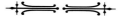

The cleaning up, repairing, remodeling, restoring, and the preservation at Huntland was all done "under the skillful expertise of Jerry Coxsey," Betsee said. In addition to managing the farming operations at Huntland, Coxsey oversaw the physical labor of six full-time workers from JSC Construction, Inc., as Betsee meticulously researched the history of the house, kennel, stables, gardens, and grounds.

Betsee and Jerry Coxsey worked together on—among many other things—restoring the wooden floors on the house's main level. The floors had all been bleached, "which made it completely blond, like mid-century modern French. I knew from preservation work that looking under the feet of the original radiators told the truth about the original floor." So Betsee had a work crew "take some of the radiators up so I could examine under the floor and we found this Jacobean oak color." Upstairs, on the second floor, the floor boards are from William Benton's original 1830s house.

Betsee insisted that the workers not use electric buffers or saws because, she said, "I wanted to keep the original fabric of the house to the extent that was possible. They had to sand by hand. Everything was going to be done to keep as much feel as I could keep. The doors were not stripped; they were sanded down [to find] the original paints and the different stains under them, and then we would find the earliest color and go to it."

Because "the core of the house was altered significantly by" Joe Thomas, she said, "we found some of his original colors that had not been sanded off the walls. We preserved some patches for posterity because we wanted known what colors he had. I chose a neutral pattern because I wanted to showcase the millwork. I think the millwork is the most important interior feature of this house. I'm told workers came over from Italy to do this. We have some pictures of them working on scaffolding in the front of the house."

Altogether, the work on the house took about three years to complete. That included getting all eleven of the working fireplaces in the house repaired and restored. It also included having Benton-period-correct silk damask drapes made to order in Italy for the rooms on the first floor, and finding and adding oriental rugs and carpets for the floors. Betsee also had all the Thomas-era plumbing and fixtures in the bathrooms and kitchens restored to pristine working order.

"I tried to restore everything I could to the oldest part of the house," she said.

As for the farming operations, Betsee Parker said in 2019 that since she acquired the property, "it has been a working farm. The farm manager here has a cattle operation and he grows different kinds of cash crops. And that was always the plan. I wanted it to retain as much feel as it could have and I felt that there was value in saving old farms for the community. I wanted to be a part of that because I knew I could do it. We have also through the years striven to gradually create a sustainable farm."

In 2018, Betsee Parker finished restoring Joe Thomas' world-famous foxhound kennel to its 1912 glory. "That was his masterpiece," she said of the kennel. "Although he did realize that he shouldn't have used a cedar shake roof on it. That was something that worked very well in New England but not down here," she said.

Two structures, the smokehouse and springhouse, had remnants of cedar shake roofs when Betsee bought Huntland in 2007. Both roofs, she said, "were completely rotted and fallen onto the ground. The roof was not even on one of the buildings; it was on the floor. Betsee and Jerry Coxsey decided, she said, to replace the roofs with standing seam tin.

"I couldn't wait" to get started preserving Huntland, she said, "I was like, 'I've got some project! I want projects.' I always liked construction. Women aren't supposed to like it and they're not encouraged to, but I'd always been drawn to historic preservation and construction projects. I wanted to learn about different types of cement and paints on walls and stains and how to sand—all of that was very thrilling to me."

Working on restoring and preserving Huntland began "as a hobby," she said, "but I found I had a knack for it. And I wanted to demonstrate that I could do it and that it would be a nice addition to the community. I really want to save it for the community for after I'm gone." Many "properties are worthy of being saved. And you're proud to be part of the heritage of Northern Virginia, such an incredibly wonderful part of the country. So I just set about doing it."

In October 2009, Betsee Parker placed Huntland and its surrounding 129 acres in a perpetual conservation and open-space easement with the Virginia Outdoors Foundation, an agency of the Virginia state government. The Huntland easement means that the property never will be subdivided and that no buildings, structures, or roads may be added—in perpetuity. Also prohibited: industrial or commercial activity—except for agricultural and equine activities and forestry.

On January 7, 2010, Betsee Parker purchased the remaining Huntland acreage—some 284 acres—from Lila Ash. Roy Ash had been preparing to sell and subdivide that acreage into ten residential sites. "I was very worried because they were trying to see if they could tap water there and cordoned off ten housing sites," she said. "I didn't want to be looking into some McMansion houses across the road from this lovely old home."

So Betsee made an offer and bought the land. "I did not speak to Mr. Ash personally, she said, "but I was told he really wanted me to have the farm because he thought I would do a good job with it. I had spoken with him about historic preservation in the past."

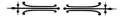

Betsee Parker has hosted many charitable events at Huntland since she began restoring the property, including a March 2018 fundraiser commemorating the restored kennel that benefitted the recently opened Masters of Foxhounds Association headquarters in the town of Middleburg. A decade earlier, in September 2008, as Huntland was being repaired and preserved, Betsee hosted a fund-raising event in a tent on the property to honor Virginia Sen. John Warner who had been named the Mosby Heritage Area Association's Heritage Hero that year.

"We have had many events here related to the history of this place," she said: "horses, horse sports, hunting, history of Virginia and Presidents Monroe, Kennedy, and Johnson. We've had carriage drives here. We've had animal rescue here." When Hurricane Florence hit the Outer Banks of North Carolina in 2018, she said, "the kennels became a rescue kennel for dogs that came up. All of them were adopted. We must have had fourteen. We had the ability to bring them back to good health and that's what we did at the capable direction of neighbor and friend France Bognon. It was wonderful."

In late December 2022, the Middleburg-Orange County Beagles moved its pack into the restored Huntland kennels. The organization, which was founded by noted horsewoman Eve Fout in 1961, encourages junior riders to appreciate the local rural landscape by participating in foxhunting meets with the beagles. The occasion marked the first time in 104 years that a pack of beagles or hounds had taken up residence in the historic Huntland kennels.

Outside of Huntland, Betsee Parker has spent many years donating her time and financial support to a wide range of humanitarian activities. In recent years, her philanthropy has centered on working on sustainable development, disaster relief, and climate change primarily in Africa, and also in the Caribbean and South Asia.

In 2005, Betsee trained and deployed a team that went to Sri Lanka in the wake of the devastating December 26, 2004, earthquake and tsunami that killed some 30,000 people. She became heavily involved in supporting sustainable development programs in 2007 when she learned about the work of Columbia University economist Jeffrey Sachs. Before long, she contacted him and became an active supporter and participant in his Millennium Villages Project.

That program, which began in 2005, worked for ten years in ten sub-Saharan countries on a range of rural development projects with the aim of reducing poverty, hunger, and disease, as well as illiteracy, environmental degradation and discrimination against women. The program integrated "many different disciplines together into an organized effort... in the poorest areas" of Africa, she said.[491]

Betsee's support of the project included serving as a delegate to the United Nations General Assembly in 2014-2018, working at the Vatican in Rome, and with the African Union. She traveled throughout Africa, spending time in Ghana, Senegal, Ethiopia, Kenya, Rwanda, Togo, Sierra Leone, and other countries meeting and working with heads of state, as well as governmental and NGO leaders. Among other things, she helped sponsor the opening of fisheries and medical clinics throughout Africa.

Her deep interest in the health and welfare of African people led to Betsee's hands-on work and philanthropy during the 2015 Ebola crisis in the West African nation of Guinea. Betsee also has sponsored and developed educational programs at the Vatican, including the Vatican Youth Symposium on Sustainable Development Goals. She serves on the Board of Directors of Sachs' nonprofit, SDGUSA, which works on similar sustainable development issues in this country.[492]

Betsee also is a strong supporter of Professor Sachs' Earth Institute's Haiti Program. The group in 2010 set up a task force to help the Haitian government with long-term, sustainable development and reconstruction efforts, including restoring ecosystems and infrastructure damaged in a devastating earthquake, and natural research management. "We are fortunate that she has chosen to support the work of our Haiti Program," the Earth Institute's Urania Mylonas said in 2010. Thanks to her donation and other funds, "the Earth Institute's important efforts in Haiti will continue to make a positive impact on the lives of the people of the country."[493]

With Betsee Parker's support, the Millennium Villages Project and its work with the UN, "has helped improve the lives and health of thousands of people," the Harvard Divinity School noted in 2016 when that institution presented her with Peter G. Gomes Harvard University Distinguished Alumni Achievement Award.[494]

Betsee Parker recently was nominated as a United Nation's Good-Will Ambassador, serving with Deputy Secretary-General Amina J. Mohammed on a global Women Rise For All Leadership initiative. Betsee was also a member of the UN's COVID-19 Verified Information Think Tank, headed by Under-Secretary General for Global Communications, Melissa Ruth Fleming.

In 2022 she was installed as Canon Emeritus of the Anglican Diocese of Southern Africa at Saint Paul's Cathedral on Saint Helena Island. She became the first woman to hold that title. Following her installation, ceremonies took place blessing the remains of enslaved people. Betsee Parker is also being considered for a King's Honour for her contributions and projects in the United Kingdom and its overseas territories.

Closer to home, Betsee Parker has provided significant funding for many charities, including the Middleburg Humane Foundation and the Buffalo Therapeutic Riding Center, Inc. She also has established scholarships, fellowships, and endowments at the Harvard Divinity School, Columbia University, Virginia Tech, Wellesley College, and the Shenandoah Conservatory at Shenandoah University in Winchester, Virginia.

For more than a decade Betsee has supported Danny & Ron's Rescue, a nonprofit, no-kill rescue organization operated by horse trainers Danny Robertshaw and Ron Danta in South Carolina and Florida. She has donated significant sums to the rescue operation, including prize money won by her show ponies and horses. "She's always been there," Danta said in 2012. "As a result of her generosity, she has quite literally saved the lives of several hundred dogs."[495]

In 2013, Betsee Parker purchased the recently restored historic Unison Store in the small village of Unison not far from Huntland. She then donated the store to the Unison Preservation Society, which since then has used the building—which was built around 1880—as a community center.

"Dr. Parker's generous gift will guarantee that the store and its half-acre of open space will continue to be the center of village and area life and activity as it has been for more than 140 years," the society's then-president Harry Bigley, said in 2013.[496] Later that year, the Unison Preservation Society presented Betsee Parker with its Outstanding Citizen of the Year award. That honor recognized her for preserving Unison Store, as well as the house at Huntland and its kennels, stables, grounds, and gardens, and for supporting the Middleburg Hunt and Piedmont Fox Hounds.

The following year, the Loudoun Preservation Society named Betsee Parker the Preservationist of the Year, recognizing her "significant contributions to historic preservation in Loudoun County." In 2023, the Land Trust of Virginia, which works with local landowners to protect and preserve open space, named her Conservationist of the Year and Landowner of the Year.

In 2015, Betsee purchased and donated the historic Allen House on the eastern edge of the town of Middleburg to the Middleburg Museum Foundation, with the understanding that it would become a local museum. "But, unfortunately, that never came to pass," Betsee Parker said, "because the foundation sold the property to the Masters of Foxhounds Association of North America the following year."

Betsee Parker remains an active horsewoman, specializing in show hunters, and has taken home many Grand Championships and U.S. Horse of the Year Awards. She has hosted hunt meets and hunt breakfasts at Huntland for all of the local fox hunts, including the Middleburg Hunt and the Piedmont Fox Hounds. A strong supporter of the National Sporting Library and Museum in Middleburg, Betsee has been an active member of the organization's Board of Directors. She also has been an officer—most recently, second vice president—of the famed Upperville Colt & Horse Show. In 2019, she became the first person to receive the President's Award, in recognition of her contributions to the future of the Upperville Horse Show. In 2021, the main hunter ring was named in her honor. And in the spring of 2023 the horse show's Wall of Honor Committee presented her with the Upperville Lifetime Achievement Award.

Betsee Parker, who recently became Baroness of Locheil, is passionate about her Scottish heritage. That includes working with the 13th Duke of Argyll, the chief of Clan Campbell, at his Inveraray Castle in the Scottish West Highlands. She has helped the Duke expand and enhance an ambitious effort to rescue and preserve an enormous archive of documents dating to the 13th century that chronicle the role of the Campbell family in Scottish and British history.

The Argyll Papers include letters, marriage agreements and other personal and business papers, accounts, charters, deeds, and surveys, along with military papers from the 15th through 20th centuries, genealogies of all branches of the Campbell family, estate archives for ten Campbell properties, and the records of the Synod of Argyll from the 17th to 19th centuries. Much of that mountain of material had been long neglected in the castle.

With Betsee Parker's support, Scottish archivists are translating and preserving the documents, most of which are written in Medieval Latin and Scottish Gaelic. The restored documents, which eventually will be accessible to researchers, "will be housed in climate-controlled rare books and scriptorium room in the castle stables," Betsee said in 2017.[497]

In 2019, Betsee Parker purchased Ackergill Castle, a 15th-century structure in Caithness, Scotland. "My clan, Clan Campbell, owned it in the 1600s," she said. "And I am a baroness of Clan Campbell assigned by the Duke of Argyll.[498] He was thrilled when I told him we got one of the castles back into the clan. Our clan sold it to Clan Dunbar in 1699 and then Clan Dunbar had it for the next 320 years. We hoisted the Campbell flag there" when the sale was complete.

Betsee characterized the castle as her newest "historic preservation project" because Ackergill Castle had been turned into a hotel and she would be restoring it as a residence. "I won't have much trouble reverting it," she said, because the previous owner "put a lot of money into it, and wanted to get out. I closed in January [2019] and I got all of the furnishings, so there is nothing for me to do except to sensitively restore some of the furniture and woodwork that has been neglected." Ackergill is among the renowned 19th-century Scottish architect David Bryce's most important projects, and includes furniture he made specifically for the castle.

Betsee Parker is not daunted by the prospect of preserving a castle. "I feel that I can take on almost anything," she said. "It's not nearly the difficult project that Huntland was. This is simple by comparison. Architecturally it may be a different form. They're using great big stones that came from the sea around there and different types of slate and shale. All of these things are very interesting, but they're not daunting. You can deal with them."

Her other significant current preservation project is the Farmer's Delight property, which Betsee purchased in October 2013 from the McGhee Foundation. When George C. McGhee, who bought the 18th-century brick farmhouse and its surrounding 89.5 acres in 1948, died at age 93 in 2005, he bequeathed the property, located not far from Huntland, to his foundation.

Farmer's Delight, which has been on the Virginia Landmarks Register and National Register of Historic places since 1973, dates from the late 18th century. Charles Green purchased the property in 1741 (the same year he bought the acreage that now makes up Huntland) from its original owner, Thomas Lord Fairfax (1693-1781), who had inherited the land in 1709.[499] The two-story Federal-style, brick manor house was built during the ownership of Col. Joseph Flavius Lane (1753-1803), who purchased the property in 1791 and renamed it "Farmer's Delight."[500]

The Lane Family owned Farmer's Delight until 1856, when the Leith Family purchased it. Henry W. Frost, Jr., who was active in the Virginia Thoroughbred Association, bought the place in 1919 from the Leith descendants and added horse stables, a dairy, and other buildings. After George McGhee and his wife Cecilia took over the property in 1948, they put an addition on one wing of the house and added a chapel, an arboretum, and terraced gardens.

George McGhee was born in Waco, Texas, in 1912, and graduated Phi Beta Kappa from the University of Oklahoma in 1933. He became an oil industry geophysicist, then received a Rhodes scholarship to Queens College, Oxford, earning his doctorate in 1937. He came back to the U.S. and made a fortune in the oil business before World War II.[501]

After the U.S. entered the war, McGhee enlisted in the Navy, serving as an intelligence officer in the Pacific. After the war, he went to work for the State Department and served as Under Secretary of State for Political Affairs and U.S. Ambassador to Turkey and to the former West Germany.

As for Farmer's Delight, Ambassador McGhee "crafted his hundreds of acres into a showplace of landscape design," his *Washington Post* obituary noted. "The property featured a maze formed by 300 boxwood plants, with the reward in a bottle of cold champagne inside the urn planted at the center."[502]

Soon after purchasing Farmer's Delight, Betsee Parker began working with architectural historian Maral S. Kalbian on restoring the main house and its furniture and furnishings. Betsee's "commitment to historic preservation and attention to detail is reflected in her restoration of Huntland and then to Farmer's Delight," Maral said. "Farmer's Delight was not in complete disrepair as Huntland was before Betsee purchased it, but Farmer's Delight still needed significant rehabilitation.

"What was so exciting was her willingness to study the house further. Experts in dendrochronology and other preservation technologies including paint restoration were able to find out more information about the house. The highly decorative paint scheme in the main core at Farmer's Delight was intact just beneath a few coats of modern paint. Not only was Betsee willing to conduct these investigations, but she also wanted to restore the original paint scheme, and she did.

"I cannot think of another house of this type in the region where so much of the original woodwork and paint was still intact—it's really remarkable."[503]

Betsee Parker received the Louis J. Malon Outstanding Preservation Achievement award from Preservation Virginia in September 2022. That award recognizes an individual who inspires others by their commitment, leadership, and vision in helping instill a historic preservation ethic in others.

Preservation Virginia—a nonprofit, statewide preservation organization—praised Betsee's leadership in preservation efforts, including "the meticulous restoration of the historic Huntland Estate and Farmer's Delight Estate in Loudoun County; and her donation of the old General Store to the Unison Preservation Society." Her "many other generous local, national, and international philanthropic efforts have resulted in the preservation and rcusc of historic placcs."

Maral S. Kalbian has been working with Betsee Parker "for more than a decade," she said in 2019. "Although we met through our shared interest in historic preservation, it did not take long for me to realize what an accomplished woman Betsee is in other areas and how deep and varied her interests are. She is well known for her international philanthropic work on sustainable development through the United Nations, and she is also a generous benefactor to many local organizations.

"I continue to be awed by Betsee's commitment to the poor of Africa, her neighbors, her roots in Minneapolis, the environment, historic preservation, and many other concerns. She once told me that as an ordained Episcopalian minister, she sees her parish as the world. I have come to see through her actions that this is true."

Notes

1   Author interview at Huntland, March 26, 2019.

2   United States Department of the Interior, National Park Service, "National Register of Historic Places Registration Form," submitted November 8, 2013; certified, December 24, 2013, prepared by Maral S. Kalbian, LLC. The Virginia Department of Historic Resources certified Huntland's application as meeting the National Register of Historic Places criteria on November 14, 2013.

3   "National Register of Historic Places Registration" form, Section 8, p. 22. See also this page on the National Park Service's website: https://www.nps.gov/nr/feature/places/13000990.htm

4   The fact-filled, extensive National Register Huntland report written by Maral S. Kalbian with Margaret T. Peters forms the basis for a large part of this book. Without the report—and without Maral's research expertise and knowledge of architecture and architectural history—this book could not have been written.

5   NRHPR, Section 8, p. 22.

6   "New Guinea Talks Open: Dutch and Indonesians Confer Secretly Near Washington" was the headline of a short article in the March 21, 1962, *New York Times.*

7   Bunker is best known for his controversial tenure, from 1967-73, as U.S. Ambassador to the Republic of (South) Vietnam, during the height of the American war in Vietnam.

8   See "Private Properties: Horse County Update," *The Wall Street Journal,* November 15, 1996, p. B18.

9   Author interview, March 26, 2019.

10   Author interview, August 31, 2020.

11   Loudoun County—named after John Campbell, the fourth earl of Loudoun, a Scottish nobleman who commanded British and colonial armed forces in North America—was carved out of the western section of Fairfax County in 1757 by the Virginia House of Burgesses.

12   Loudoun County, Virginia, Deed Book K, 422 and 423, May 5, 1777, "Hancock to Johnston, Leases."

13   Loudoun County Deed Book K, 422 and 424, "Deeds of Lease and Release," May 5, 1777. The same document notes that that land was part of a large tract "patented by Charles Green, late of Fairfax Co." in 1741. A search of the Deed Books did not turn up any information on the property prior to 1741 or when the land came into George Johnston's hands.

14   Loudoun County Deed Book Deed Book K, 423 and 427, "Hancock to Johnston, Release."

15   Loudoun County Deed Book B, 180, George Johnston, "Last Will and Testament," November 27, 1776.

16   Bronaugh family personal information from the hand-written "Family Record" in the family's Holy Bible, Library of Virginia, "Bronaugh family Bible records, 1779-1884," System number 000492338. According to the entry, Elizabeth Hope Mitchell was born "at Hayes in Montgomery County, Maryland," on August 18, 1779.

17   Loudoun County, Virginia, Deed Book 2-N, page 80, March 21, 1811, shows that the 150 acres was conveyed to William Bronaugh by Hugh and James Johnston after they "advertised" to sell the land "at Public Sale to the highest Bidder." The Deed Book also notes that this is the "same land conveyed to George Johnston by Simon Hancock & Mary, his wife."

18   Loudoun County Deed Book, 3 Z, p. 252, January 3, 1833.

19   His obituary in the Aug. 4, 1881, edition of *The Mirror* of Loudoun County, Virginia, reads in its entirety: "Mr. Wm. Benton, of his county, died on last Thursday, aged 92 years. He was born in Lincolnshire, England, on December 25, 1788, and came to this country in 1801. He was very much respected by all who knew him." Benton Family genealogies often refer to the fact that William Benton was born in "the village of Lisbon in Lincolnshire." However, no primary source evidence has been found to confirm this.

20   "Death of Mr. Wm. Benton," the Leesburg, Virginia, *Washingtonian,* August 1881.

21   National Archives, "Declaration for a Pension," War of 1812, S.C. 7074, William Benton, April 10, 1871.

22   The Battle of New Orleans took place on January 8, 1815, after Great Britain and the U.S. signed the Treaty of Ghent, ending the War of 1812, but before word reached the United States. The Senate ratified the treaty on February 15. President Madison signed papers that officially ended the war on February 18.

[23] See, "Willis Family," *William and Mary Quarterly*, Vol. 6, No. 4, April 1898, p. 210.

[24] Byrd Charles Willis was quite a character, who—in his own words—was "fond of pleasure, and as remarkably averse to everything like business." He had an arranged marriage in 1800 at age nineteen, then moved with his bride to the family farm of Willis Hill, where he was "an idle fellow, fond of fox hunting, racing, and convivial parties" and "paid no attention to plantation business." He joined the Army and took part in the War of 1812, serving in the Regular Army's 20th Infantry Regiment. In 1835, he sold his interest in the farm and moved to Florida. When he died in 1846, Willis left behind nine children. See, Byrd Charles Willis and Richard Henry Willis, *A Sketch of the Willis Family of Virginia...* (Whittet and Shepperson, 1898), pp. 62-66.

[25] James Monroe to Byrd Willis, November 17, 1917. James Monroe Museum, The Papers of James Monroe, Box 49.

[26] Judge Jones (1727-1805) was the brother of James Monroe's mother, Elizabeth Jones Monroe, who died in 1772 when the future President was fourteen years old. After the death of James' father, Spence Monroe, two years later, Judge Jones served as executor of the estate and became James Monroe's guardian. Charles Carter Jr. (1732-96) was a close friend of George Washington's and a grandson of Robert "King" Carter (ca. 1664-1732), the Virginia-born British colonial figure who owned some 295,000 acres of land, mostly on Virginia's Northern Neck.

[27] *The Washingtonian*, Feb. 6, 1810; the Richmond *Enquirer*, October 27, 1809.

[28] See United States Department of the Interior, National Park Service, "National Register of Historic Places Nomination Form," Oak Hill, October 10, 1966, continuation sheet 17, page 3.

[29] See letter from Grace Benton, September 15, 1962, Thomas Balch Library, Family Files, No. 499.

[30] George Morgan, *The Life of James Monroe* (Small, Maynard, 1921), p. 429.

[31] National Park Service Oak Hill Nomination Form, *op. cit.*

[32] Richmond *Dispatch*, August 13, 1881.

[33] President James Monroe to William Benton, May 8, 1818. James Monroe Museum, The Papers of James Monroe, Box 49.

[34] President James Monroe to William, Benton, November 30, 1818. Dartmouth College Rauner Library, MS 818630.

[35] James Monroe to William Benton, January 22, 1821, College of William and Mary, Swem Library, Jay Johns Papers, 1918-1974.

[36] Elizabeth Morgan, "Oak Hill," Works Progress Administration of Virginia Historical Inventory, February 19, 1937.

[37] Although he gave suggestions to other Virginians as they contemplated building their homes, the only structures that Thomas Jefferson, a self-taught architect, completely designed were his homes at Monticello and Poplar Forest, the Virginia State Capitol Building in Richmond, and the grounds and buildings at the University of Virginia in Charlottesville.

[38] Thomas Jefferson to James Monroe, June 27, 1820. *Founders Online*. National Archives, last modified June 13, 2018.

[39] James Monroe to William Benton, January 13, 1821. Library of Congress, James Monroe Papers, 1758-1839, William Benton Correspondence, 1788-1881.

[40] National Park Service Oak Hill Nomination Form, *op. cit.*, continuation sheet 19, p. 5.

[41] *Genius of Liberty*, Nov. 50, December 24, 1822, p. 3.

[42] James Monroe to William Benton, July 18, 1820. Morristown National Historical Park and Library, James Monroe Letters.

[43] James Monroe to William Benton, August 3, 1822. Morristown National Historical Park and Library, James Monroe Letters.

[44] James Monroe to Samuel Gouverneur, October 10, 1823. New York Public Library, James Monroe Papers, 1772-1836. MSS 2035. Samuel Gouverneur (1899-1865) in 1820 married James Monroe's daughter Maria, who also was his first cousin. He served as his father-in-law's private secretary and later as executor of his estate.

[45] William Benton to James Monroe, January 20, 1824. James Monroe Museum, The Papers of James Monroe, Box 49.

[46] From Loudoun County land records sited in Virginia Historic Landmarks Commission Survey Form, "Historical Background," File no. 53-107, 1983. County tax records cited in the form show "buildings" assessed at $5,000 were on the property.

[47] It is likely that William Bronaugh, who was one of the seven original 1787 trustees of the town of Middleburg, was the father of Jeremiah William Bronaugh, who in 1833 would sell the land that became Huntland to William Benton.

[48] "Copy of Award for W. Benton," March 20, 1824. James Monroe Museum, The Papers of James Monroe, Box 49.

[49] James Monroe to unknown (possibly William Noland), March 26, 1824. James Monroe Museum, The Papers of James

Monroe, Box 49. Noland later served as Commissioner of Public Buildings in Washington, D.C.

50 Loudoun County Deed Book, 6A/334 (1870). Also see Huntland, "National Register of Historic Places Registration" form, Section 8, p. 24. William Benton "had [New Lisbon] built for Uncle James Benton," according to a February 22, 1974, letter from Grace Benton, a great granddaughter of William Benton. Copy of letter courtesy of Betsy Leith Kelly.

51 "Young Snow Ball," *Genius of Liberty*, Vol. 11, No. 10, March 1827, p. 3.

52 An advertisement placed by Joseph Lane in the May 26, 1796, *Columbian Mirror and Alexandria Gazette*, offered the "Pot House and Land" for sale or rent. "This Pot House," the ad said, "includes the Kiln House (both being in one range, of one elevation and under the same roof" with "a room laid off, with fire place, &c, for the accommodation of a family. Every necessary and convenience for the Potter's Business are inviting; and the great demand for Earthen Ware, and the rapid consumption, encouraging." Joseph Flavius Lane (1756-1803), a lieutenant colonel in the 1793 Whiskey Rebellion, had built nearby Farmer's Delight, a Georgian-style brick home on five hundred acres, in 1799. The house is one of Loudoun County's oldest brick dwellings. The architectural historian Maral S. Kalbian is at work on a detailed study of the history of the property, which Betsee Parker purchased in 2013 and has restored and preserved.

53 According to Loudoun County land tax records, William Benton added $1,500 in improvements in 1833 and 1834 to the 171.5-acre parcel of land (New Lisbon) he had purchased in January from William Bronaugh. As there are no recorded significant improvement increases in the next decade, it can be inferred that those expenditures went toward building the house that would become known as Huntland. See Loudoun County Deed Book 4E/381 (1836) and Huntland, "National Register of Historic Places Registration" form, Section 8, p. 24.

54 U.S. Federal Census, 1830, William Benton, Bloomfield, Loudoun, Virginia.

55 "Wheat Drill," *The Southern Planter*, July 1857, Vol. 17, No. 7, p. 406.

56 "Agricultural," *Genius of Liberty*, Vo. 11, No. 27, July 10, 1827, p. 3.

57 See Loudoun Museum, "Loudoun History," www.loudounmuseum.org/loudoun-history Schoharie County, New York, and the entire Delaware/Maryland/Virginia Peninsula also make that claim.

58 U.S. Federal Agricultural Census for Loudoun County, 1850 and 1860 (Southern District).

59 U.S. Federal Census, William Benton, Sr., Southern District of Loudoun County, for 1830, 1840, 1850, and 1860, and Slaves Schedules, 1850 and 1860. Also see Huntland, "National Register of Historic Places Registration" form, Section 8, p. 24. The slave schedules listed the date ranges—not exact ages—of the enslaved people.

60 See James Monroe to William Benton, January 3, 1818. University of Virginia Alderman Library, Special Collections, Monroe Papers, Box 2.

61 Loudoun County Deed Book 3B:054, August 25, 1820. Also see Lori Kimball and Wynne Saffer, "References to James Monroe's Slaves...." January 25, 2012, Balch Library.

62 Bureau of the Census, "Population of United States in 1860...." 1864, pp. 517 and 518.

63 Virginia never enacted a law explicitly prohibiting the education of enslaved perople. However, beginning with the first slave rebellions in the early 1800s, the Virginia General Assembly made it more difficult for enslaved people to learn to read and write by passing laws that prohibited the "gathering of slaves for the purpose of education." See Antonio T. Bly, "Slave Literacy and Education in Virginia," Virginia Humanities and the Library of Virginia, *Encyclopedia Virginia*, https://www.encyclopediavirginia.org/Slave_Literacy_and_Education_in_Virginia

64 Sharon Peterson, a McQuay-family descendant, in an August 1, 2019, interview for this book with Maral S. Kalbian, recalled hearing from relatives that some of her enslaved ancestors lived at Huntland (then New Lisbon).

65 The filled-in tunnel exists between Pot House Road and the main house, but it has not been excavated. Therefore, no definitive conclusions can be made about when the tunnel was constructed or its original use. The tunnel could have been built by Joe Thomas as part of a heating or delivery system. See Huntland, "National Register of Historic Places Registration" form, Section 8, p. 26.

66 "Meeting of Stockholders," *Alexandria Gazette*, Aug. 20, Aug. 23, Sept. 4, 1867. Also see U.S. Department of the Interior, National Park Service, "National Register of Historic Places Registration Form," Little River Rural Historic District, 2013, Section 8, pp. 99-100.

67 The Whig Party peaked in 1840 when William Henry Harrison won the presidential election and the party held a majority in the House and Senate in what pundits called the "Whig Wave." But after Harrison died a month after he took office, the new president, John Tyler, vetoed nearly every piece of legislation the Whigs favored. Henry Clay, the Whig presidential candidate in 1844, lost the election to Democrat James K. Polk. Gen. Zachary Taylor won the presidency for the Whigs in 1848, but the party broke into factions after Millard Fillmore assumed the presidency following Taylor's death two years later. Many southern Whigs joined the Democratic Party; most northern Whigs joined the Republican Party when it formed in 1854.

68 Quoted in Benjamin F. Hall, *Republican Party and Its Presidential Candidates* (Miller, Orton & Mulligan, 1856), p. 265.

69 For a history of the founding of the American Colonization Society, see Marc Leepson, *What So Proudly We Hailed: Francis Scott Key, A Life* (St. Martin's Press, 2014), pp. 78-84.

70 Quoted in "Public Dinner: To the Hon. Charles F. Mercer," *Leesburg Genius of Liberty,* Jan. 11, 1840. Mercer was the first president of the company. Due to funding issues, only seven miles of the canal were built and the project was abandoned in 1857.

71 James M. Benton to William H. Benton, Aug. 15, 1856. Copy of private letter courtesy of David Benton.

72 National Archives, State of Virginia, Loudoun County, "Certificate of Identity and Oath of Service," William Benton, November 21, 1850.

73 Department of the Interior, "War of 1812 – Survivor's Pension," William Benton, February 14, 1871. Copy of document courtesy of David Benton.

74 See John Devine, Wilbur C. Hall, Marshall Andrews, Penelope Osburn, and Fitzhugh Turner (editor), *Loudoun County and the Civil War: A History and Guide* (Virginia Civil War Centennial Commission), 1961.

75 At Antietam, Gen. George McClellan's 80,000-man Army of the Potomac went head to head with Lee's Army of Northern Virginia in what became the bloodiest one day in American history. Nearly 22,000 Americans were killed, wounded, or went missing that day. The Battle of Antietam ended in a stalemate, but one that forced Lee to retreat to Virginia.

76 The Battlefield Trust describes the cavalry battles of Aldie, Middleburg, and Upperville as "some of the largest and costliest cavalry actions of the Civil War." Those "vicious battles" cost the Confederates some 600 casualties and the Union some 900—"roughly the same amount of losses suffered at [the July 9, 1863, Battle of] Brandy Station, which is considered the largest cavalry battle of the war." See Battlefield Trust, "Civil War: 10 Facts: Middleburg," https://www.battlefields.org/learn/articles/10-facts-middleburg

77 A grandson of Chief Justice of the United States John Marshall (1755-1835), who lived in Fauquier County.

78 Ann Peterson to Betsee Parker, December 16, 2010. Copy of letter courtesy of Betsee Parker.

79 Edwin Havens to Nell Havens, December 4, 1864, Edwin R. Havens Papers, 1838-1926, Michigan State University Archives and Historical Collections, Civil War Collections, LC00016, Box 2, Folder 3. Thanks to Lee Lawrence for uncovering the letter.

80 Diary entry in Lee Lawrence, editor, *Dark Days in Our Beloved Country: The Civil War Diaries of Catherine Hopkins Braun* (Piedmont Press and Graphics, 2014), p. 105.

81 National Archives of the United States, Compiled Military Service Records, James M. Benton, Company F, 6 Virginia Cavalry.

82 See Richmond (Va.) *Dispatch,* June 25, 1857, p. 2.

83 Letter from Grace Benton, September 15, 1962, Thomas Balch Library, Family Files, No. 499.

84 *Ibid.*

85 An unsigned advertisement in the July 21, 1832, *Genius of Liberty* newspaper in Leesburg—most likely written by Rev. Haynes—announced a search for a teacher for "the school house on the land of William Benton about half way between Middleburg and Union, in Loudoun County." Said teacher, the ad said, would need to be "well recommended for moral conduct and qualified to teach Reading, English Grammar, and Geography, together with the Latin language...." Lodging for the teacher, could be had "at a convenient distance from the school house, on moderate terms." New Lisbon Female Institute advertisement, *Alexandria Gazette,* January 18, 1861. Rev. Haynes placed the same ad at least ten other times in that newspaper in January and February of 1861.

86 An advertisement with the headline, "Education! Lisbon Institution, Loudoun County, Virginia," appeared in several newspapers in the first six months of 1845, including the May 8, 1845, issue of the Charles Town, West Virginia, *Virginia Free Press.* The article also noted that the school was "established in 1839."

87 Writing in the *Alexandria Gazette,* December 16, 1844, p. 3.

88 See *Alexandria Gazette,* January 2, 1851.

89 The 1885 "Virginia School Report" by the Commonwealth's Superintendent of Public Instruction characterized the school as "large and popular."

90 "New Lisbon Female Seminary," *Winchester Virginian,* September 13, 1854.

91 Advertisement, *Alexandria Gazette,* September 29, 1853, p. 3.

92 Biographical details from George Braxton Taylor, *Virginia Baptist Ministers,* Fourth Series. (J.P. Bell Company, 1913), pp.

416-417, and John K. Gott, *A History of the Middleburg Baptist Church,* Part One (Middleburg Baptist Church, 1997), pp. 40-41.

93   *The Clarke Courier,* April 8, 1880.

94   *A History of the Middleburg Baptist Church, op. cit.,* p. 49.

95   The 1850 Federal Census lists Benjamin Hyde Benton as a "Preacher," living with his wife Margaret in Middleburg in a household headed by Fayott Swart, a merchant, along with his wife and three young children. William Baswell, a blacksmith, also is listed as a member of the Swart household.

96   1840 United States Federal Census, Jonah Hood, Loudoun Virginia, roll 554, p. 144.

97   United States Patent Office, "Benjamin H. Benton, of Middleburg, Virginia. Improvement in Surveying-Instruments," December 12, 1842.

98   Ads in, for example, *The Monongalia Mirror* (Morgantown, West Virginia), February 4, 1854.

99   Advertisement in the Charles Town, West Virginia, *Spirit of Jefferson* newspaper, March 20, 1855, p. 4.

100   "Loudoun Agricultural School," *The Country Gentleman,* December 27, 1855, p. 26. Caldwell was not exactly an unbiased observer. In January 1856 he was listed as one of the principles when the Institute formerly incorporated in the Commonwealth of Virginia. The others were Benjamin Benton, James Gulick, Hamilton Rogers, Joseph L. Russell, Samuel Simpson, James R. Simpson, William Gulick, and Harmon Bitzer. See "Acts of the General Assembly of Virginia Passed in 1855-6..." p. 226.

101   *Alexandria Gazette,* July 23, 1856.

102   *Alexandria Gazette,* December 2, 1857.

103   *Alexandria Gazette,* December 14, 1858. Now known as Institute Farm, the property and main building still exist on a 512-acre tract of land. A group of members of the National Beagle Club, which had begun in Boston in 1887, bought the 512-acre property in 1916. The main building was renovated in 2015, and the property is used today for National Beagle Club activities, and is listed on the Virginia Landmarks Register and the National Register of Historic Places.

104   "New Market – Edinburg – Education," *The Daily State Journal,* May 5, 1873.

105   Personal advertisement in the Washington *Evening Star,* February 8, 1883 and the *National Republican,* March 10, 1883.

106   "Benton's Body Found," *National Republican,* June 14, 1883, p. 2

107   "The Body of Prof. Benton Found," *The Evening Star,* June 10, 1883.

108   *Ibid.*

109   In his will, written on June 19, 1866, William Benton left his son James Monroe Benton "the Lisbon Farm... on which the same James now resides." He left his son, William H. Benton, "the tract of land on which I reside called Spring Hill Farm." Copy of hand-written will provided by David Benton.

110   Eugene Scheel, *The History of Middelburg and Vicinity* (Piedmont Press, 1987), p. 78.

111   Letter from Grace Benton, September 15, 1962, Thomas Balch Library, Family Files, No. 499.

112   "Two Weddings," *Alexandria Gazette,* December 11, 1882, p. 2.

113   Beginning in 1844, many Methodist Episcopal churches in the South decided they could not abide by the church's General Conference's anti-slavery stance, and broke off and formed their own denomination, the Methodist Episcopal Church, South.

114   In the *Alexandria Gazette,* May 31, 1872.

115   "Camp Meetings," *Alexandria Gazette,* August 19, 1872, p. 2.

116   Legal Notice, *Alexandria Gazette,* July 22 and August 9, 1873.

117   Quoted in the *Alexandria Gazette,* August 21, 1873, p. 3.

118   "Camp Meeting," *Alexandria Gazette,* August 25, 1874, p. 2.

119   "Camp Meeting—Man Shot, &c.," *Alexandria Gazette,* August 19, 1875, p. 2.

120   "Alexandria Annals," *The Washington Post,* August 20, 1878, p. 3.

121   "Loudoun Camp-Meeting," The (Baltimore) *Sun,* August 16, 1898, p. 8.

122   As reported in the Fredericksburg *Free-Lance,* August 25, 1904, p. 3.

123   "Methodists of Virginia: Great Camp to Open Soon in Benton's Woods," *The Sun,* August 5, 1904, p. 8.

124   The SCV was formed in Richmond in 1896; the Daughters of the Confederacy in Nashville in 1894.

[125] *Alexandria Gazette*, August 21, 1901, p. 2.

[126] "Loudoun Camp-Meeting," Richmond *Times-Dispatch*, August 22, 1909.

[127] Elizabeth F. Morgan, "Survey Report, Camp Meeting and Its Site, Benton's Woods," Virginia Historical Inventory Project, Virginia Conservation Commission, Division of History, U.S. Works Progress Administration, Feb. 28, 1938, p. 3.

[128] Loudoun County Deed Book 7 P, August 9, 1898, p. 490, recorded August 11, 1898.

[19] Loudoun County Deed Book 7 S, January 1, 1900, recorded January 23, 1900.

[130] Leith family documents provided by Betsy Leith Kelly. Annie Leith obituary, *The Washington Herald*, December 1, 1921, p. 12.

[131] "Application of Annie A. Leith," No. 28088, January 9, 1900. Mutual Fire Insurance Company of Loudoun County Records, 1849-1954. Accession 41374. Business records collection, The Library of Virginia, Richmond, Virginia.

[132] See Henry D. Kingsbury and Dimeon L. Deyo, eds., *Illustrated History of Kennebec County Maine, 1625-1892* (H.W. Blake & Co.), Part II, p. 735. Also see Captain Joseph B. Thomas' obituary in *The Boston Post*, January 14, 1891, p. 5.

[133] Petitioner's Exhibits 76 and 77, Commonwealth of Massachusetts, September 28, 1870, and July 7, 1872.

[134] Cesar J. Ayala, *American Sugar Kingdom: The Plantation Economy of the Spanish Caribbean: 1898-1934* (University of North Carolina Press, 1999), p. 32.

[135] The equivalent of around $21 million in 2020. "Sugar Trust's New Plan," *The Boston Daily Globe*, October 31, 1890, p. 2. American Sugar Refining Company officially incorporated in January of 1891 in New Jersey. Founded by Henry O. Havemeyer, it began with $50 million in capital. At the time of Havemeyer's death in 1907, American Sugar controlled more than 95 percent of the sugar processing in the United States.

[136] "Obituary, Captain Joseph B. Thomas," *The Boston Post*, January 14, 1891, p. 5.

[137] *Class of 1879 Harvard College Secretary's Report, No. VIII* (The University Press, 1914), p. 303.

[138] Testifying before the Special U.S. House of Representatives Committee on the American Sugar Refining Co. and Others," July 18, 1911. The U.S. Government had sued the Sugar Trust in 1892 under the 1890 Sherman Antitrust Act, alleging that the conglomerate had gained "nearly complete control of the manufacture of refined sugar in the United States." The case went to the U.S. Supreme Court, which dismissed the suit, ruling that "there was nothing ...to indicate any intention to put a restraint upon trade or commerce...." See *United States v. E. C. Knight Company*," 156 U.S. 1 and 17, decided January 1, 1895. A federal grand jury in 1909 indicted American Sugar and its officers—including its president Washington B. Thomas—on charges of conspiracy, tax evasion, and restraint of trade. If proven, those charges likely would have resulted in the breakup of American Sugar, but prosecutors failed to prove their case. The 1911 House special committee investigation made headlines with allegations of price-fixing and other monopolistic practices, but they did not result in any legal action against the Sugar Trust.

[139] When asked by the Special Committee what his net worth was when he became a director of American Sugar in 1873, Washington Thomas replied: "possibly $200,000 or $250,000, something like that." That would be the equivalent more than $7 million in 2023. According to the 1900 U.S. Census, Washington B. Thomas lived with his wife Caroline and their two daughters in an expansive house on Beacon Street in Boston. They employed two butlers, a handyman, and seven women listed as "servants." He was a member of six private clubs in Boston, the Somerset Club, Algonquin Club, Eastern Yacht Club, Myopia Hunt Club, Essex Country Club, and Brookline Country Club—as well as the Brook, Metropolitan, and University Clubs in New York.

[140] *The New York Times*, October 5, 1905, p. 1.

[141] Ayala, *op. cit.*, p. 45.

[142] "Thomas, Washington, Butcher," *Who's Who in New England, 2nd Edition* (A.N. Marquis & Co., 1916), p. 1,059.

[143] "To Fly the Blue Flag: Mr. Thomas Named as Commodore of Eastern Yacht Club," *New York Daily Tribune*, January 28, 1909, p. 5.

[144] *Class of 1879 Harvard College Secretary's Report, No. VIII*, p. 304.

[145] Washington, D.C., *Evening Star*, May 30, 1929, p. 22

[146] According to the 1880 U.S. Census, the household consisted of the Thomas family, as well as Katie Hammel, a Canadian cook; two maids, Marion McClosky and Jennie Bagley; and Leander Bagley, their coachman.

[147] On December 6 1901, for example, the Thomases give a "small dance" for their son Joe—then a freshman at Yale home for Christmas break—at Delmonico's. "There was a cotillion and some pretty favors," an article in the society pages of *The New York Times* noted. "It was a small dance. Only fifty or sixty in all were invited, and they were of the younger set." "What is Doing in Society," December 7, 1901, p. 9.

148 "Personality and Comment," *The Spur* magazine, April 1, 1934, p. 32.

149 "Moosehead's Private Camps," *The New York Times*, June 11, 1905, p. X6.

150 See "Taxes Hit Big Estate," *The New York Times*, May 3, 1921, p. 15.

151 According to *Who's Who in New England of 1909*, Joe Thomas was sent to Paris to attend the progressive *Ecole Monge* elementary school, which was founded in 1871. A profile of Thomas in the April 1, 1934, issue of *The Spur (op. cit.)* magazine refers to his "schooldays in Paris." And the August 16, 1937, "Personality Sketch" of Joe Thomas prepared by Elizabeth F. Morgan for the Works Progress Administration's Virginia Historical Inventory notes that he was "educated at Ecole Mongle [sic] in Paris" and "Berkeley School, New York." However, the official *History of the Class of 1903 of Yale College* (Yale University, 1906, p. 270) makes no mention of Paris, saying that Joe Thomas attended the Blake School in New York City before beginning Yale in 1899.

152 "Personality and Comment," *op. cit.*

153 *History of the Class of 1903, op. cit.*, p; 270.

154 "Early Training for the Yale Track Team," *The New York Tribune*, July 6, 1901, p. 10.

155 "Paris Wants Polo Team," *The New York Times*, May 29, 1903, p. 14.

156 "Where They Excel," *The Pittsburgh Gazette*, June 15, 1903, p. 2.

157 *History of the Class of 1903, op. cit.*, p; 270.

158 "The Poultry Show Opens," *The New York Times*, January 31, 1900, p. 9. *The Spur* magazine profile (op. cit.) refers to his interest in "fancy poultry."

159 Freeman Lloyd, "The Russian Wolfhounds, or Borzoi," *American Kennel Gazette*, October 1831.

160 Bo Bengston, "The Hound Classic," *Dogs in Review*, July 2017, p. 98. The "ancient" type of Borzoi Joe Thomas sought, Bengston said, actually was "the modern type that dedicated Russian breeders had [by the early 1900s] been perfecting for many years."

161 Grand Duke Nicholas Nikolaevich of Russia (1856-1929)—whom *The Washington Post* called "the leading dog enthusiast in the vast empire of the czar," ("Gossip of the Elite World in Moods of Gray and Gay," August 19, 1914, p. 7)—commanded the Russian Imperial Army when World War I started in 1914. He survived the Russian Revolution and died in exile in France.

162 Joseph B. Thomas, *Observations on Borzoi: Called in America Russian Wolfhounds: In a Series of Letters to a Friend* (Houghton Mifflin, 1912), p. 40.

163 "A $5,000 Dog Lost and Found," *The New York Times*, March 9, 1904, p. 1.

164 "Russian Sheep Dogs: Breed of Big Woolly Fellows to be Seen in This Country," *The New York Times*, December 19, 1904, p. 9.

165 Barbara Austen, "Wolfhounds for Sale in Simsbury," Connecticut Historical Society, November 7, 2012.

166 Joseph B. Thomas, *Observations on Borzoi*, p. v.

167 "Russian Wolfhound Club," *Forest and Stream*, February 27, 1904, p. 170.

168 "Steve Tillotson, writing in *Our Afghans*, 2012, www.afghanhoundtimes.com/ovalley.htm

169 *Simsbury Free Library Quarterly*, Fall 2014, p. 7.

170 "Will Shoot Wolves, Mountain Lions," *The Hartford Courant*, November 21, 1906, p. 8.

171 "Wyoming Branch for Wolfhounds," *The Hartford Courant*, January 31, 1907, p. 8.

172 Bengston, *op. cit*, p. 99.

173 Among other business endeavors, Joe Thomas headed the American College Stores Corporation, which provided merchandise to college co-op stores. Its clients included the co-ops at the University of Michigan in Ann Arbor and Amherst College in Massachusetts.

174 "Back with Polo Ponies," *The Hartford Currant*, October 15, 1909, p. 14.

175 Horace A. Laffaye, *Polo In the United States: A History* (McFarland, 2011), p. 56.

176 "Chief Joseph's Potlash," *The Hartford Currant*, May 18, 1906, p. 1.

177 "In True Indian Style," *The New-York Tribune*, June 17, 1906, p. C2.

178 "Pastoral Ball on Fair Grounds," *The Hartford Currant*, September 29, 1906, p. 17.

179 "Joseph B. Thomas, Jr., Simsbury," *Legislative History and Souvenir of Connecticut, Vol. VI., 1908-1908.* (William Harrison Taylor, 1908), p. 277.

[180] Christopher Gray, "Streetscapes: The Frederick Sterner House, at 139 East 19th Street; An Architect Who Turned Brownstones into Gems," *The New York Times*, June 29, 2003.

[181] "J.B. Thomas Jr., Buys 19th Street Houses," *The New York Times*, April 5, 1910, p. 16. Among the apartment house's residents: the famed muckraking journalist Ida Tarbell, the society painter Cecilia Breaux, and the stockbroker and art collector Chester Dale.

[182] Gina Wouters and Andrea Gollin, eds., *Robert Winthrop Chanler: Discovering the Fantastic* (The Monacelli Press, 2016), p. 32. "Robert Chanler was the quintessential artist of the Gilded Age, with a stable of wealthy patrons," Stephen Van Dyke of the Cooper Hewitt museum wrote. Educated at the Ecole des Beaux-Arts in Paris and in Italy, he decorated his E. 19th Street house "in his style, and filled the basement with caged monkeys, sloths, and toucans, and the pool with crabs, seahorses, eels, and turtles," which he used as inspiration for the animals he painted on his screens. "The Fantastic Beasts of Robert Winthrop Chanler," https://www.cooperhewitt.org/2017/04/03/cooper-hewitt-short-stories-the-fantastic-beasts-of-robert-winthrop-chanler

[183] "At the Opening of the Winter Academy," *Town & Country*, December 10, 1910. The magazine reported that Joe Thomas "has displayed much originality and energy in his disposal" of the two other E. 19th Street brownstones. "Each residence is being made a house beautiful but with a view to the harmony and character of the block as a whole. In this plan to make an attractive residential section, he has commercial as well as artistic success in view."

[184] A. Henry Higginson and Julian Ingersoll Chamberlain, describe Col. Dulany as "the father of fox-hunting in the Piedmont Valley" in their 1908 book, *The Hunts of the United States and Canada: Their Masters, Hounds and Histories* (Franklin L. Wiles), p. 144.

[185] Dulany (1820-1906) also founded the oldest continuously run horse show in the U.S., the Upperville Colt & Horse Show, in 1853. He gave up foxhunting when the Civil War began, joined the Confederate States of America Army, and went on to command a regiment of the 7th Virginia Cavalry. He inherited Welbourne, which dates from the 1770s, from his father John Peyton Dulany (1787-1878), who had purchased it around 1819. Welbourne today is a bread-and-breakfast run by descendants of Col. Dulany.

[186] Walter A Dyer, "Country Life in Loudoun County," *Country Life in America*, February 1908, p. 428. Dyer (1878-1943), edited *Country Life in America* from 1906-1914. His work included many magazine articles and novels about dogs. The latter include *Pierrot: Dog of Belgium* (1915), *Gulliver the Great and Other Dog Stories* (1916), *The Dogs of Boytown* (1918), *Many Dogs There Be* (1924), and *All Around Robin Hood's Barn: a Canine Idyll* (1926).

[187] A.C. Rowantree, "Hunting in Virginia," *Town and Country*, November 9, 1912, pp. 22-23, 42.

[188] Mayme Ober Peak, "Virginia's Piedmont Hunting Section," *Spur*, October 15, 1920, p. 44.

[189] Smith (1865-1945), a self-made millionaire industrialist, and Higginson (1876-1958), an heir to a huge banking fortune, were nationally known foxhunters in Massachusetts. Smith had first fox hunted in Upperville in 1889, and came to believe that Middleburg-Upperville area "was the best [fox] hunting country in the United States," as he wrote in an unpublished biography in the collection of the National Sporting Library in Middleburg. Also see Martha Wolfe, *The Great Hound Match of 1905* (Lyons Press, 2016), p.78, and Andrew C. Baker's "Southern Landscapes in the City's Shadow," a 2014 Rice University doctoral dissertation which contains an excellent, concise summary of the Great Hound Match and its implications on foxhunting in the Virginia Piedmont.

[190] Baker, *op. cit.*, pp. 48 and 56.

[191] Now known as the National Steeplechase Association, the organization was founded in 1895.

[192] "Joseph B. Thomas, Hunting Diaries, 1913-1929, Biographical Note," Archives & Manuscript Collections, National Sporting Library.

[193] Burrland was home to the Noland family beginning in the mid-19th century. Major Burr Noland gave the property to his son, Cuthbert Powell Noland, and his wife Rosalie Haxall, as a wedding present in 1879, after which the couple named the place "Burrland" in his honor. They had seven children, including Charlotte Haxall Noland, who would go on to found Foxcroft School in 1914. Charlotte Noland ran a summer camp called a "Farmette" at Burrland in the early 1900s. See U.S. Department of the Interior, National Park Service, National Register of Historic Places Registration Form, "Burrland Farm Historic District," Janet G. Murphy, January 1997, Section 8, pp. 10-11.

[194] Advertisement in *Bit and Spur*, February 15, 1908, p. 6.

[195] "Burrland, Middleburg: Loudoun Co., Virginia," *Bit and Spur*, August 1, 1910, p. 44.

[196] "About People," *Bit and Spur*, January 1, 1912, p. 14.

[197] See the Burrland Farm Historic District National Register of Historic Places Form, *op. cit.* An ad in the October 26, 1912, issue of *Town and Country*, touting "America's Only Real Fox Hunting Country Inn at 'Burrland Hall' in Middleburg" contained contact information for a "pamphlet and full particulars": C.L. Bohanan at 132 E. 19th St. in New York City—the address of the house Joe Thomas owned and had turned into an apartment building.

[198] "Westbury: Polo Tournament at Great Neck Chief Even on Calendar," *The New York Times*, June 16, 1912, p. X3.

[199] "Fire Destroys Seven Narragansett Villas," *The New York Sun*, July 28, 1912, p. 1. The article contains an account of a fire that destroyed seven villas on "one of the picturesque estates of Narragansett Pier." Joe Thomas was among a group of volunteer firefighters, the article, reported, "who are spending the summer at the pier" who "rushed to the aid of the local department and rendered valuable service."

[200] "Inaugural Meeting, March 9, 1912," *The Minute Book of the American Foxhound Club*, Archives & Manuscript Collections, National Sporting Library, American Foxhound Club Archive, 1912-1977.

[201] Joseph B. Thomas to Henry T. Oxnard, April 5, 1916. Archives & Manuscript Collections, National Sporting Library.

[202] Annie Leith did not move completely out of New Lisbon until January 12, soon after buying a 37-acre property at North Fork in Loudoun County. See Loudoun County Deed Book 8P/254, January 12, 1912.

[203] Loudoun County Deed Book 6W/327 (1885); 8P/158 (1912).

[204] Loudoun County Deed Book 7U/118 (1901).

[205] Loudoun County Deed Books 8U/434 (1914) and 8X456 (1915).

[206] N. Frank Neer, Jr., "Facts from Virginia," *Bit and Spur*, November 1, 1912, p. 41.

[207] N. Frank Neer, Jr., "Hound Haven at Huntland," *Bit and Spur*, May 1, 1913, p. 40.

[208] Joseph B. Thomas, *Hounds and Hunting Through the Ages* (The Derrydale Press, 2001), p. 140.

[209] *Ibid.*, p. 137.

[210] *The Chase, Field Sports, Rural Games and other poems by William Somervile* (James Ballantyne & Co., 1812), p. 88 and pp. 3-4.

[211] *Hounds and Hunting Through the Ages, op. cit.*

[212] *Ibid.*, p. 142.

[213] Kitty Slater, *The Hunt Country of America*, revised edition (Arco, 1973), p. 31.

[214] Loudoun County Land Tax Books, 1913. The improvements were added to the original 272-acre parcel that contained the house and the new kennel.

[215] Claude H. Haga, "The Use of Cement Grout and Field Stones in Interesting and Economical Construction," *Concrete-Cement Age* magazine, January 1914, p.7.

[216] Claude Haga died in his mid-thirties on Feb. 2, 1915, at Sibley Hospital in Washington, D.C., following brain-cancer surgery. Newspaper obituaries (*Washington Times*, February 4; Washington *Evening Star*, February 5; and *The Washington Post*, February 3) gave differing ages (35 and 37) and the number of his children (five and six). The Star obit also reported that "the plans for the remodeling of the Virginia State Capitol in Richmond were his work." However, the architect in charge of the 1904-06 renovation of the Capitol was John Kevan Peebles (1866-1934) of Norfolk, who added two new wings to Thomas Jefferson's iconic building. Haga, then in his mid-twenties, may have worked for Peebles' firm.

[217] See the entry for Read & Morrill, Inc. in *Sweet's Catalog of Building Construction for the Year 1913, Vol. 2*, p. 48. Morrill studied architecture in the U.S. and Paris, and while working for the federal government designed several early 20th century government buildings in Washington, D.C., before turning to home designing using reinforced concrete, according to the self-published book, *The Morrill Moulded Concrete Houses* (1919).

[218] Haga, *op. cit*, p. 6.

[219] "Huntland," a detailed marketing brochure prepared by Joe Thomas in 1920 when he put the property on the market.

[220] Quoted in Christopher Oakford, "Restoring a Foxhunter's Legacy," *Covertside* magazine, Spring 2016, p. 21.

[221] *Hounds and Hunting, op. cit.*, p. 149.

[222] "Huntland," *op. cit.*

[223] Thomas, *op. cit.*, p. 141.

[224] Julian Street, *American Adventures: A Second Trip 'Abroad at Home'* (The Century Co., 1917), p. 173.

[225] Slater, *op. cit.*, p. 33.

[226] Thomas to Oxnard, *op. cit.*

[227] Oakford, *op. cit.*, p. 22.

[228] United States Department of the Interior, National Park Service, Huntland nomination, *op. cit.*, Section 7, p. 5.

[229] Huntland marketing brochure, p. 4.

230 The firm designed many notable structures, primarily large estates on Long Island. They include the McClintock Laboratory at the Cold Spring Harbor Laboratory (1914); the estate of George W. Bacon, Thatch Meadow Farm, in St. James (1914); Julian Peabody's Southern Colonial-style residence, Pond Hallow Farm, in Westbury, which contains a circular staircase strikingly similar to the one in Huntland's entrance hall (1915); the Milburn Estate at the Old Westbury Equestrian Center (1916); the Reginald Fincke, Sr. estate in Southampton (1924); as well as the Washington, D.C., home of Admiral Cary Grayson (1926); and the historic Post Office in Mineola, New York (1935).

231 "Country Houses of Character," *Country Life*, November 1919, p. 32.

232 United States Department of the Interior, National Park Service, "National Register of Historic Places Registration Form," submitted November 8, 2013, *op. cit*, Section 7, p. 9. The nomination's author, Maral S. Kalbian, did unprecedented, extensive research into the changes Joe Thomas made to Huntland.

233 *Ibid*, Section 7, p. 10.

234 *Ibid*.

235 Huntland marketing brochure, p. 4.

236 Much of the decorative mural wallpaper that Joe Thomas added throughout the house was created by Zuber & Cie, a world-renowned, French-based wallpaper and fabric company. Only some of this wallpaper is still intact at Huntland.

237 Garrick (1717-1779), a renowned English actor and playwright, extensively remodeled a large elegant villa in Hampton on the Thames River southwest of London. "Adam-style" refers to a neoclassical type of interior design practiced by Robert Adam and his two brothers. Adam, in fact, redesigned the exterior of the Garrick Villa at Hampton.

238 "From New Lisban [sic] to Huntland Tradition," *The Pink Sheet*, January 1988, p. 4. An award-winning journalist and author, McClary is best known for her best-selling 1972 novel, *A Portion of Foxes*, which is set in Hunt Country and tells the tale of the misadventures of a mysterious newcomer who buys an old estate. Michael Korda, who edited the book, called it "a kind of '*Gone With the Wind*' of fox hunting" in his book, *Horse People: Scenes from the Riding Life* (Simon & Schuster, 2003), p. 28.

239 Nomination, *op cit.*, Section 7, p. 5.

240 Claude H. Haga, "The Use of Cement Grout and Field Stones in Interesting and Economical Construction," *Concrete-Cement Age*, January 1914, p. 7. According to neighbor Don Bevors, his grandfather helped in the construction of stone walls at Huntland in 1918.

241 "Two Cottages with solid Concrete Walls, Built Near Middleburg, Va., *Concrete-Cement Age*, January 1915, p. 18.

242 Maral S. Kalbian interview with John D. Beavers, March 25, 2023.

243 Huntland marketing brochure.

244 Haga, *op. cit*, p. 8.

245 Nomination, *op. cit.*, Section 8, p. 29.

246 "Sportsmen to Banquet," *The Washington Post*, March 12, 1913, p. 2.

247 "Must Have Horses," *The Washington Post*, April 3, 1913, p. 1.

248 "All Fox-Hunters to Form Association," *Richmond Times-Dispatch*, August 9, 1913, p. 6. It appears that the association did not come to fruition.

249 "First Tuesday Dance: Green Decorations for St. Patrick's Day at Joseph B. Thomas's Home," *The New York Times*, March 18, 1914.

250 "3,000 see Mauretania Go: Big Ship Crowded—Voyage Starts with Music and College Yells," *The New York Times*, April 29, 1914, p. 6.

251 See "F.J. Gould is Married," *The New York Times*, July 9, 1910, p. 1 and "Former Helen Kelly Secures Decree in Paris from Albanian Prince Whom She Married Here in 1917," *New York Herald*, October 11, 1922, p. 9.

252 "Ralph Hill Thomas, B.A., 1905," *Bulletin of Yale University, Obituary Record of Yale Graduates, 1914-1915*, 11th Series, July 1915, p. 864. The headline on his January 2, 1915, obituary in *The New York Times* read: "Ralph Hill Thomas Dead. American Sugar Refining Co. Official Who Married Mrs. F.J. Gould."

253 "Thomas Memorial Lectures," *Yale University Catalogue*, 1918-1919, p. 130.

254 Dr. Dudley Allen Sargent, a pioneering physical education instructor, started the school in 1881.

255 Biographical details from a 1970 Foxcroft School publication, "Charlotte Haxall Noland, 1883-1969" edited by Mary Custis Lee deButts and Rosalie Noland Woodland.

256 "20th Anniversary Celebration of Foxcroft" speech, courtesy of the Foxcroft School Archives. The sleeping porch

arrangement, with students' beds separated from their shared study rooms and bathrooms, remains a feature of dormitory life today at Foxcroft.

257 Author interview, May 25, 2018.

258 Nancy Perkins Lancaster, Class of 1915, Oral History Recording, Foxcroft School Archives, Recorded April 26, 1975.

259 "Miss Fargo Engaged," *The New York Times*, January 22, 1915, p. 11.

260 "Miss Clara Fargo," *Town & Country*, February 1, 1915, p. 34.

261 William George Fargo, the Mayor of Buffalo, N.Y., from 1862-66, served as president of American Express and later as the Director of Wells Fargo Express. The city of Fargo, North Dakota, was named after him in 1871.

262 According to her obituary in *The New York Times*, April 27, 1970, p. 33. Now known as The Spence School, the institution was founded in by Clara Spence in 1892.

263 "Miss Fargo Meets Society," *The New York Times*, November 28, 1908, p. 9.

264 "Junior League in Musical Comedy," *The New York Times*, February 17, 1909, p. 9.

265 Prizes at Tea Dance," *The New York Times*, December 25, 1913, p. 9.

266 "Dance for Day Nursery," *The New York Times*, February 9, 1914, p. 7.

267 "Hunting Notes," *The Spur*, December 1, 1914, p. 35.

268 "Joseph B. Thomas Weds Miss Fargo," the *New York Tribune*, February 16, 1915.

269 *Vogue*, May 1, 1915, p. 40; *Harper's Bazaar*, April 1915, p. 21.

270 "Five O'clock Tidbits," *The Spur*, May 15, 1915, p. 23.

271 Caption below a full-age photo of Clara by Arnold Genthe (1869-1942), the German-born photographer best known for his portraits of notables of the day, including many socialites, actresses, and literary figures. *Vogue*, December 15, 1915, p. 62.

272 "A Toast to 100 Years," *Stream Ripples*, the newsletter of the Fauquier and Loudoun Garden Club, November/December 2015. The hundredth anniversary celebration of the club took place in the ballroom at Huntland where Betsee Parker displayed a bust of Clara Fargo Thomas.

273 Slater, *op. cit.*, p. 38.

274 LBJ Library Oral History Collection, Transcript, Isabel Brown Wilson Oral History Interview I, February 19, 1988, by Michael L. Gillette.

275 In fact, in her oral history, Isabel Wilson explained that what she said about Miss Charlotte and Joe Thomas was a "story" she and her family heard, that "didn't know if it's true or not."

276 1910 U.S. Federal Census, Mercer, Loudoun Virginia, Roll T624-1633, p. 5B. Under the category "Color or race," the African Americans were listed as "Mulatto." Daniel C. Sands' occupation was "Farmer."

277 "Society Forms Club to Foster Dalmatian Dogs," *Philadelphia Enquirer*, April 17, 1905, p. 2.

278 "Foxhounds: American Foxhound Club's Show," *The Dog Fancier* magazine, March 1913, p. 12. The event took place at the North Avenue Casino in Baltimore.

279 "Virginia Fox Hounds Run Wild in Show," *The New York Times*, February 23, 1913, p. 41.

280 Thomas Atkinson, "Daniel C. Sands, Jr.: Master of the Middleburg Hunt—and One of America's Noted Fox Hunters," *The Chronicle* magazine, June 18, 1954, p. 16. National Sporting Library, Archives and Manuscripts Collections, MC0040, Box K 07, Folder 3.

281 See, for example, "Daniel Cox Sands, MFH of the Middleburg and Piedmont Hunts (1875-1963)," *Museum News* (the official publication of the Museum of Hounds and Hunting), May 2004, p. 1.

282 *The Spur* magazine praised Sands' leadership of the Piedmont Hunt, saying that, under his leadership, its pack "became the finest in this country." "Five O'clock Tidbits," *The Spur*, May 15, 1915, p. 23.

283 An image of the broadside is reproduced in the book *The Lure of Loudoun: Centuries of Change in Virginia's Emerald County* by Noel Grove and Charles P. Poland, Jr. (Loudoun Museum, 2007), p. 136, and credited to the National Sporting Library. However, the original could not be located in the NSL Archives.

284 Daniel C. Sands, Jr. to A.C. Reid, April 3, 1916, National Sporting Library, Archives and Manuscripts Collections, Piedmont Fox Hounds Archives 1915-1930, Correspondence 1916-1938, Box MC009.

285 Joseph B. Thomas to Henry T. Oxnard, April 5, 1916, *Ibid.* Henry Thomas Oxnard (1861-1922) made a fortune in the beet sugar refining business. In 1904, he served as president of both the American Beet Sugar Co. and the American Beet Sugar Association and he and three brothers owned five beet refineries, including one in Chino, California. In 1898, the

brothers had built a refinery in a rural area near Chino known as Rancho Colonia. A town soon grew up around the factory. In 1903, it incorporated and named itself the City of Oxnard in honor of Henry and his brothers. See the City of Oxnard's official history, https://visitoxnard.com/about/history; Henry Oxnard's obituary in *The New York Times*, June 9, 1922, p. 5; and "Henry T. Oxnard at Home," *San Francisco Sunday Call*, July 10, 1904, p. 5.

286 Henry T. Oxnard to F.J. Bryan, April 29, 1916, National Sporting Library, Archives and Manuscripts Collections, MC 0040, Box K 11, Folder 29.

287 In her 1973 Texas Woman's University M.A. Thesis, "An Historical Survey of Foxhunting in the United States, 1650-1970," Sherri L. Stewart wrote: "By 1915, Thomas had financial control of both hunts and asked Mr. Sands to relinquish his Mastership of the Piedmont and serve only as Master of the Middleburg. Mr. Sands took great offense, resigning from both hunts. During the season of 1915-16, Mr. Thomas was Master of both hunts. During the following season Middleburg was without a Master. Mr. Sands was Acting Master for the season of 1917-18 and was listed as the Master in 1919. That same year, Mr. Thomas resigned from the Piedmont in the Spring and Mr. Sands again resigned as Master of the Middleburg."

288 Harry Depuy died at age 40 on July 4, 1920, in a hospital in New York City from "apoplexy following a nervous breakdown caused by overexertion while undergoing training during the war," according to the *Obituary Record of Graduates Deceased during the Year Ending July 1, 1920* (Yale University, 1921), p. 157.

289 Military information from Thomas' World War I Discharge Card; *The Yale Alumni Weekly*, October 25, 1918, p. 128; and the *Army-Navy-Air Force and Defense Times*, September 7, 1918, p. 266.

290 Walter L. Goodwin to Eugene Gatewood, August 30, 1918, National Sporting Library, Archives and Manuscripts Collections, Piedmont Fox Hounds Archives, *op. cit.*

291 Eugene Gatewood to Walter L. Goodwin, September 5, 1918, *Ibid.* Carver (1878-1951) worked as Joe Thomas' Huntsman from 1911-1932. In his 1928 book, *Hounds and Hunting through the Ages*, Joe described Carver as "the most clever huntsman within my ken"; an "indefatigable enthusiast in breeding, training, and hunting grounds"; and a "bold rider" who "has probably seen more of hound work than any living American huntsman..." (Derrydale Press edition, 2001), p. 102).

292 Joseph B. Thomas to E.C. Gatewood, May 14, 1919. National Sporting Library, Archives and Manuscripts Collections, MC 0009, Folder 38.

293 *Ibid.*

294 "American Holsteins Arriving in France," *Holstein-Friesian World* magazine, October 18, 1919, p. 50.

295 Alan Fox to the U.S. Department of State, May 3, 1920, attachment to Joe Thomas' May 7, 1920 passport application. Fox was a partner in the New York law firm of Trowbridge & Fox.

296 "Bastille Day Links France and America," the *New-York Tribune*, July 14, 1918, p. 8.

297 "Give Play for Milk Fund," *The New York Times*, July 11, 1918, p. 9.

298 Joe is listed as president and director of Cornucopia Mines in the 1915-16 *Directory of Directors of the City of New York* (p. 688), and as President in the 1919 *American Mining Manual* (p. 270).

299 *American Mining Manual, op. cit.*

300 Joseph B. Thomas to E.C. Gatewood, January 16, 1920. National Sporting Library, Archives and Manuscripts Collections, MC 0009, Box K04, Folder 39.

301 Kitty Slater, *The Hunt Country of America Revisited*, revised edition, *op. cit.*, p. 44.

302 The same ad appeared in the April and May 1920 issues of *Country Life.*

303 Norman Fine, editor, *The Derrydale Press Treasury of Fox Hunting* (Derrydale Press, 2003), p. x. Also see Denison B. Hull, *Thoughts on American Fox-Hunting* (David McKay, 1958), p. 115.

304 "400 in Society Dance at Grasslands Ball," *The New York Times*, December 6, 1930, p. 19. The international event took place for only two years at Grassland. It then moved to Richard K. Mellon's Rolling Rock Hunt Meet course in Ligonier, Pennsylvania. Since 1983, the International Gold Cup has been held at the Great Meadows racecourse between Warrenton and The Plains, in Fauquier County, Virginia.

305 See "Biographical Note," National Sporting Library, Archives and Manuscripts Collections, Joseph B. Thomas Hunting Diaries, 1913-1929, MC0008.

306 Thomas, *Hounds and Hunting, op. cit.*, p. 142.

307 *Ibid*, p. 184.

308 "Taxes Hit Big Estate: Executor Asks Time for Joseph B. Thomas, Who Owes $209,942," *The New York Times*, May 3, 1921, p. 15.

309 National Sporting Library, Archives and Manuscripts Collections, MC 0040, Box K11, Folder 35, p. 88.

310 "Purcellville," *Richmond Times-Dispatch*, March 26, 1922, p. 2.

311 United States Census, 1920, U.S. National Archives and Records Administration, GS Film Number 18212033. The employees listed as servants were Mary O. Sullivan (born in Ireland), age 40, and Susan Fournier, (France), 27. The nurse, Mary McInerney, 49; cook, Margaret Martin, 32; and maid Margaret Ward, 37, also were born in Ireland.

312 In the caption of a full-page photograph of Clara, "Mrs. Joseph B. Thomas," *The Spur*, July 1, 1920, p. 33. Four months earlier, *Vogue* magazine also ran a full page photo of Clara, commenting: "She is a well-known hostess, and her evening musicals are of notable success." *Vogue*, March 1, 1920, p. 72.

313 "J.B. Thomases Aid Needy Artists with Amusing Soiree," *The New York Tribune*, January 5, 1925.

314 See "Many Purcellville Prize Winners Listed," *The Evening Star*," September 10, 1926, p. 13, and "Smith's Clydesdales Win at Loudoun Show," *The Washington Post*, September 11, 1926, p. 2.

315 See Virginia Lee Warren, "Campanile: A Pseudo-Norman Palazzo with a Special Cachet," *The New York Times*, March 3, 1968, p. 80. The "cachet," Warren wrote, "is the list of tenants who have lived there." That list includes the actresses Mary Martin, Ethel Barrymore, and Greta Garbo; the playwright and composer Noel Coward; the architect Edgar J. Kaufman; *New York Herald-Tribune* publisher Walter N. Thayer; and the critic Alexander Woollcott.

316 *Hounds and Hunting, op. cit.*, p. 10.

317 S.W. Cousans, "For the Hunting Library," *The Spur*, March 1, 1929, p. 43.

318 "Hunting Dogs Find New Historian of Their Efforts," *Chicago Daily Tribune*, February 9, 1929, p. 11.

319 "With Sportsmen Afield and Afloat," *The Wall Street Journal*, May 21, 1929, p. 3.

320 *Cincinnati Enquirer*, April 13, 1924, p. 36.

321 "Newsy Murals," *The New Yorker*, December 2, 1933, p. 14.

322 See, Virginia Gardner, "Tribune Mural Depicts Battle for Free Press," Chicago *Tribune*, June 22, 1936.

323 "Mural Traces Beauty through History," *The Washington Post*, August 7, 1935, p. 11.

324 "'Beauty' Mural Exhibited," *The New York Times*, October 15, 1935, p. 10.

325 "Joseph Thomas, A Sportsman, 75," *New York Times* obituary, July 15, 1955, p. 21.

326 Nina Carter Tabb, "The Hunting Log," *The Evening Star*, March 25, 1936, p. B-2.

327 That is the arrangement that the May 3, 1921, *New York Times* article referred to: that Joe had "mortgaged a $215,000 stock farm in Loudoun County" to raise the funds to pay off his debt to his mother's estate.

328 Loudoun County Deed Book 9Z/134 and 136 (1927) and 9Z/150-151 (1927). The deed was recorded on June 22, 1927. The Robinsons paid at total of $115,000 cash and took a mortgage for $85,000, at six percent, paying in five annual installments.

329 Quoted in Slater, *The Hunt Country of America Revisited*, revised edition, *op. cit.*, pp. 203-204.

330 "Famous Huntland Sold to Kentuckian: Former Washington Woman Will Be Chatelaine of Old Colonial Estate," *The Washington Post*, May 29, 1927, p. R4. In 1923, Hilleary sold Thomas Jefferson's Monticello for its owner, the real estate and stock speculator Jefferson M. Levy, to the Thomas Jefferson Memorial Foundation, the nonprofit that owns and operates Monticello today. See Marc Leepson, *Saving Monticello: The Levy Family's Epic Quest to Save the House That Jefferson Built* (University of Virginia Press, 2003), pp. 213-215.

331 "Wedding at Aiken, S.C., of Washington Interest," Washington *Evening Star*, April 11, 1921, p. 8.

332 On her May 29, 1924, passport application, Gwendolyn Robinson listed her occupation as "housewife," and her permanent residence as Tulsa. Also see "Denys-Robinson," *Louisville Courier Journal*, April 3, 1921, p. A8.

333 "Gwendolyn Denys Massey, 1894-1979," Norwich Terrier Club of America, *The Norwich & Norfolk News*, Issue 39, 1980.

334 See "Adds to Virginia Holdings," *The New York Times*, November 14, 1929, p. 53.

335 Loudoun County Deed Book 10F/63 (1930).

336 The Talmages were members of the Piping Rock Club, a country club on Long Island that Joe Thomas sometimes frequented. In May and August of 1929, after the couple bought Huntland, Hunt Talmage entered a hunter named Angel Girl at the annual Keswick Hunt Club horse show near Charlottesville, Virginia, and at the Charles Town Horse Show and Fair in West Virginia. See "Keswick Hunt Club Show Entries Many," *The Washington Post*, May 30, 1929, p. 3 and "Horse Show Ends at Charles Town," *The Washington Post*, August 10, 1929, p. 18.

337 New York Municipal Archives, "New York City Municipal Deaths, 1795-1949," Thomas Hunt Talmage, FHL microfilm 1,322,904.

338 New York State Archives, "New York Abstracts of World War I Service, 1917 1919," Form No. 724, November 22, 1919, Talmage, Thomas H.

339 American Consular Service, American Consulate General, "Report of Birth of Children Born to American Parents," Jacqueline Talmage, April 5, 1928.

340 Loudoun County Deed Book 1OL/263 (1933).

341 See *Richmond Times-Dispatch*, January 20, 1936.

342 "1,884 Cows Given Tests in Loudoun: June Record Production Hits High of 1,311,707 Pounds of Milk," *The Washington Post*, July 11, 1931, p. 18.

343 See Washington *Evening Star*, September 4, 1936, p. B-2. Hardin, whom one gossip columnist described as "lean, saturnine, [and] sporting," moved from Washington, D.C., into one of the Huntland cottages after his wife, Nancy Hale Hardin, sued him for divorce late in 1935. He left Huntland and moved to Newstead Farm in Upperville after marrying Katherine Bliss Boker in the summer of 1937. See Washington *Evening Star*, January 1, 1935, p. A-9; and December 5, 1935, p. B-13; and *The Washington Post*, July 27, 1937, p. 12.

344 President Franklin D. Roosevelt created the Works Progress Administration by executive order in 1935 to provide government public works jobs. Part of the WPA included work for writers such as Elizabeth Morgan, as well as actors, musicians, playwrights, and other artists.

3245 Elizabeth F. Morgan, "New Lisbon Survey Report, 1936" Works Progress Administration of Virginia Historical Inventory, December 29, 1936.

346 "Residents Back from Florida Visit," *The Sunday Star* (Washington, D.C.), March 7, 1937, and "In the Hunt Country," *The Evening Star*, March 22, 1937.

347 When the property sold in 1938, the deed of trust noted that the sale was "subject to the right of Raymond F. Tartiere and Gladys H. Tartiere, his wife, to harvest and remove any growing crops on any portion of the land hereby conveyed which may have been seeded prior to May 10th, 1938." Loudoun County Deed Book 11/B, 66, (1938).

348 See, Gladys R. Tartiere obituary, *The Washington Post*, March 5, 1993, and "Tartiere Family Papers, 1920-1950," Biographical Note, U.S. Holocaust Memorial Museum Archives.

349 In 1961, Gladys Tartiere leased Glen Ora to newly elected President John F. Kennedy and his wife Jacqueline, to use as a weekend country getaway. Jackie Kennedy, an avid horsewoman, had spent time in Middleburg as a young woman. The Kennedys visited Glen Ora often during the next two years, and offered to buy the property from Gladys Tartiere, who declined. When the lease ended in the fall of 1963—not long before JFK was assassinated—the Kennedys bought another large Hunt Country horse farm, built a house there that Jackie designed, and renamed it Wexford.

350 Loudoun County Deed Book 11/B, 66, (1938). *The New York Times* reported that the selling price was "about $100,000." "Virginia Estate Sold: Property Includes 413 Acres in Hunting Section," *The New York Times*, August 8, 1938, p. 31.

351 Loudoun County Deed Book 11/F, 390, (1939).

352 "Boston Man Buys Huntland Estate," Washington *Evening Star*, May 14, 1938, p. B-2.

353 "Huntland Estate Sold to McLeods [sic] of Boston," *Loudoun Times-Mirror*, May 12, 1938.

354 January 13, 1948, p. B2.

355 Interview with author and Maral S. Kalbian, July 1, 2018.

356 According to the 1940 U.S. Census Population Schedule for the Loudoun County Mercer District.

357 Nina Carter Tabb, "The Hunt Country," *The Washington Post*, June 26, 1939, p. 8.

358 Nina Carter Tabb, "The Hunt Country," *The Washington Post*, May 26, 1940, p. S2.

359 "Boston Man Buys Huntland Estate," op. cit. Also, Nina Carter Tabb, "Atkinsons Will Entertain at Eggnog Party Today," *The Washington Post*, December 24, 1944, p. S2.

360 U.S. Department of Veterans Affairs, BIRLS Death File, "Colin Macleod."

361 Nina Carter Tabb, "Down Virginia Way," *The Washington Post*, August 30, 1942, p. S4.

362 Nina Carter Tabb, "Atkinsons Will Entertain at Eggnog Party Today," op. cit. Jane Thomas and Peter Greenough (1917-2006), a *Boston Globe* and Cleveland *Plain Dealer* columnist and editor, had three children. After their divorce, in 1956, Greenough married the opera singer Beverly Sills. See Peter B. Greenough, obituary, *The New York Times*, September 8, 2006, p. A27.

363 The sale to the Prophets closed on January 7, 1946, but the MacLeods stayed in the house through February. Ann and Sandy met in October that year and were married in December. Sandy MacLeod died on December 12, 1977, at age 62. In the summer of 2019 Ann MacLeod, at 97, made her annual trip from Upperville to Saratoga to take in the races.

[364] Robert Copeland, "A $728,000,000 Snack," *Nation's Business*, February 1944, p. 79.

[365] Nina Carter Tabb, "'Sport of Kings' Attracts Crowd to Middleburg for Annual Events," *The Washington Post*, April 28, 1946, p. S2.

[366] Loudoun County Deed Book 12/T, page 443, February 6, 1948. The deed was recorded on April 1, 1948. Fred Prophet died on March 12, 1959, at age 74, in Santa Barbara, California.

[367] "Huntland Farm Sold Near Middleburg," *The Washington Post*, January 29, 1948, p. B9.

[368] "Large Virginia Estate Sold," New York *Herald Tribune*, February 1, 1948, p. D2.

[369] Deborah C. Pollack, *Vintage Miami Beach Glamour: Celebrities & Socialites in the Heyday of Chic* (History Press, 2019), p. 98.

[370] "Bill Returning Citizenship to Woman Goes to Senate," Washington *Evening Star*, February 1, 1952, p. D-5.

[371] "Genevive Cambon and Alain deBriel to Wed Tomorrow, New York *Herald Tribune*, November 29, 1950, p. 31.

[372] Alfred W. Knowles served as one of the horse trainers at Huntland from 1952-59, according to his September 12, 1989, obituary in *The Washington Post*.

[373] "Bill Returning Citizenship to Woman Goes to Senate," Washington *Evening Star*, February 1, 1952, p. D-5.

[374] Private Law 713, Chapter 441, For the Relief of Priscilla Ogden Dickerson Dillson de la Fregonniere, 48 U.S. Stat. 797, June 16, 1952, HR 2920.

[375] Author interview, January 21, 2019.

[376] Loudoun County Deed Book 341, page 362, December 3, 1954.

[377] Slater, *The Hunt Country of America Revisited*, revised edition, *op. cit.*, p. 38. The count and countess made headlines in April of 1956 when Margaret Truman—the daughter of President Harry Truman—and her husband Clifton Daniel, spent their two-week honeymoon at their spacious home in Nassau. Priscilla de la Fregonniere died on February 22, 1979.

[378] LBJ Library Oral History Collection, Frank Oltorf Oral History, Interview I, August 3, 1971, by David G. McComb, p. 23: "I never did any lobbying on any legislation, or tried to get business buy using any of the Texas delegation."

[379] Robert T. Pando, "Oveta Culp Hobby: A Study in Power and Control," Florida State University College of Arts and Sciences, dissertation, 2008, p. 128.

[380] The luxurious, Beaux Arts-style Carlton Hotel—now the St. Regis Hotel Washington, D.C.—was built in 1926 on 16th Street within sight of the White House.

[381] LBJ Library Oral History Collection, George R. Brown Oral History Interview I, April 6, 1968, by Paul Bolton, p. 21.

[382] LBJ Library Oral History Collection, Frank Oltorf Oral History, Interview I, *op. cit.*, p. 23.

[383] LBJ Library Oral History Collection, Isabel Brown Wilson Oral History Interview, February 19, 1988, by Michael L. Gillette.

[384] The de la Fregonnieres sold Huntland to George Brown in 1954. In June 1957 Herman Brown became co-owner; a year later Alice Brown and Margarett Brown joined their husbands as deed holders of the property, along with about 125 additional adjacent acres they purchased.

[385] LBJ Library Oral History Collection, George R. Brown Oral History Interview I, *op. cit.*, p. 1.

[386] LBJ Library Oral History Collection, George R. Brown Oral History Interview II, August 6, 1969, by David G. McComb, p. 1.

[387] Details from the Texas State Historical Association biographies of George and Herman Brown, "Handbook of Texas Online," and from the Brown & Root history on the company's website at http://www.brownandroot.com/about/history

[388] Isabel Brown Wilson Oral History Interview February 19, 1988, *op. cit.* Also see John McMillan, "Remembering Isabel Brown Wilson, '53," *Smith College News*, April 9, 2012. In 1997, Isabel Wilson, her sister Maconda Brown O'Connor, and their cousin Louisa Stude Sarofim donated $14 million to Smith through the Brown Foundation—one of the largest gifts in the college's history. The college named its museum and art building the Brown Fine Arts Center in honor of the family.

[389] Joseph A. Pratt and Christopher J. Castaneda, *Builders: Herman and George R. Brown* (Texas A&M University Press, 1999), p. 178.

[390] "Over the Countryside: News of Hounds, Horses and People," *Loudoun Times-Mirror*, December 5, 1963.

[391] According to their granddaughter Cyndy McGee, in a June 25, 2014, post on the "Half Pudding Half Sauce" blog, http://halfpuddinghalfsauce.blogspot.com.

[392] LBJ Library Oral History Collection, Transcript, Frank Oltorf Oral History Interview I, *op. cit.*, p. 26.

[393] Pratt and Castaneda, *op. cit.*, p. 177.

[394] Kitty Slater, "The Hunt Country," *The Washington Post*, December 2, 1956, p. F20.

[395] LBJ Library Oral History Collection, Transcript, Frank Oltorf Oral History Interview I, *op. cit.* George Brown said his brother Herman, who was fifteen years older than Johnson, thought of him like "a younger brother. He felt like he was more or less one of the family, and he treated him very much like me, his [actual] younger brother... He really loved Lyndon and Lyndon loved him." LBJ Library Oral History Collection, George R. Brown Oral History Interview I, *op. cit.*, p.24.

[396] In *The Path to Power: The Years of Lyndon Johnson* (Knopf, 1982, p. 579), the first volume of Robert Caro's mammoth LBJ biography, he quotes from a May 2, 1939, letter in which George Brown wrote to Lyndon Johnson, about their relationship. "I hope you know, Lyndon," Brown wrote, "how I feel reference to what you have done for me and I am going to show my appreciation through the years to come with actions rather than words if I can find out when and where I can return at least a portion of the favors."

[397] Dan Briody, *The Halliburton Agenda: The Politics of Oil and Money* (Wiley, 2005), p. x.

[398] Caro, *The Path to Power, op. cit.*, p. xvi.

[399] Robert Dallek, *Lyndon B. Johnson: Portrait of a President* (Oxford University Press, 2004), p. 64.

[400] LBJ Library Oral History Collection, Walter Jenkins Oral History, Interview IV, Mary `13, 1962, by Michael L. Gillette, p. 26.

[401] See Pratap Chatterjee, *Halliburton's Army: How a Well-Connected Texas Oil Company Revolutionized the Way America Makes War* (Nation Books, 2009), p. 17.

[402] LBJ Library Oral History Collection, Robert E. Waldron Oral History, Interview I, January 28, 1976, by Michael L. Gillette, p. 5.

[403] LBJ Library Oral History Collection, Claudia "Lady Bird" Johnson Oral History, Interview XXXVI, August 1994, by Harry Middleton, p. 5.

[404] Mary Margaret Wiley, who was born in Waco, Texas, came to Washington in January 1954 to work as a receptionist in Senate Majority Leader Johnson's Capitol Hill office not long after graduating from the University of Texas. She soon became LBJ's private secretary and accompanied him many times on his outings to Huntland and elsewhere. Wiley stayed in that job until the summer of 1962 when she married longtime LBJ friend and confidant Jack Valenti, who headed the Motion Picture Association of America from 1966-2004. Robert Earl (Bob) Waldron, from the small East Texas town of Arp, came to Washington in 1955 to work for Rep. Homer Thornberry. A few years later he took a job as an LBJ Senate aide and later as his secretary. After leaving that position, he operated his own design firm, Bob Waldron Interiors in Washington, D.C., from 1968 until his death in 1995.

[405] LBJ Presidential Library, "Lyndon B. Johnson's Daily Dairy Collection," Saturday, July 20, 1960.

[406] *Ibid*, Sunday, March 12, 1961.

[407] LBJ Library Oral History Collection, Mary Margaret Valenti Oral History, Interview VII, September 21, 1988, by Michael L. Gillette, p.1.

[408] LBJ Library Oral History Collection, Transcript, Robert E. Waldron Oral History Interview I, *op. cit.* p. 54.

[409] The Texas-born William S. (Bill) White (1905-1994) met and befriended Lyndon Johnson after World War II when he was *The New York Times*' chief Congressional correspondent. White left *The Times* in 1958 to write a syndicated newspaper column. *The Taft Story*, his 1955 biography of Republican Sen. Robert A. Taft, won a Pulitzer Prize. See his *New York Times* obituary, May 2, 1994, p. B-9.

[410] LBJ Presidential Library, "Lyndon B. Johnson's Daily Dairy Collection," Sunday, April 23, 1961.

[411] Earlier that year, LBJ had given three-year-old Caroline Kennedy a small pony named Tex, which she rode on the South Lawn of the White House, at Glen Ora, and later at Wexford in Middleburg. See "Caroline Kennedy Shares White House with a Menagerie," *The New York Times*, June 26, 1961, p. 33.

[412] Quoted in Alfred Steinberg, *Sam Johnson's Boy: A Close-up of the President from Texas* (Macmillan, 1968), p. 413.

[413] John F. Kennedy Presidential Library and Museum, JFK Library Oral History Program, George Smathers Interview, May 27, 1982, pp. 28-31.

[414] Steinberg, *op. cit.* Also see Robert Caro, *The Years of Lyndon Johnson: Master of the Senate* (Knopf, 2002), p. 619.

[415] William S. White, *The Professional: Lyndon B. Johnson* (Houghton Mifflin, 1964), p. 204.

[416] Robert E. Gilbert, "Lyndon B. Johnson's Physical and Psychological Pain: the Years of Assent," *Presidential Studies*

Quarterly, Summer 1996, p. 698. Gilbert, a Northeastern University Political Science Professor, specialized in presidential health issues. This account of the July 2, 1955, heart attack is based primarily on the detailed reporting of the incident by Robert Caro in *Master of the Senate, op. cit.*, pp. 619-624, and the words of Frank Oltorf from his 1971 LBJ Library Oral History Interview, *op. cit.*, pp. 27-32.

417 Lyndon B. Johnson, "My Heart Attack Taught Me How to Live," *American Magazine*, July 1956. Also see Caro, *Master of the Senate, op. cit*, p. 621 and Merle Miller, *Lyndon: An Oral Biography* (Putnam, 1980), p. 101.

418 Other sources say that George Brown called Dr. Gibson. According to George Smathers, once Clint Anderson saw that Johnson was having a heart attack, he "rushed to George Brown and told him, 'Call a doctor, or there's a good chance we'll read in the papers tomorrow that the Senate majority leader expired in the house of George Brown.'" See Steinberg, *op. cit.*, p. 415.

419 LBJ Library Oral History Collection, George R. Brown Oral History Interview I, *op. cit.*, p. 22. The drink, Brown said, "did relieve it a little bit, but he pain came right back."

420 Oltorf said that LBJ asked Dr. Gibson if he'd ever be able to smoke again after the heart attack. Dr. Gibson said he wouldn't. Then Johnson "gave a great sigh and said, 'I'd rather have my pecker cut off."

421 LBJ Library Oral History Collection, Lady Bird Johnson Oral History Interview XXXVI, August 1994, by Harry Middleton, p. 7.

422 Quoted in William Theis, "Johnson Gains after Close Call," *The Washington Post*, July 7, 1955, p. 25. In a 1970 interview, Dr. Cain said that LBJ "was not actually in shock at any time." LBJ was "quite ill," he said, "His blood pressure was down.... but he was not in shock. [He] had a severe heart attack and was given superb care." LBJ Library Oral History Collection, James Cain Oral History Interview I, February 22, 1970, by David G. McComb, p. 9.

423 Both letters courtesy of James W. Gibson, Jr. Dr. Gibson kept the LBJ letter in a frame in his office.

424 James W. Gibson, Jr., email to author, September 9, 2019.

425 Also known as West or Western New Guinea, West Papua, West Irian, Irian Jayay, and Papua. The nation of Papua New Guinea makes up the eastern half of the island of New Guinea. The country was a German colony until World War I, after which neighboring Australia occupied it. The island was the scene of brutal fighting during World War II; after the war, eastern New Guinea became an Australian territory known as Papua New Guinea. It remained that way until winning independence within the British Commonwealth in 1975.

426 John F. Kennedy to Jan de Quay, telegram, April 2, 1962. John F. Kennedy Presidential Library, President's Office Files, "Netherlands Security, 1961-1963," Box 122a, pp. 7-10.

427 After graduating from Yale in 1916, Ellsworth Bunker went to work for his father George Raymond Bunker's company, National Sugar Refining Company. Coincidentally, Joe Thomas' grandfather, father, and uncle made their fortunes with the American Sugar Refining Company.

428 "Talking Points Paper, The Secretary and the Netherlands Prime Minister, March 2, 1962." John F. Kennedy Presidential Library, President's Office Files, "Netherlands Security, 1961-1963," Box 122a, p. 4.7-10.

429 See, for example, "Ex-U.S. Envoy Names to Aid in Dutch Dispute," *The New York Times*, March 17, 1962, p. 10.

430 "New Guinea Talks Open: Dutch and Indonesians Confer Secretly Near Washington" was the headline of a short article in the March 21, 1962, *New York Times*.

431 "Site of Talk Near Capital," *The New York Times*, March 20, 1962, p. 7.

432 Howard B. Schaffer, *Ellsworth Bunker: Global Troubleshooter, Vietnam Hawk* (University of North Carolina Press, 2003), p. 96.

433 David Webster, "Self-Determination Abandoned: The Road to the New York Agreement on West New Guinea (Papua), 1960-62," *Indonesia 95*, April 2013, p. 19.

434 The Association for Diplomatic Studies and Training Foreign Affairs Oral History Project. Ambassador Michael Newlin Interviewed by Thomas Dunnigan, October 10, 1997, p. 8.

435 John F. Kennedy to Her Majesty Juliana Queen of the Netherlands, August 16, 1962. John F. Kennedy Presidential Library, President's Office Files, "Netherlands Security, 1961-1963," Box 122a.

436 "New Guinea: Settlement at Huntlands, *Time*, August 10, 1962. Other observers called it the New York Agreement as the final details were hammered out at the UN in New York City.

437 Schaffer, *Ellsworth Bunker, op. cit*, p. 107.

438 Quoted in Schaffer, *Ellsworth Bunker, op. cit*, p. 96. The UN agreed to the plan, then transferred West New Guinea to the Indonesians on May 1, 1963. The Indonesian military ran the 1969 plebiscite, in which just 1,026 members of local legislatures took part, none of whom voted for independence. Pro-independence Papuans and many outside observers believe that the Indonesia government unfairly manipulated the plebiscite.

[439] LDJ Presidential Library, Vice President Lyndon B. Johnson Daily Diary, Saturday, April 7, 1962. Thomas, a law partner of another close Texas lawyer friend of LBJ's, Ed Clark, helped run the Vice President's Texas TV and radio stations, and served as a trustee for the Johnson Family Foundation. See Alfred Steinberg, *Sam Johnson's Boy, op. cit.*

[440] "Thomas G. Corcoran, Aide to Roosevelt, Dies, *The New York Times*, December 7, 1981, p. D-18.

[441] Geraldine Williams had worked as a secretary for Lyndon Johnson since his days in the U.S. Senate. LBJ and Lady Bird hosted her wedding reception at their home on 52nd Street, NW in Washington after Williams married the conservative newspaper columnist Robert Novak on November 10, 1962.

[442] Gene Locke, described by one reporter as "a genial, slightly rumpled Rotarian," resigned his post in Vietnam to run, unsuccessfully, for governor of Texas in January 1968. He had received the Presidential Medal of Freedom from LBJ in 1967. Locke died at age 54 on April 28, 1972. See "Eugene Locke, Texas Lawyer, Johnson Aide in Saigon, Dead, UPI, *The New York Times*, April 30, 1972, p. 67.

[443] Vice President Lyndon B. Johnson Daily Diary, Sunday, January 20, 1963.

[444] Adam Bernstein, "Leonard Marks, USIA Director in the Vietnam War Era," *The Washington Post*, August 15, 2006, p. B6.

[445] Marks advised Johnson in 1967 to withdraw all American troops from Vietnam, but to continue "military support" in the form of "arms and money" to South Vietnam, he said in 1976. LBJ disregarded that advice. However, after he left the presidency Johnson told Marks that he knew the advice was correct, but "couldn't do anything about it" at the time. See LBJ Presidential Library, Oral History Transcript, Leonard H. Marks Interview II, January 26, 1976, by Michael L. Gillette, pp. 28-29.

[446] Kitty Slater, "Over the Countryside: News of Hounds, Horses and People," *Loudoun Times-Mirror*, December 5, 1963.

[447] LBJ Presidential Library, Mrs. Lyndon B. Johnson Daily Diary, August 8, 1966.

[448] LBJ Presidential Library, Audio Diary and Annotated Transcript, Lady Bird Johnson, 5/13/1964, p. 2.

[449] In an admiring review in the May 31, 1964, *New York Times Book Review*, the author and former JFK speechwriter Sidney Hyman called the book "a frank, compelling biography that was not an 'authorized' campaign biography," but rather "the work of a professional of one kind taking the measure of a professional of another kind."

[450] LBJ Presidential Library, Oral History Transcript, J. Willis Hurst Interview, May 16, 1969, by T.H. Baker, p. 3.

[451] Julia Sweig, *Lady Bird Johnson: Hiding in Plain Sight* (Random House, 2021).

[452] Loudoun County Deed Book 0824, page 1969, dated August 8, 1975. In 1990, the property transferred to another Brown family entity, High Hunt, Inc. See Loudoun County Warranty Deed 08429, Deed Book 1087, p. 974, May 15, 1990. It then was conveyed back to Highland Management the following month: Warranty Deed 10870, Deed Book 1091, p. 877, dated June 14, 1990.

[453] The Foundation donated some $1.67 billion from 1951-2018 according to its FY 2017-2018 Annual Report. http://www.brownfoundation.org/templates/brownfoundation/Assets/2018-annual-report-1.pdf

[454] Author interview, September 15, 2018.

[455] Commonwealth of Virginia, Department of Health, Division of Vital Records, Marriage License, State file number 85-04243, August 5, 1985. Martin Kersey Spilman served as the minister of the Middleburg United Methodist Church from 1983-85.

[456] See Kitty Slater, "The Hunt Country," *The Washington Post*, December 2, 1956, p. F20.

[457] R.H. Melton, "Methodical Robb Proves to Be a Master at the Art of Politics," *The Washington Post*, October 28, 1988.

[458] Email to author, March 18, 2019.

[459] "Private Properties: Horse County Update," *The Wall Street Journal*, November 15, 1996, p. B18.

[460] See Cheryl H. Shepherd, United States Department of the Interior, National Park Service, "National Register of Historic Places Inventory—Registration Form," Green Pastures [Ardarra's former name], October 1, 2001, section 7, page 1.

[461] "Llangollen Farm Sold for $5.3 Million," *The Washington Post*, September 14, 1989, p. B16.

[462] See Clay Latimer, "Financial Wizard Roy Ash Starred at Litton Industries," *Investor's Business Daily*, March 12, 2015; and the obituaries by Dennis McLellan, "Roy L. Ash Dies at 93; Former Litton President, Budget Director," *The Los Angeles Times*, January 12, 2012, and Douglas Martin, "Roy Ash, Powerful Budget Director for Nixon, Dies at 93," *The New York Times*, January 12, 2012.

[463] Latimer, *op. cit.*

[464] Quoted in David Reed, "Charles B. Thornton Dead at 68; Was a Litton Industries Founder," *The New York Times*, November 26, 1981, p. 74.

465 James E. Hewes, Jr., "From Root to McNamara: Army Organization and Administration," U.S. Army Center of Military History, 1975, p.85.

466 McNamara famously applied statistical analysis to Vietnam War policymaking as Secretary of Defense—with disastrous results. He resigned as Secretary of Defense in disgrace in 1968.

467 McLellan, *op. cit.*

468 "Remembering Roy Ash: One of Largest Single Donors to HKS Dies at 93," Ash Center for Democratic Governance and Innovation, *Communiqué*, Spring 2012, p. 3. Northrup Grumman acquired Litton Industries in 2001.

469 Felicia Paik, "Buyers and Sellers," *The Wall Street Journal*, March 20, 1998, p. W-11A.

470 Betsee Parker interview, March 26, 2019, *op. cit.*

471 Peter Whoriskey and Michael Laris, "In Loudoun, Farming Serves as a Potent Symbol," *The Washington Post*, July 23, 2001, p. A-12.

472 Sara Fleishman, "A Thoroughbred of a Price," *The Washington Post*, January 27, 2007. The Ashes, according to the article, listed Huntland with the Middleburg real estate firm Armfield, Miller & Ripley.

473 Nancy DeMoss' husband, Arthur S. DeMoss, made a fortune with his insurance company, National Liberty Corporation, which sold policies via television advertising that featured the TV host Art Linkletter. Soon after Arthur DeMoss sold the company in 1979, he died at age 53. Nancy DeMoss then became CEO of the Arthur S. DeMoss Foundation, which runs the multimedia Power for Living evangelical Christian campaign. The Foundation, based in West Palm Beach, Florida, also funds entities in the U.S. and overseas "that are harder edged," *Time* magazine reported in 1999, "targeting abortion and gay rights and promoting a vision of a Christian America...." See David Van Biema, "Who Are Those Guys?" *Time*, August 1, 1999.

474 Author interview, March 26, 2019.

475 Rosie Uran graduated from Foxcroft in 2021 as a National Merit Scholar.

476 See foundation press release, "Southwest High School Foundation Announces $250,000 Contribution from Alumna, Dr. Betsee Parker," November 20, 2018.

477 Ibid.

478 Along with graduating with honors, she received the Templeton Prize in Writing and was runner-up in the Truman Political Science Prize.

479 In 2021, the Upperville Horse Show Committee voted to name the ring in her honor. She is the only woman athlete in the sport at the national level to have an arena named after her.

480 See "Biographical Sketch," Irwin Uran Memoirs, 2001-2003 (SC 0087), Thomas Balch Library, Leesburg, Virginia.

481 U.S. Armed Forces Information School, *The Army Almanac: A Book of Facts Concerning the Army of the United States* (Government Printing Office, 1950), pp. 545-547.

482 Irwin Uran, "My Autobiography," unpublished series of letters sent to author in 2002. Also see Irwin Uran Memoirs, 2001-2003, *op. cit.*

483 Quoted by Peter Pae, "Motel Dweller," *The Washington Post*, May 25, 1977. In a section in his unpublished "My Autobiography" written in January 2003 called "My Purpose in Life," Irwin Uran wrote that he had given more than $70 million "to many various charities" during his lifetime to "many churches and synagogues... food kitchens, shelters of all types, orphanages, homes for pregnant poor young girls," and to "colleges to establish psychological counseling services," as well as to "town governments for their needy, underprivileged, homeless people, battered women, sick, and to juvenile delinquents for their rehabilitation into society." He wrote that he also donated money to libraries, museums, police and volunteer fire departments, animal shelters and animal hospitals and to needy individuals. "I come from a family where 'helping people' is part of life's meaning," he wrote. "As long as I live and I have the means, I will continue to help the poor, needy, sick, helpless, downtrodden people. 'It is in giving that we receive.'"

484 Quoted by Susan Saulny, "Millionaire Bestows a Sudden Blessing," *The Washington Post*, October 4, 1998.

485 Quoted by Dana Hedgpeth, "Donor's Latest Benefits Library; Gift for Holocaust Material," *The Washington Post*, May 9, 1999.

486 See Dana Hedgpeth, "Town's Santa Strikes Again; 3 Group Get Gifts from Philanthropist," *The Washington Post*, December 12, 1999.

487 Quoted in Kimberley Christine Patton and John Stratton Hawley, eds., *Holy Tears: Weeping in the Religious Imagination* (Princeton University Press, 2005), p. 277.

488 Quoted in "My Parish Is the World," *Harvard Divinity School News*, April 1, 2016.

145

489 Deed of Gift of Easement, October 1, 2009, between Dr. Betsee Parker and the Virginia Outdoors Foundation.

490 The Mosby Heritage Area Association, now known as the Virginia Piedmont Heritage Area Association, is a Middleburg nonprofit historic preservation group that focuses much of its efforts on local history education events for children and adults.

491 Quoted by Joanne Maisano, "An Extraordinary Neighbor," *Middleburg Life*, August, 2017.

492 The group has adapted the UN Sustainable Development goals "to the U.S. context," with the goal of "good jobs for all, healthcare for all, investing in America's children, putting people's interests over special interests, ensuring equal opportunity for all, providing sustainable infrastructure, and ensuring a clean and safe environment." See https://www.sdgusa.org/about. In 2022, the Columbia University School of International and Public Affairs instituted The Parker Fellows program in her honor.

493 "Dr. Betsee Parker Donates to the Haiti Program," Earth Institute, Columbia University, April 7, 2010

494 "My Parish Is the World," *op. cit.*

495 "Dr. Betsee Parker Interview, Danny & Ron's Rescue, YouTube, May 23, 2012.

496 Speaking during ceremonies at the Unison Store on April 21, 2013, when Betsee Parker turned it over to the Unison Preservation Society. The building had been operated as a country store since the early twentieth century, but shut its doors in 1990. The vacant store had been in severe decline when the society formed in 2001. Coe and Maria Eldredge, who live nearby, bought the Unison Store in 2002, and immediately worked to stabilize the building, which "was in terrible condition," Coe Eldredge said in 2019. "It still had a few [decades old] canned goods on the shelves." Using the federal Historic Rehabilitation Tax Credit program, Eldredge—whose company, University Group, designs, builds, and renovates homes, office buildings, and light commercial spaces—completed the $300,000 renovation project in 2004. (Author interview, November 26, 2019).

497 "An Extraordinary Neighbor," *op. cit.*

498 Betsee Parker is the 17th Baroness of Lochiel, a title created in 1608 by King James I of England, formerly King James VI of Scotland.

499 Robert "King" Carter (ca 1664-1732), the richest man in colonial Virginia, managed the property for Lord Fairfax, who lived in England until moving permanently to Virginia in 1742.

500 Details on Farmer's Delight's history from Virginia Department of Historic Resources, National Register of Historic Places, "Farmer's Delight, July 2, 1973, VLR 053-0121, and National Park Service, National Register Information System ID 73002033

501 According to his obituary in *The New York Times*, July 24, 2005.

502 Adam Bernstein, "George C. McGhee Dies; Oilman, Diplomat," *The Washington Post*, July 6, 2005. Also see Wolfgang Saxon, "George Crews McGhee, 93, Oil Prospector and Diplomat, Dies," *The New York Times*, July 24, 2005.

503 Author interview, November 26, 2019.

Acknowledgements

Betsee Parker came up with the idea for this book and I am extremely grateful to her for asking me to write the history of Huntland. She provided me with a wealth of information, guidance, and encouragement throughout the two-plus years I worked on researching and writing the book.

I couldn't have written this book without the help of architectural historian Maral S. Kalbian. She has worked closely with me from the very beginning, primarily with research, as we spent many, many hours digging up information on every aspect of Huntland's history from the 1830s to the 2010s. She also provided much-needed information about all things architectural—not to mention being an excellent copy editor and proofreader. And shepherding the finished manuscript through every step of production and into the book you have in your hands.

As always, I depended on the professionalism and expertise of librarians and archivists as I searched for primary-source materials and the best secondary sources to put together this house history. Archivist Allen Fisher at the LBJ Presidential Library in Austin, Texas, helped guide me through the library's extensive collections, primarily the oral histories and vice presidential and presidential diaries. He also patiently answered my questions and provided excellent advice about the best Huntland sources at the Library.

Thanks, too, to Jarod Kearney, the curator at the James Monroe Museum and Library in Federicksburg, Virginia, for guiding Maral and me through the James Monroe letters in their collection. I received valuable help with other Monroe materials from Sara Bon-Harper, the Executive Director of James Monroe's Highland in Charlottesville; Laura Schieb, a Reference Specialist at the Rauner Special Collections Library at Dartmouth College; Reference Librarian Regina Rush and her colleagues at the University of Virginia's Albert and Shirley Small Special Collections Library; Susan Stein, Senior Curator at Monticello; and Ellen Satrom and Jason Coleman at the University of Virginia Press.

John Connolly, the George L. Ohrstrom, Jr. Head Librarian at the National Sporting Library and Museum in Middleburg, and Erica Libhart, the Marsh Technical Services Librarian, kindly made an entire room at the library available for Maral and me to go through their extensive collection of material on local foxhunting. Thanks also to Library of Virginia reference archivist Amanda Morrell in Richmond, the architectural historian Margaret T. Peters, as well as Foxcroft School Archivist and Assistant Librarian Kerri Gonzalez and Academic Dean Alex Northrup for digging out archival material dealing with Joe Thomas and Charlotte Noland.

And to former Foxcroft head of school Mary Lou Leipheimer, who shared her memories of Miss Charlotte. Alexandra Grissett, the Library Director of the Thomas Blach Library, the repository of Loudoun County's local history in Leesburg, and Balch research librarian Maria Christina Mairena and Library Associate Bryan Fisher helped enormously guiding us through their collections.

As has been the case with all of my books, I greatly depended on my friend Sheila Whetzel, the former branch manager of my local library, the Middleburg (Virginia) Library, and her staff, for help with intra-library loans, but also for myriad other research tasks.

Two William Benton descendants—David Benton and Michael Benton—generously provided me with copies of letters and other family documents. My old friend Denis Cotter, the former chair of the Loudoun County Library Board of Trustees, helped dig out documents and provided general encouragement throughout the research and writing. My long-time friend Childs Burden, who has encyclopedic knowledge of Civil War history in Loudoun County (and many other places), offered excellent suggestions for the section in the book on what happened in and around Huntland during that conflict. My colleague Lee Lawrence generously shared her knowledge of the war's local impact—along with some great LBJ Texas tales.

I also received much-needed advice and support from other fellow members of the Virginia Piedmont Heritage Area Association Board of Directors, as well as the VPHA staff. Colleagues and fellow members of Biographers International Organization shared research and other publishing advice and encouragement.

Thanks to Middleburg-area friends who had first-hand knowledge of Huntland and kindly shared it with me, especially Jimmy Hatcher, Trowbridge Littleton, Ann McLeod, and Betsy Leith Kelly, who sat down for interviews. And to Jimmy Gibson, Jr. for filling me in on how his father saved LBJ's life after his heart attack at Huntland, and especially for kindly letting us use the thank-you letter LBJ sent to his father, one that has never before appeared in print. And to Chuck and Lynda Robb for their memories of long-ago visits to Huntland.

Special thanks to Janna Murphy Leepson, who for the umpteenth time graciously allowed me an inordinate amount of time to work on this book. You are the wind beneath my wings.

Index

Names with an asterisk (*) identify owners of New Lisbon/Huntland before its purchase by William Benton, Sr., and his naming it New Lisbon. Names with a double asterisk (**) identify the owners of the property known as New Lisbon and Huntland.

In Memoriam

To the memory of:

Leah Coxsey

Laura Ham

**Jerry Scott Coxsey
(1961-2016)**

*master craftsman, sterling
farm manager, and ardent
preservationist.*

**Maximilian "Max" Schaefer
(2001-2019)**

*scholar, athlete, and
lover of history.*